Yesterday's Faces

Yesterday's Faces

A Study of Series Characters in the Early Pulp Magazines

Volume I — Glory Figures

Robert Sampson

Bowling Green University Popular Press
Bowling Green, Ohio 43403

Copyright © 1983 by Bowling Green University Popular Press

Library of Congress Catalogue Card No.: 82-73597

ISBN: 0-87972-217-7 Clothbound
0-87972-218-5 Paperback

Covers reprinted by permission Blazing Publications, Inc., for *The All-Story*, copyright 1908, Frank A. Munsey Co., renewed 1936, renewed 1964 by Popular Publications, Inc.; *Argosy* and *Argosy All-Story Weekly*, copyright 1920, Frank A. Munsey Co., renewed 1948 Popular Publications, Inc., *Adventure*, copyright 1918 Ridgway Corp., renewed 1948 Popular Publications, Inc. Covers reprinted by permission Conde Nast Publications, Inc., for *Detective Story Magazine*, copyright 1917, Street & Smith Corp, renewed 1945; *Love Story Magazine*, copyright 1921, Street & Smith Corp., renewed 1949; *Sea Stories*, copyright 1922, Street & Smith Corp.; *People's* and *The Popular Magazine*, copyright 1906, 1916, Street & Smith Corp., renewed 1934, 1944. *The Monthly Magazine* was copyright 1905 by Story-Press Corp; *Hopalong Cassidy's Western Magazine* was copyright 1950 by Best Books, Inc.

Cover art by Gary Dumm

For Diane, who hasn't read one yet

Contents

Acknowledgments....

For permission to quote from copyrighted material I wish to thank the following individuals:

Paul Bonner and the Conde Nast Publications Inc. for permission to quote from various Street & Smith dime novels, *The Popular Magazine* and *Detective Story Magazine,* as indicated.

Miss Penelope Wallace for permission to quote from the works of Edgar Wallace and, in particular, from *The Council of Justice.*

Dodd, Mead and Company for permission to quote from Max Brand's *The Seventh Man, The Untamed* and *The Night Horseman.*

My particular warm thanks are extended to the following collectors, enthusiasts and friends who helped, without complaint or dismay, as this work expanded through the years.

To Edward T. LeBlanc for permission to quote from indicated issues of the *Dime Novel Round-Up* and for his helpful assistance concerning the dime novel series characters.

To J. Randolph Cox, who supplied innumerable obscure volumes from his personal library and read, without complaint, against a rising tide of pages; my warmest appreciation for his continued assistance and support.

To Richard Minter, who dug the raw material from those storehouses where old pulp magazines go, and who has exercised his memory in support of this work for years.

To Fred J. Siehl, who made available copies from his collection of *Argosy, All-Story*, and the rest, when they could be located no place else.

To Edward Keniston, Graphic Services, for heroic support in preparing the photographs.

To the Huntsville Public Library, whose amusing policies concerning use of reference materials necessitated constant use of other library facilities, thereby substantially enriching the accuracy of this text.

And to Wooda Nick Carr, whose original idea it was that started all this work, although neither of us anticipated how difficult it would be to reach the 1930s from the dime novels.

1

Introduction

The era of the pulp magazine extended from 1896 to about 1957. It is a bubble, then, in the stream of literature. The magazines were created and terminated by conditions of the market place. For some sixty years, it was profitable to clothe one branch of popular literature in a distinctive format. After sixty years, it was not. At that point, the fiction changed its clothing and proceeded on.

Fiction endures.

Fiction also evolves. It is a living tissue. It undergoes constant, if minute, change. Over extended periods, these changes accumulate. Suddenly a new type of story or a novel new character jets up, clothed in flame, overawing the reader. Commentators genuflect and squint long into the future, predicting wonders. Through all these excitements, the long snowfall of magazine fiction continues, week after month after decade, changing inexorably to its own internal logic.

Change leaves its track. Given time enough and a fondness for solitary labors in private libraries and public collections, you can work out how the old magazines changed through the years. Here was introduced a new narrative technique. Here editorial formats decisively altered. At this point, a new face gleamed forth, after which similar faces swarmed.

The eager mind seizes upon these and reads miracles of predestination in trifles.

The pulp magazines dealt in fiction that was, by reason of the audience and the medium, heightened beyond normal experience. The drama was intense, the colors vivid, the pace exhausting. The characters moving through these prose dreams were heightened, too. Most were cast in quasi-heroic mold and moved on elevated planes of accomplishment. The least of them was Fortune's Child. The most successful blazed with grandeur more than human.

Sixty years of fiction-making created immense numbers of characters. Most glimmered briefly and vanished. After them crowded others, equally ephemeral. Seen largely, they present a glinting splendid sweep of faces, constantly changing over those sixty years.

Certain characters rose above their casual origins. Various factors, now difficult to measure, brought them intense popularity. They touched the hidden heart of the times. They stirred other writers to imitation. Themselves based on successful characters of the past, they fused old ore to new metal.

They opened new possibilities and sent excited shocks across the fabric of fiction. They directly influenced the conventions of the day—a new character or a new role, a different way of presenting action, a fascinating variant in narrative structuring. And, almost incidentally, they brought to general use certain assumptions and attitudes that lay implicit beneath the stuff of the writer's work.

Change, you see. Usually slow, occasionally accelerated by momentary popularity. All of it filtering into the literary convention of the period, and thus slowly entering American literary tradition—that tradition being the summation of transient conventions, each regarded, in its time, as immutable.

This book, and its companion volumes, are concerned with the slow boiling and shaping of many literary conventions over many decades. That should not terrify the casual reader. If the purpose is abstract, the material used is concrete, vivid, audacious. We plan to move among the series characters of the pulp magazines. We will walk with giants—men and women of accomplishment; heroic figures undaunted by action, prone to dangerous encounter.

In coming chapters, we will follow main lines in the development of these series characters. For clarity, they have been grouped as types: deductive geniuses, criminals, westerners, adventurers to places close and far, and those who tread supernatural and fantastic ways, questing marvels.

Taken as a whole, the scene is a chaos of faces, authors, titles, editors—a scintillation of detail.

Beneath the dazzle lies order. One literary convention melts to another, secretly connecting characters widely dispersed in time. Tomorrow's paperbacks reflect yesterday's dime novels. Part of our pleasure will be to follow these changes through time, meeting many of the characters who played so bright a role in shaping the literature of the pulps and, consequently, our literature of today.

In this volume, we will begin with the dime novels and several early series characters who influenced the direction of pulp fiction at its source. Later volumes will lead through the 'Teens and 'Twenties, examining characters that played distinctive parts in preparing for the vast upsurge of 1930s series characters.

Enough material presents itself to cram a library. We must select, since we can touch only a fraction of the existing characters. Inevitably, your favorite character will have been omitted. Or, more ignominiously, reduced to a reference.

In dealing with such massed material, hard to locate and expensive to secure, certain errors of reference may have slipped in. If errors are found, in spite of this researcher's zeal, please write and advise, so that they can be corrected. The subject is vast. The single person, facing it alone, is small, indeed, and chronically in need of help. Yours would be appreciated.

To it now.

The past reopens. Other times take shape.

From the first pages, almost familiar faces look out at us. Strangers they seem. Yet we know them well. The present is stripped of its masks. From across almost eighty years, we look again into yesterday's faces.

Robert Sampson
Huntsville, Ala.
February 1983

I—The Feast Incomparable

1-

The news distributor's truck came in early morning, through light silver as a new dime. It was a square machine, fat and high, painted brown. It came growling along the street, veering to the curb at intervals, like a great smooth animal pausing to sniff.

At each stop, a little brisk man plunged from the rear of the machine. As a matter of pride, he contrived to be in mid-air before the truck quite stopped. As his heels crashed on the bricked street, he was already reaching back inside, snatching out packages of printed material—newspapers, magazines, comic books—all compacted by double strands of silver wire to packages the size of a suitcase. These he whacked to the pavement. He straightened grinning. He shouted an inarticulate syllable forward to the unseen driver, then swarmed up into the rear of the truck among the undelivered bundles.

Growling, the truck wallowed away into traffic, a curious vehicle to purvey wonder.

But wonder is not at all choosy about its vehicles.

2-

In early morning, you would pass the bundles stacked untidily in store doorways. Wraps of faceless newsprint protected the exteriors and, from the open sides, you could see the bright magazine spines burn and glow. These burned and glowed in your heart all through the morning, as you sat jittering in the pasty sniff of school.

While you waited, a door opened off down the street and the store absorbed the packages. Shears clipped the silver wires. A pencil flitted down the enclosed checklist. Within the hour, the miracle was complete—the silver wire gleamed now in the back-alley trash can; the newsprint wraps had vanished; and fresh new magazines, in stacks lovingly squared and trued, waited on shelves cunningly sited just inside the front door.

The afternoon ritual was this: You leaned the bicycle against the brick wall. You came idling forward to the

5

doorway, anticipation like iced white fire in you. The glass door was partly blocked by the cardboard figure of a highly lipsticked young lady and her glass of Coke. Open the door. Just inside towers a wire rack holding sheaves of comic books, the big square ones—*Whiz, Action, Shield, Famous Funnies, Detective*. On the covers, people in brightly colored clothing did strange things.

Beyond the rack, the splendor of the magazine stand unfurled its bright complexities, a feast incomparable. High up on the rack stood those magazines favored by adults, whose tastes were so strangely different: True detective magazines, movie magazines, magazines showing well-bred women smiling and featuring stories by Paul Gallico. News magazines, men with creased faces stern on the covers. *True Confessions. Sports Afield. Liberty.* Lower down, the big magazines, *Colliers, Life, Saturday Evening Post.*

At the bottom of the racks, occupying the same position in the display that they occupied in the eye of the community, piled stacks of fresh pulp magazines: *Astounding, Unknown, Famous Fantastic Mysteries, Argosy, Amazing.* At their side, astonishingly laid out in public for sale to any casual reader, shone piles of the single-character pulps:

The Shadow
Doc Savage
The Spider, The Avenger
The Whisperer, Captain Future. The Wizard, The Ghost Detective. The Phantom Detective.

The covers glowed with a sleek, deep shine. Under your fingers, they felt smooth and cool. Inside, the off-white paper released a delicious odor, sweet as open sky. The magazine lay solid in the hand, a firm presence of paper and illustrations, marvelously promising.

You selected your personal issue, setting aside copies with covers scored by the silver wire. You bought one or two or four according to a rigid set of priorities and your ability to pay. There were always more titles than purchasing ability.

Then the long ride home, holding the issues gingerly cover to cover, preserving them from the wet imprint of fingers. If less persnickety, you rolled the magazine up, rammed it into a back pocket. Or carried copies shuffled up together with

Captain America or *Blue Beetle* comics.

Understand—the pulps were read at levels more formal than that accorded the comics. The comics were scanned with an intensity that should have browned the paper. But comic reading was essentially a public rite, as pulp reading was essentially private. The comics were communal property. You gathered up your stack and carried it off to sit with your peers, all in a pack, turning pages in a hypnosis of togetherness. Finish your stack. Grab up those good issues that the other guy has. Over a month, twelve kids each read a comic five-six times. That frightful concentration shreds covers. The issues dog-ear, crumble. Staples tumble out. Ungracious mothers consign stray pages to the garbage can. But the wire rack down at the corner bulged with more copies than you could ever buy. Everybody owned a boxful stuck under his bed or left casually on a rain-swept porch. Comics were ordinary as grass. You felt only minor regret at their demise.

Pulps were different. Concealed in a respectful box upstairs, the copies of *Doc Savage* accrue. Here are preserved the adventures of The Shadow, that grim vengeance figure, the spines of his magazines alternating red and dark blue. And here the savage *Spiders* wait, a dripping dagger on each blood-red spine, frenzy scarlet inside.

Once read, these magazines are laid safe into that box, preserved from the erosion of pets or little brother. For the pulps are intensely personal. No social reading here. Stories 86 pages long cannot be easily shared with others. The vapid narratives of Batman, hit hit hit, are speedily over. But G-8 and His Battle Aces fly, chapter after chapter, against incredible menace in German skies.

You open this crisply tight lovely issue. Work through the pages, intensely examining each illustration, moving methodically back into the letters column. Scan that, seeking for those diamond-dusted names of novels fortunate others have read—names only now you have learned. Anticipation builds, a stronger heat at the nerves. Glance over the short stories. Then, no longer able to hold back, in one exquisite leap, quickly to the front of the magazine.

One final breath.

Eyes touch the first words of the new novel. And feel, once

again, the blind forward rush into the story, the plunge through that deep doorway, yourself melting out, dissolving into the fiction, into that real world, grandly alive between the bright covers once a month twice a month ten cents a copy "The Trail of Fear," "The Council of Evil," "Red Skies for the Squadron of Satan," "Devils of the Deep," "The Wasp"....

This one-to-one relationship printed the pulps in our hearts. At least once a month, you spent several hours focused intensely on a single story. You learned the characters. You drenched yourself in the details of their violent lives. You incorporated them into the structures of your world. You did this as precisely as you incorporated those familiar radio voices as facts of your life or the equally familiar faces on Saturday theatre screens.

Whether those familiar names within the magazine were of actual people, whether their adventures occurred in the real world—these problems did not bother you. Enough that the people became familiar facts of your daily experience, as uncritically accepted as the doors and tables at home. The question of unreality never came up. They simply were.

True enough, the world between magazine covers and the world around you diverged perceptibly. In the pulp world, guns pounded frequently and urgent things happened very close together. In the comic books, people charged from violence to violence—by ropes and leaps and thunderbolts—and large numbers of folk got socked on the jaw very often. You felt an intrinsic difference between these adventures and the flowing of your own life. Already you had developed certain precise feelings about your place in the surrounding world. Without much effort you could detect certain improbabilities in the pulp world, even as you detected the superficial slovenliness of the comic book world. You sensed the cardboard without ever refining your emotional judgment to words. It was not necessary. Even when playing Superman, the worlds were not really confused. Your parents may have feared otherwise, but they underestimated you.

The fiction did possess intense vitality.

It was much more accessible than the world of adults. You could usually make out why a magazine character did something; but the actions of adults were often not understandable at any level of experience available; they were simply beings incomprehensible of unilateral will.

So, not surprisingly, the magazines exerted considerable leverage on you, and their images, their excitement, the joy of them was absorbed unwittingly, like light, down into the deep foundations of the heart.

3-

You became a collector by accident. Because the pulps were personal treasures, you laid them back. Most of them. Some were suitable for reading only once, after which the issue lost its urgency and could be loaned or lost or accumulated in a brown paper bag and carried across town for trade at the used magazine store.

Saturdays, when the wind lay fair, you could go sniffing after back issues in the second-hand stores that littered the town. 1940 was the tag-end of the Depression. Then, as now, you could assess rather nicely the condition of the national economy by counting the number of active second-hand sales places. Call them Flea Markets, or Treasured Trash, or Jake's Book Exchange, their appearance, like fungus on the economic loam, argued hard days and dollars being stretched.

So today. And so in 1940. The stores, like a shabby belt, circled the center of town. Within the belt, paint cracked away in great dry flakes. The signs were hand-painted, the rents trivial because the property couldn't be rented anyhow. Inside, ceilings stained with trespassing rain. The rooms smelled of old clothing sold unwashed, mixed with a deep frying stink from the back room, and, too frequently, the cucumber odor of rats.

In these soiled places, if you searched carefully, you could find wonder hidden among stacks of depression glass (YOUR CHOICE—1¢ EACH), spoons with remarkable handles, knives that wouldn't cut, rusty scales, tools innocent of care. Here stacked mounds of print dresses, and someone else's underwear, and dead shoes, all mixed with enameled pans and hymnals without covers and hats without dignity.

Littered through this shambles were the pulps.

You looked first for stacks of them. Otherwise you pawed

for them under the clothing, or pulled out boxes of them, gone ragged and funny, from under the rack of old coats. You methodically lifted rows of tin pans to check the titles beneath. You sorted through cardboard boxes heaped by the door, the magazines thrown in whichever way they fell, and don't recoil at the scratchy flight of a brown bug across your wrist.

You searched through the soiled remnants of other lives to turn up occasional gold. From beneath a heap of ladies' blouses came a pair of 1938 *Shadow Magazines*, hardly creased. From a box jammed in beneath book shelves (but somehow coated densely with brown dust) came that 1934 *Doc Savage,* showing the great man ripping free of a net, and in that blighted place, joy foamed cold along your nerves.

But finds of aged magazines were rare. You could locate them, more usually, for two years back, perhaps three. But you had no real hope of seeing those older issues, whose titles appeared, distant and inaccessible, in the magazine letters column. Only once in a while, only rarely, almost never, did you stumble into that special store that offered really old copies.

If you were of independent means, quite indifferent to money, you could write away to Street & Smith or Popular Publications, or one of those wonderfully remote places. By enclosing 15¢ a copy, you could receive issues as much as a year and a half old, delivery in about a week. These magazines appeared fresh and new, untarnished by their burial in the vaults of far-off warehouses.

Nonetheless, buying by mail or searching second-hand stores were acts of fierce dedication. Few readers were so single-minded. Content with today, they read the current issue and patiently endured the dragging hours until the brown van rolled through early morning. It happened regularly, that visitation. It would continue always. It always had.

4-

"Always," that inflexible word, requires qualification.

The pulp magazine had an observable life of about sixty years. It first appeared as a distinct type with the December 1896 issue of *The Argosy*, a magazine with a hectic past. That particular issue combined, for the first time, a ten-cent cover price, pulp paper pages, and cover-to-cover fiction, almost 200 pages of it.

Only the dime novels (at that time priced at five cents) offered entire issues of fiction. But these were no more than 32 pages long. Although printed on pulp paper, they were pamphlets, rather than magazines and, therefore, only the spiritual ancestor of the pulps. *The Argosy* was the founder and from its special characteristics, generations of magazines followed.

Some sixty years later, around 1957, after two world wars and astonishing social changes, the final pulps were issued. The form had seen extended life, although, after all, it had not been around always.

So many years bred change. Between that first *Argosy* and the final pulps lie profound cultural and technical chasms, for 1896 was a different world and its readers read with different eyes. As that world insensibly evolved toward 1957, time's formidable pressures altered magazine format, transformed the fiction, modified beyond recognition the art of publishing.

Readers' taste changed too. Pulp paper pages preserve a sixty-year record of fashions in popular fiction. Since the magazines depended on mass sales, and were inordinately sensitive to readers' volatile enthusiasms, the fiction is an intimate record of the past. In it you can trace what the reader admired, what fads gripped his fugitive fancy, what social and political beliefs heated his view of the world. It is all there in the fiction, clearly visible to literary geologists tunneling the old pages.

At the time the pulp magazine took form, popular fiction had reached one of those brilliant periods that shake the present and imprint the future. Suddenly, years of silent preparation end. Suddenly white bursts light the sky and the heart is dazzled. Suddenly in the final quarter of the nineteenth century appeared an extraordinary surge of novels. These deeply influenced the popular fiction magazines of the next century, establishing themes, characters and kinds of fiction that, in various forms, resonate through contemporary pages.

Perhaps 1883 is an appropriate beginning. In that year *Treasure Island* was published. In 1885 it was followed by *Huckleberry Finn* and *King Solomon's Mines*. The next year,

1886, *Kidnapped* and *She* were published, and, in 1887, *A Study in Scarlet.* Then came *A Connecticut Yankee in King Arthur's Court* (1889), *The Sign of Four* (1890), and *The Wrecker* and *The Adventures of Sherlock Holmes* (1892).

Other superb books appeared throughout the 1890s, among them *Lilith* (1893), *The Jungle Book* (1894), *The Time Machine* and *The Red Badge of Courage* (1895), *The Invisible Man* (1897), *In The Midst of Life* and *The War of the Worlds* (1898), and *The Amateur Cracksman* (1899).

The early 1900s continued as brilliantly. *The Wonderful Wizard of Oz* appeared in 1900; and, in 1901, came *The First Men In the Moon, The Purple Cloud,* and *Raffles.* The following year, 1902, saw publication of *The Hound of the Baskervilles, The Virginian,* and *Just-So Stories.*

It was a rich period. Within about twenty years were written most of H. G. Wells' scientific romances, much of the Sherlock Holmes series, many of the H. Rider Haggard adventure novels, and the bulk of Robert Louis Stevenson's novels.

It was one of those vast upwellings of energy which comes without warning and transforms whatever it touches. In this case, the minor literary forms of detective and crime fiction, and science-tinged fantasy were abruptly thrust into prominence. And a new audience discovered the excitements of adventure fiction, its romantic core plated with realistic description. By the early 1900s, each of these forms had grown vividly distinct. Each was vigorously evolving.

None of these forms had been spontaneously created from air. Not at all. Each had been tried, tested, polished through generations of fiction. In particular, each had been a part of the newspaper and dime novel fiction published in England, France, and the United States.

At this point, we again acknowledge the past. The dime novels, themselves, fused two strong lines of popular fiction. The first of these, the frontier novel, had been popularized by James Fenimore Cooper from 1820 to the mid-1840s. The second line, which had appeared somewhat earlier, was that of the English penny dreadfuls and bloods, energetic pamphlets that sweat luridly over escapes, dangers, and dooms. These rubbed elbows with boys' fiction papers and a wealth of sensational newspaper fiction. Through all these pages, echoes of the earlier gothic novels boomed and muttered.

The dime novels began, in America, during the Civil War. Reaching their golden age during the early 1900s, they promptly faded and, by 1915, most were gone. Their appeal was widespread and simple. They offered continuous action in fascinating locales. Stories were decorated by large lumps of melodrama, blatant and purple and unashamed. Characters were sketched, rather than detailed, for this was a literature of event, not much given to counting the soul's filaments.

Contemporary influences heated their pages. The dime novels reveled in new inventions, Indian battles, masterful men with weapons. They mixed imagination with newspaper headlines and poured out strongly visualized adventures to sizzle through slender pamphlets with illustrated covers and doubtful reputations. Over the years, they offered a variety of story types—frontier and western, sports, detective and mystery, fantasy, world-wide adventure, and, occasionally, love. These story types would be continued in the pulp magazines.

The final dime novels and the first pulp magazines overlapped during the 1900-1915 period. (Refer to Table I.) One publication form gradually superseded the other, but the fiction adapted itself to the new format and hurried on.

Initially the pulps contained a wide range of fiction. The intent was to publish a magazine that contained something for the entire family, a sort of Universal Divertisement enthralling Grandmaw, Dad, and Little Teddie. At least in part. At least some of the time. Like a patent medicine, the magazine was everybody's dose. Buy *The Argosy* or *The Popular Magazine* (1903) or *All-Story Magazine* and *Monthly Story Magazine* (both 1905), or *People's Favorite Magazine* (1906), and in each there would be fiction to snare you.

The story types were the same that had buoyed up the dime novels for so long—sports, cowboys and horses, detectives, secret service aces, eccentric adventures; here fumbled dubious inventors, wabbling at the edge of science fiction; here shone grand Irish lads, fighters all; here love-struck couples peered wanly; and here a story determined to be humorous clumped about, grinning glassily.

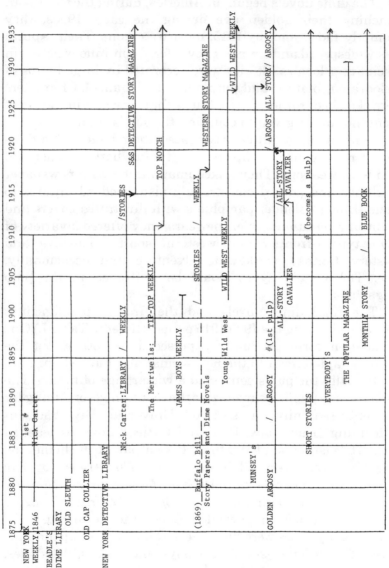

TABLE I: Dime Novel and Popular Magazine Interactions At Turn of Century

These earliest magazines seem aimed rather heavily toward 14-year old boys. But that imprecision was soon corrected, as editors learned the composition of their audiences. You note that the second issue of *Popular* (December 1903) contained two sports serials and other short fiction sized to a boy's taste. But fifteen months later, the February 1905 magazine offered a serial part of Haggard's *Ayesha* (the sequel to *She)*, plus a second serial by H. G. Wells, both solidly adult offerings.

Each general fiction magazine developed its own style, and its own readership. It was dynamic evolution in the marketplace. At the same time, publishers began experimenting with more specialized magazine forms. These were single-theme publications that spoke to a limited but intensely interested group of buyers. Probably the earliest of these magazines was the *Railroad Man's Magazine* (1906), with stories celebrating the steam locomotive era. In 1910 the *Adventure* magazine began its lengthy run, taking the world as its stage and action as its theme.

Other specialized magazines began to appear. In 1912 came the notorious *Snappy Stories,* prancing like a naughty kitten. It was followed in 1916 by *Pep*—filled with scandalous fiction about girls who flirted and stared boldy about. It was candy wrapper prose that giggled of secret revelations to come. If they never came, no one seemed to notice. The magazines endured and multiplied.

On a less tipsy level, other single-theme magazines rose from the ashes of burnt-out dime novels. The lead was taken by Street & Smith, whose *Tip-Top Weekly,* the dime novel showcase for Frank Merriwell, went through a series of cautious title and format transformations, then blended into the *Top Notch* magazine. In 1915 *Nick Carter Stories* slipped soundlessly into the *Detective Story Magazine*—the first popular publication dedicated entirely to detective, crime, and mystery fiction. It was soon followed, in November 1917, by *Mystery,* a slender pamphlet issued twice a month. Somewhat later, the Buffalo Bill dime novel was absorbed by *Western Story Magazine* (1919), the first of the all-western fiction pulps.

Following the first World War, single-theme magazines burst forth with shouting energy: *The Black Mask* (1920),

Action Stories and *Love Story Magazine* (1921), *Sea Stories* (1922) and *Weird Tales, Detective Tales, Sports Story Magazine* (1923).

Eager competitors instantly duplicated successful titles. No sooner was it determined that buyers waited anxiously for love stories or western fiction or detective magazines than crowds of each came rushing forth. The failure rate was high. But there were frequent successes—and each success generated groups of similar magazines, eager to share the gold.

In 1926 Hugo Gernsback published *Amazing Stories*, the first science-fiction magazine. Science fiction—or rather fantasy lightly seasoned with laboratories and professors— was a long-time fiction staple. The *All-Story Magazine* published quantities of it, as did the short-lived *Thrill Book* (1919) and *Weird Tales*. Gernsback himself had included science-fiction serials in many issues of his *Electrical Experimenter* (1913, becoming *Science and Invention* in 1920). The term "science fiction" not having been invented, the stories were called scientific romances or interplanetary romances or scientification. They were all fantasy. In these stories, science is treated like the unexpected guest who is joyously received, loudly praised—and hustled out the door before dinner is served.

The year of *Amazing Stories* was also the year that the pulps discovered war fiction. This occurred through one of those cross-fertilizations common between the pulps and other forms of popular entertainment. In this case, it was a play, *What Price Glory*, which opened on Broadway in the Fall of 1924 and became a stunning success. Obviously if war could be mined by the stage, the fiction magazine should also profit. Thereafter *War Stories* (1926), *Battle Stories* (1927), *Over the Top* and *War Novels* and *Under Fire* (1928).

It is not recorded that any war stories writer was inhibited by not knowing which end of the gun went bang. If he could spell "rifle," "trench," "Boche" and knew two words of French to work into the dialogue he could churn out war fiction pleasing to every reader. The heroes, to a man, were tough individualists, casually contemptuous of military discipline and massed German machine guns. The shadow of Sergeant York lay over them, and they prospered wonderfully, for a brief period, until the fad burnt itself out.

The air-war magazine endured much longer. This highly specialized publication first appeared in 1927, the year that Lindbergh flew non-stop to Paris. The immediate consequence of that flight (and one not often celebrated) was to establish the unwritten requirement that every lead character in a pulp fiction series could handle an airplane brilliantly.

In addition to Lindbergh's feat, the year 1927 also saw the release of the motion picture *Wings* and publication of Elliott Spring's book on World War I combat flying, *Nocturne Militaire*. (Springs, who had published *Diary of An Unknown Aviator* anonymously the preceding year, had been a combat pilot and wrote with authority.)

Whether these events were causes or effects, 1927 was filled with nostalgia for wartime skies. This resulted in a burst of all-fiction magazines—*Wings* (as in the motion picture) and *Air Stories*, both in 1927. And, the following year, *War Birds, Sky Birds* and *Air Trails*. In 1929 there was that hyper-specialized offering, *Zeppelin Stories*, and afterward, *Flight, Flying Novel, Eagles of the Air*, and so on and on through the 1930s into the Second World War. Even Gernsback, prophet of the future, entered the competition with the 1929 *Air Wonder Stories*, an indigestible combination of aviation adventure and science fiction.

With the exception of Elliott Springs, Arch Whitehouse and a tiny number of others, the writers of air-war fiction were a singularly uninformed group. Tedious reality rarely spoiled their stories. They borrowed from Rickenbacker's *Fighting the Flying Circus* (1919) and articles from the Sunday supplements and let their imaginations soar, chattering with machine guns and flaming Fokkers. As usual, readers soaked up these fantasies with enthusiasm.

By the end of the 1920s large numbers of specialized magazine titles flooded the market. Numerous publishers now competed for the readers' small change, among them Clayton, Street & Smith, Doubleday Page, Red Star News, Dell Publishing, Munsey, Consolidated Magazines, Magazine Publishers, Pro-Distributors Publishing, Butterick Publishing and a swarm of others. For there was money in inexpensive magazines. The fiction gushed forth merrily, ten cents a copy, and an even better issue offered next month.

Gangster magazines enjoyed brief popularity: *Gang World, Complete Gang Novel, Gangland Stories, Gangster Stories, Racketeer Stories*—and such related titles as *Speakeasy Stories, Cabaret Stories* and *Prison Stories,* a natural enough sequence.

Ever more magazines appeared to exploit the war: *Submarine Stories, War Aces, Battle Aces, Spy Stories, Navy Stories.* Others offered adventure in all sorts of places—*Tropical Adventure, Danger Trail, Romance* (it had little to do with love), *Oriental Stories, Far East Adventure, Excitement...*

Fight Stories carried you into the boxing ring. *Fame and Fortune* revealed how the worthy made their pile. *Scotland Yard* revealed the real story behind the headlines, or so it claimed. *Paris Nights* revealed other matters. *Ghost Stories, College Stories* and *Miracle Science and Fantasy Stories* each clutched for a bit of an increasingly fragmented audience.

The pot boiled frantically. But even this was merely prelude to the 1930s' explosion of titles.

From the shrill tumble of the 1930s certain major lines stand out. Most prominent among these were the single-character hero magazines, the weird menace magazines, development of the sex-exploitive titles, and emergence of the space opera as a major science fiction form. During the same period, the general fiction magazines were severely reduced, while detective and western fiction magazines, and the maturing fantasy and science fiction magazines, claimed a substantial bite of the market. The 1920s had formed major subjects and themes; in the 1930s these were exploited in a reeling dazzle of titles.

The first major line to be exploited was that of the single-character publications. In 1931 *The Shadow, A Detective Magazine,* reintroduced the periodical devoted to the novel-length exploits of a major lead character. This form had not been seen in mainstream fiction for about fifteen years, ever since the *New Buffalo Bill Weekly* had melted into pulp format. No sooner had *The Shadow* proved itself (it began twice-a-month publication in 1932) than single-character magazines leaped up on every side. During 1933 were introduced *Doc Savage* (adventures of a superman), *Nick Carter Magazine* (the famous detective in contemporary stories), *The Spider* (a deadly justice figure warring on crime), *The Phantom Detective* (a disguise master warring on crime), *G-8 and His Battle Aces* (a superspy in World War I air-war fantasies), *The Lone Eagle* (more air combat against the Germans) and *Pete Rice* (sheriff in a West that curiously combined yesterday and today). (Refer to Table II.)

Fewer characters appeared in 1934. *Secret Agent X* was a disguise master battling weird crime. *Bill Barnes* told of the adventures of a contemporary aviator. *Operator 5* began as a secret-service series, then converted to fantasy war, and *The Masked Rider* rode the Old West fighting against odds for justice.

All these magazines featured a novel about one glorious individual and his interesting assistants. The stories were vigorous, violent, improbable and unqualified fun. They brimmed with machine guns and gangsters, pseudo-scientific devices, and ice-cold master criminals given to costumes and mass murder. The scene was contemporary—most frequently New York City, although Chicago is often mentioned.

The single-character magazines managed magnificent diversity with rather limited story materials. The central situation is simply stated: An extraordinarily gifted man, fighting outside the law, battles an immense criminal organization directed by a mysterious genius of crime. Endless variations are played. The heroes are variously costumed, disguised, blood-soaked or non-lethal; customarily they are aided by a few close friends who fumble and blunder realistically. Together these representatives of justice and stability face what amounts to criminal insurrection. Very large and organized criminal groups use advanced technology to ravage society. The normal protection offered by police and the law instantly collapses and only that single hero, his name on the masthead of the magazine, stands between society and the coming of the night.

It was perhaps inevitable that the pulps would experiment with single-character villain magazines. They did so without much success. *Wu Fang* (1935) and *Yen Sin* (1936) borrowed heavily from the Fu Manchu series. *Dr. Death* (1935) combined the mad scientist and mad magician into a single character

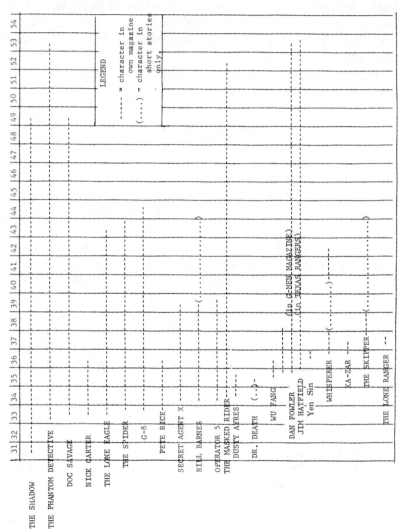

TABLE II - THE INITIAL WAVE OF SINGLE-CHARACTER PULPS

with equal lack of success. All faded swiftly.

After 1935 the single-character magazines dropped off sharply, not to regain favor until the end of the 1930s. But other magazine types enjoyed a flare of popularity, particularly those which exploited sex.

In 1934 *Spicy Detective, Spicy Adventure, Spicy Mystery Stories* demonstrated that out among the bushes skulked a large audience for breathless adventure featuring expanses of unclothed female flesh. The stories edged as close to rape as a second class mailing permit would allow. Erotic violence dabbled the prose and from the paragraphs rose a heavy panting. The good work was continued by *Spicy Western* in 1936.

Equally strong sexual elements appeared in a group of magazines roughly identified as the weird menace pulps. These included *Dime Mystery Magazine* (begun in 1932 and editorially redirected in 1933), *Terror Tales* (1934) and *Horror Stories* (1935). They routinely brought pitiful girls to torture, humiliation and the threat of mutilation. Gothic backgrounds dominated. Through the stories marched tribes of maimed madmen, dwarfs, deformed monsters and foreign crazies, all lusting to slice up fresh screaming young girls. In this mad world rape was the least of all possible crimes.

More reasonable emotions between the sexes were shared in the love story pulps. These experienced a distinct upswing in 1936. *Love Book Magazine, Love Fiction Monthly, Love Story* and *All Story Love* (which was the genial old *All-Story Magazine* in drag), all came out that year. Love stories were important business and through the 1930s and 1940s the titles were legion: *Sweetheart Stories, Ten-Story Love, Thrilling Love, Popular Love, New Love.* Some curious romantic hybrid magazines were created including *Saucy Romantic Adventures, Range Romances* and *Underworld Romances,* proving that love shines in all climes, on all types.

Unlike the love pulps, the magazines that exploited moving picture and comic page characters appeared only to vanish. The *Movie Action Magazine* (1935) compressed low-budget moving pictures into brief awful narratives. In 1936 the *Buck Jones Western* failed to cash in on the Buck Jones name. *Flash Gordon Strange Adventures, Dan Dunn* and *Tailspin*

Tommy attempted to move their title characters to the printed page with grim results. However, *The Lone Ranger* (1937) transferred from the radio to eight magazine issues, and these later formed the nucleus of a successful boy's book series.

During the later 1930s, fantasy magazines secured a modest audience. *The Witch's Tales* (1936) and *Eerie Stories* (1937) failed rather quickly, and were followed into oblivion by *Uncanny Tales* (1938) and *Strange Stories* (1939). However, in 1939, the brilliant *Unknown* (later *Unknown Worlds*) redefined fantasy and thrust it forward into the contemporary world. Counterpointing that sparkling new approach was a pair of magazines dedicated to the reprinting of fantasy novels and short fiction that was mainly drawn from the early Munsey magazines: *Famous Fantastic Mysteries* (1939) and *Fantastic Novels* (1940) were living fossils but they were more successful than most new fantasy publications.

The outstanding success of the late 1930s was science fiction. *Astounding Stories* and *Thrilling Wonder Stories* (both products of the early 1930s) were joined by a wild cascade of new magazines. The rush began about 1938 with *Marvel Science Stories* which came and went. However, in 1939 several long-lived titles appeared, including *Startling Stories, Planet Stories* and *Fantastic Adventures*. These relied heavily on a bouncy art form called "space opera," whose first stirrings may be found in mid-1920s *Weird Tales*. Space opera was horse opera tricked up fancy and taking place on worlds of crushing improbability. It was high foolishness that owed a lot to Burroughs and a little to Robert Howard, a highly physical writer of black imagination, whose best work appeared in *Weird Tales* during the early 1930s.

A swarm of lesser titles swirled up, brightly sparkling, their numbers constantly replenished. *Dynamic Science Fiction, Comet, Stirring Science Stories, Future Fiction, Super Science Stories*—their titles spin out like spider silk. Most had vanished by the late 1940s. But just as the science-fiction fad seemed crumbling away, it was renewed by the publication of *Galaxy* (1950), a literate digest-sized magazine. There followed a vigorous burst of digest science fiction magazines, and the final failure of their pulp counterparts.

Popular as were the love and science fiction pulps, they

were consistently outsold by the detective action magazines. We speak of these magazines as if the stories they published were all of a kind. This was far from the case, however. Detective action includes a number of distinct story types, including hardboiled, atmospheric melodrama and realistic thriller.

The most famous of these, the hardboiled story, had developed in the *Black Mask* of the late 1920s. The style proved highly infectious, altering the prose tone of *Flynn's Weekly Detective Fiction* (later *Detective Fiction Weekly*) and *Dime Detective* (1932). The 1935 *Detective Tales* also featured hardboiled stories, although the vigor of the style was, by then, much diluted.

Almost in parallel with the hardboiled story developed a second form of detective action fiction. This employed melodrama instead of understated action, stressed atmosphere and purple emotion rather than objective descriptions and unsentimental iciness, substituted action for character development, rather than displaying character subtleties of character through action. In most essential characteristics, atmospheric melodrama was the antithesis of the hardboiled style. Yet in the end it became the most popular, for it led directly into the single-character pulps.

Detective Dragnet (1928, and later *Ten Detective Aces*) incubated this story form. It continued through *All Detective* (1932) and is found in such later magazines as *Ace Detective* and *Thrilling Detective*.

Other pulps developed stories which featured minimal characters in pounding action. Violence, corpses, hammering guns, unending movement through often incoherent adventures. The stories grew ever more improbable as the detective action story was increasingly seduced by those spectacular doings in the single character pulps. Soon every detective, even those brainless as a papier-mache skull, matched wits with costumed killers, all of whom seemed to be that nice lawyer down the street. These stories were epidemic in *Clues, Popular Detective, Super Detective, Strange Detective* and some dozens of other titles.

In 1935 began a rash of G-Men magazines, capitalizing on the publicity given J. Edgar Hoover's boys. These included *The*

Feds, G-Men (later retitled *G-Man Detective*), a curious hybrid titled *Public Enemy* (later *Federal Agent*) and the wild shoot-'em-up *Ace G-Man*. G-Men short stories appeared everywhere they could be inserted.

From 1937 on it became clear that the old forms were chipping away. The private detective stereotype was heavily kidded in *Private Detective* and the later *Hollywood Detective*. Flashes of humor sparked among the bloodstains, as increasingly eccentric (not to say peculiar) detectives pranced through *Clues, Crime Busters* (later *Mystery*), *Strange Detective Mysteries* and *Dime Mystery* (which, in turn, had given up weird menace).

During the early 1940s, the magazines began emphasizing more realistic characters in less fantastic adventures. Human motives and real emotion were introduced in fiction less gripped by formula. The change was noted in such long-established titles as *Detective Story* and *Shadow Mystery*, and in freshly established titles, among them the splendid *New Detective*. The change was, however, slow and incomplete.

At the end of the 1930s, the single-character magazine flared up once more. (Refer to Table III.) *The Avenger* (1939) was followed in 1940 by *The Ghost Super Detective, The Whisperer, The Wizard* and *Captain Future* (which was pure space opera). Other magazines featured single characters without placing their names on the masthead, as *Jungle Stories* (1939) which featured Ki-Gor, a Tarzan copy; and *Black Book Detective*, home of The Black Bat, a costumed crime fighter. *Detective Novels* presented Jerry Wade (1939) and The Crimson Mask in alternating issues; and in *Double Detective*, the Green Lama held forth. Other single characters appeared during 1941, but death was on the form and few survived for long.

By then the Second World War had struck at the heart of the pulp magazines. They were battered by shortages of printing materials, shortages of personnel and a slow breakdown of the distribution system. The first 25¢ pocket books were being mass merchandised, beginning a deep erosion of the pulp market. And perhaps readers were at last tired. That gaudy violence which had captivated the public for a decade had grown stale and forced. The shock of the

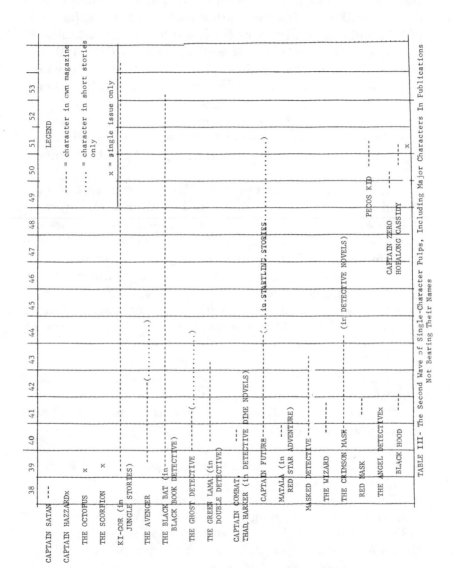

TABLE III - The Second Wave of Single-Character Pulps, Including Major Characters In Publications Not Bearing Their Names

Depression had created a reading public whose tensions found some trifle of release in the heartless action of pulp fiction, and in the iteration by that fiction that social woes were the result of criminal conspiracy. Now the hot colors of these fantasies bleached before the glare of war. Readers entered military service. The world shook. And the pulps, gripped by wartime restrictions, withered slowly. How painfully they attempted to rally. They trimmed their pages, improved their artwork, smoothed down their narrative styles. Some magazines became digests; others reduced their frequency of publication. But costs increased and through the long twilight, the numbers of pulps shrank.

In 1943 *Argosy* became a slick. *Blue Book* followed near the end of the decade. *Range Romances* continued, and *Western Action, Smashing Detective, Famous Detective, Sports Novels, Sweetheart Love Stories, Dime Western, Love Short Stories, Startling Stories.* There were others. But few now, few.

In the final hours, a tiny scattering of single-character magazines made a last frail effort: *Captain Zero* (1949), a reluctant hero who was cursed with invisibility each midnight; *Hopalong Cassidy* (1950), *Sheena, Queen of the Jungle* (1951), the last single-character pulp to be introduced.

But it was too late. One day you could find only digest-sized magazines and paperbacks. The fine old pulp format, suddenly obsolete, became suddenly extinct.

The art of pulp fiction, as it had done before, donned new bright covers and continued.

5–

Throughout the pulp era, clouds of series characters passed through the magazines. Some occupied their own single-character publication. But most were content with a reference on title page or department. They appeared in almost every type magazine, with the possible exception of the love pulps, which had other matters to attend to.

By definition, a series character performs in a group of stories—whether novels, novelettes or short stories. He returns again and again. His name may appear on the magazine cover. He develops a cadre of faithful readers who express to the editor their profound delight. The very announcement that the character will appear in the next issue will boost sales, thus demonstrating that the magazine has succeeded in establishing a tangible link with that fickle, faceless beast of a public out there.

At some point the character has managed to touch the hidden minds of his readers, and he will endure. For a while.

But unanticipated perils menace the most successful character of the best selling magazines.

By ceaseless repetition the writer may exhaust himself and sink into a calloused formula, while the character slowly loses his gleaming flecks of originality. Or the magazine editor leaves, compromising at a stroke all those characters which he felt suitable for public consumption—for the next editor will hold other views. Or the magazine itself may founder and only powerful, highly admired characters successfully switch magazines. Most lethal of all, the reader may tire, for public taste is transient and fads pass and fashions change.

Whatever the cause, series characters did not usually continue over long periods. More typically, they appeared in short bursts of stories, five or six to a group. After which the series melted silently into the sand. Perhaps reader outcry might generate a second series or even a novel. But beyond these modest limits, few series characters endured. Of all the continuing characters featured in the pulps, only Herbert New's Diplomatic Free Lances (in *Blue Book*) and Burrough's Tarzan and John Carter consistently bridged the generations.

Any long-run character satisfies specific needs. At the obvious level, his adventures have those characteristics endearing to editorial hearts—Action, Thrills, Excitement, Novelty, Gripping Drama. All these apply at the surface, up where the story dashes along full of foam and the fine flat crack of sidearms.

At less accessible levels, series characters appeal in other ways. They communicate directly with the reader about matters involving his most powerful emotions. They reinforce his deep beliefs. They provide a proxy, identifiable as the reader himself—or as he would be if only he had a little more time and luck. And the character responds to problems which haunt the public's awareness.

These are not necessarily real problems. The public mind is not subtle. It hits at symptoms and leaves the sickness unmedicated. It hates gangsters, tolerates Prohibition. It deplores corruption, and votes back The Good Old Boys. But regardless. The perceived problem is the one that gets attention.

It is not necessary that the character perform in the present. The record of historical fiction demonstrates otherwise. So series characters have been placed, with equal facility, in the past or in the future. The setting makes no difference. All series characters are really contemporary men. They reflect the public spirit of their day. For if the character were really a man of his stated period, he would not be popular. You might understand a few of his actions. But his motives would be all askew and his mode of thought would seem as unreal as a night with King Neptune—as would be right and proper for men embodying worlds so different from our own.

As long as a series character is a mirror reflecting the face of contemporary society, however obliquely, he can be called Ruggh the Caveman or Lllllllz the Futurian. No matter. He is the key to the Present. If he were popular in 1895 or 1941, it is either because he addressed matters pertinent in those years, or he represented something of worth to those years. If he remains popular today, it is because he still has something to say about our present situation.

For this reason, long-term characters have a well-remarked tendency to change. If a character is to remain successful for any length of time, there must be always something more to be revealed about him. He must develop and change, for it is not possible to continue spilling out the same bag of tricks.

So partially by design, partly by chance, the character will gently alter. His habits, friends, the events of his life reflect the years' slow change. And further change results from the alteration of society, itself aswim in history.

Granted that a character can adjust endlessly to the vagaries of public taste and still not survive. Today's wonder is tomorrow's quaint relic. But the inner equations always prevail. If a character does not adjust to changing social needs, as felt by the reader, he is done for. He can ignore fads and buzz words. But he must respond to what the reader senses is important—whatever that is and however that is discovered.

Change is not always due to abstract forces. More immediately, one series character influences others. Success is the great factor. If a character meets strong public acceptance, similar characters thrust up like flowers in a landscape. Each differs mildly from the original, none by much. Each, in turn, influences later characters. And so the chain lengthens and grows complex—to the mute despair of researchers gingerly testing the lines of succession.

Weaving through the whole bright array of the pulp magazines lie immensely complex lines of influence and modification. Long chains of characters evolved, each within the circumscribed limits of their specialized fields. Within each of these fields, further specialization occurred, lines evolving within lines. But no line and no character was exempt from outside influences. A character in fantasy adventure might strongly influence characters in western and mystery fiction, setting up curious eddies and cross currents which broke away into their own specialized forms. And from radio and moving pictures, successful plays and popular books, came powerful forces of change. The pot boiled violently and the soup was never the same.

At first look the field is a chaos of magazines, authors, series characters, the marketplace in full cry. But under the sparkling confusion is order. There is chronological development. Characters do fall in a reasonable sequence. Themes and special character types may be traced back through the years to the first grand originals, whose shadows are long indeed.

It's true that beginnings are elusive. It depends upon your angle of view as to whether a beginning is new or merely an extension of the past. In fiction this is particularly true, for what is new also stands on the past and is a part of it.

But within certain limits, new characters did rise suddenly up to shake their worlds. Their appearance decisively changed their special sectors of popular literature, giving these direction and form that persisted through the decades.

This book, together with its subsequent volumes, will examine a few of these influential figures and the development of the particular type of story that they represent. We will, for example, look closely at the beginnings of the Justice Figure— a figure who administers justice where society fails, who defends society when it cannot defend itself. We begin with Edgar Wallace's Just Men, whose influence came to full flower in the 1930s, three generations after their appearance.

We will also follow the development of the deadly western gun-fighter from the Buffalo Bill dime novels through Clarence Mulford's books and short stories about Hopalong Cassidy, two figures whose presence deeply stamped the course of pulp western fiction.

We will examine the history of Nick Carter, whose dime novel adventures established the prototype of the urban private detective and the direction of the action detective story. And we will meet Jimmie Dale, a reluctant, dual-identity demi-criminal, a bent hero, whose adventures launched a library of imitators and whose influence extends to the present.

Unique figures all. Their personalities ring through the years of the pulp magazines. Each represents a specialized story type. Each announced dozens of others, detectives, jungle men, cowboys, avengers, filling the pulps with movement and color and a vitality blazing fresh and joyous all these years.

6–

Sixty years of change and growth. Faces beyond number. Their personalities shine like polished metal in the sun, their names, fondly remembered, gleaming from old pages.

They were your friends yesterday. The characters who contributed iron to the structure of your life. Familiar names, familiar faces. Not all of them certainly. You couldn't know them all. But every face, every character, one way or another, is in your life. Somehow or other, each has contributed.

In some lost paragraph, in a magazine unrecorded, in yesterday's memory, they still endure. A breath recalls them. They stand, solid and competent at your side, ready for that fury of action which ignites in the next paragraph.

So we begin.

It was a long time ago.

It was 1900....

1900

A nation of little towns scattered along networks of dirt roads, endlessly intersecting through woods and uncleared fields. Railroads webbing the country, spawning communities at every crossing. The cities and their amenities clung by the railroad. Ten miles from the tracks equalled a full day's journey by horse and buggy over weather-sensitive roads.

Off past the horizon, the far Wild West glimmered in its pale terminal blaze. The buffalo were decimated—and the redskin. Almost extinct were the border towns and free-wheeling gunmen of harsher days. Most bandit gangs were broken now, but memories of the James Boys, the Daltons, remained hot and juicy. And such marshals as Bill Tilghman still carried their worn pistols apurpose.

The national population, some 75,000,000, concentrated on the East Coast and around the Great Lakes, spread thinly elsewhere. Immigrants still poured into the cities—the Germans, Italians, the Balkan peoples, the Irish, creating vast ethnic enclaves that would endure fifty years.

The economic pyramid, curiously malformed, rested on the farmers and the laboring poor, for there was an immense surplus of labor, willing and cheap. The middle class was small, capped by a tiny tip of intensely wealthy in these days before the income tax—that 1913 innovation of the dreamer Woodrow Wilson.

Average income was then about $500. Children aged ten and older could work 14 hours a day toward the American Dream and earn 30¢ doing so. Women sewing the same hours could earn 40¢ a day. At day labor, a man could earn 50¢, although if he were skilled at the building trades, his earnings might rise to $1.

How inexpensive, then, a schooner of 5¢ beer?

Unions were still to come. But already voices rose in protest of these hours and these wages. During the next ten years, the country would be stirred by the name Debs and the Social Democrats and their sinister theories, and labor problems would shock newspaper readers, who would wonder whatever it was that ailed the country.

Horses clattered on brick city streets, mingling with bicycles, trolley cars, the infrequent automobile—these still toys of the very rich and very sporty. The Model T was eight years away; the first gush of the Ford production line lay six years beyond that. In the golden present, the horse powered the country and, incidentally, heaped the streets with manure and its attendent companions of stench, flies and disease.

For the past twenty years, science and technology had heaved hugely under the surface of the daily world, birthing unevaluated marvels. Edison had established the world's first industrial research park, in 1876, at Menlo Park, New Jersey. 1888 saw the foundation of the Institut Pasteur in France and the completion, in California, of Lick Observatory, equipped with a telescope having a 36" lens. The element Helium was discovered in 1895, the same year that Marconi transmitted the first telegraph message. Sir Ronald Rose isolated the mosquito as the carrier of malaria. That was in 1897, and the following years saw the isolation of radium and new applications of the electro-magnetic theory.

Looking forward from 1900, vast accelerations of technology impended. Who could dream those coming metal shapes? Optimism ran high. In spite of bank panics, trusts and sinister economic moans, the coming years were good to see. Man's questing mind, winged by science, could, it seemed, conquer all obstacles. Scientific advancement, gushing riches, would free man, cure social ills, glorify mankind.

Thus began the public's star-flecked love affair with science, that fickle wench, dazzling among her laboratories and high-voltage equipment, where white-coated geniuses created new worlds from glass tubes, copper wires and that magical fluid electricity.

Shining prospects, indeed. As yet the population lighted homes with gas or oil. They observed the daily ritual of emptying the Necessary in each bedroom. The privy was a customary outbuilding for both poor and well-to-do. In the homes of the rich, a few electric lights burned. There was, perhaps, running water in the kitchen.

Telephones (chancy objects full of mystery) could be found in businesses and homes of the wealthy. By 1905 public phone booths would be scattered through the town. Phone lines would rise above the horses of commerce and rushing messengers carrying telegrams—for the telegram was an instantaneous way to send messages, more rapid even than the postal service, which provided five to seven commercial deliveries daily.

By night the streets flickered with gas light, if lighted at all. The wise pedestrian kept to crowds or secured himself in a carriage or remained locked secure in his home. For the night was full of toughs. Policemen in conical helmets and clubs and strong arms maintained low levels of order. The police force itself suffered from corruption and amateurism. Record keeping was primitive. Finger-printing was not an official technique. Photography was barely used, although the French method of head measurement for identification was applied. The Pinkertons, loudly publicized, caught train robbers and outlaws and inflamed public imagination via the dime novels and the *Police Gazette*. Every boy yearned for the desperate adventures of a detective, as described in a weekly torrent of 5¢ novels.

The people of the setting? The men lived armored in stiff shirts, detachable stiff collar, detachable cuffs, waistcoat, suits of wonderfully dense material and plug hats. (Or they pulled on overalls, heavy blue shirts and heavier shoes.) They smoked cigars and spit tobacco juice prodigiously at the public spitoon. The women lived encased in layer after layer of clothing, sternly drawn in at the waist—which possibly accounts for their recorded swoons and faints. Women did not smoke, paint, straddle a horse nor guffaw. Skirts concealed the enticing ankle, although dress at formal affairs might properly display the bosom's cleavage. A proper lady scrupulously observed the separation of the sexes, would not consider addressing a man alone, an act of indiscretion to besmirch her reputation for purity. Purity was highly regarded.

In 1900 no cure was yet available for the common cold, cancer, toothache or childhood diseases. In spite of which, myriads of patent medicines proclaimed otherwise. The available medications were nostrums from the Civil War period—opium, morphia, mercury—the latter causing amazing changes in tooth enamel. Strange whispers rose from Europe of treatment by hypnotism. Already the psychoanalytic heresy, not yet translated into English, brought bi-lingual medical men snarling to their feet. In the United States, doctors were making astonishing advances against Yellow Jack. But medical science awaited the deadly accelerations of the Great War, fourteen years off, still quite invisible.

The national digestion engulfed fried pies, potatoes, breads, doughnuts, salt and pickled meats. Fresh fruit and vegetables came available only in late Spring to mid-Autumn. The Christmas orange thrilled palates drained of Vitamin C. They drank tea, water, not much coffee as yet. Wine was more popular than whisky, and beer was sluiced down by workers in an astounding number of saloons (where ladies could be accommodated if they entered by the side door). While ominous rumblings sounded from the Prohibition forces, the dry life lay almost twenty years in the future.

Vaudeville flourished. Also public readings and magic lantern shows. Silent movies would arrive in 1903, "The Great Train Robbery" evidence of wonders to come, with sound films twenty years distant. In the cities, you could attend the opera, or drama, or musicals—or the burlesque, if your impulses were depraved. You could dance sedately to violins and harp, less modestly to the strains of a ragtime orchestra replete with violins and clarinets. The Foxtrot, that immoral jiggling together of couples, would not appear until 1912.

All manner of things to come. The first airplane flight in 1903; combat aircraft by 1915. Exploration of the Poles by men on dog sleds. US Steel consolidating in 1901. Shortly Woolworth would offer 5¢ and 10¢ bargains. A&P would begin that long expansion toward product uniformity.

Fourteen years to European war: submarines, zeppelins, death in French mud, trenches, machine guns. Seventeen years to the US entry into the war, the Marne, the Argonne Forest.

Peace at last. Leave in Paris. Home at last. Back to a depressed job market, the invention of rayon, and, in 1920, the introduction of installment buying.

A decade of coming wonders.

Chapter II—Glory Figures

1-

Beadle's Boy's Library of Sport, Story and Adventure.
Brave and Bold. Buffalo Bill Stories. Rough Rider Weekly.

His body shot by the detective, clinging for life in midair, and it struck the rocky bed of the canyon far below, with a sickening thud.

Young Sleuth in The Lava Beds of New York or The Tenderloin District by Night.

"Curse him! He thought he'd got Jesse James, did he? Well, Jesse James isn't getting caught by any such cheap mutt as that," said the world-famous desperado.

Frank Reade Library 43, "Lost In the Land of Fire or, Across the Pampas in the Electric Turret."

The knife was descending. It had almost reached Chick when Nick's revolver spoke, and a bullet... crashed its way through the brute's wrist; and at the same instant, Nick leaped forward and felled him to the ground with a terrific blow to the jaw.

Suddenly a whirlwind caught the disabled vessel and whirled it around and dashed it broadside against some object....

Diana, the Arch-Demon or Nick Carter's Run of Luck.
Fred Fearnot's Narrow Escape or the Plot That Failed.
Plucky Bob or The Boy Who Won Success.
King of the Wild West's Test of Honor or Stella In Bondage.

"Hold on. I know this is a smuggler's craft, and, boy though I am, I'll run her under the guns of yonder cruiser."

But the Indians were not checked in the least. They rode forward like a swarm of bees.... And they fired volley after volley as they came.

Diamond Dick Weekly. Golden Hours. Secret Service.

Bowery Boy Library: The adventures of a poor waif whose only name is "Bowery Billy." Billy is the true product of the streets of New York. No boy can read the tales of his trials without imbibing some of that resource and courage that makes the character of this homeless boy stand out so prominently.

Pawnee Bill, with his knife covered with blood, was dealing death blows to the invading Indians.

Might and Main. All-Sports Library. Tip-Top Weekly.

Frank Merriwell and his brother Dick are known and loved by over one hundred and fifty thousand of the best boys in the United States. They are both clean-cut, vigorous fellows who dare to do right no matter what the consequences.

He was handsome in face as well as in figure, and the flowing chestnut hair that hung over his shoulders set off his countenance like a picture in a frame.

Crashleigh, The Corsair or the Diamond Demon.
Old Cap Collier 639, "The Headless Man or Clear Grit's Great Case."
Old King Brady and the East River Mystery.
The James Boys Among the Boomers.

Optic Carter Stratemeyer Ellis Patten Alger Buntline Brereton Dey Merriwell Leslie LeBlanc Munro Tousey Enton Ingraham.

"Never!" cried the woman. "Take that! We die together!" and hurled the bomb straight at....

2-

For nearly eighty years, they bought dime novels.

They bought them in smoke-scented railway stations, in candy stores and billiard halls, from street stands. Generation to generation appeared the familiar stacks, always available, always new, luring the reader's change.

Splendid then. Splendid now. You finger gently through your own copies—some are nearly one hundred years old now and inclined to be sensitive along the edges. They are simply enough made—folded sheafs of paper, stapled once or twice through the fold. They feel strangely thin to the fingers, bending bonelessly as you read, wraiths of paper. But essentially sturdy. That paper lasted.

Color burns from the covers: red, blue, bright yellow, rich tones of orange and brown. Color came late to the dime novels—about the mid-1890s. Before that, covers—usually the only illustrated part of the publication—displayed complex black and white drawings of fierce action:

The helpless vessel stunned by waves.

Ferocious redskins tomahawking frail flowers of femininity.

Ferocious men pistoling other ferocious men.

Rescuers sprinting toward those in peril from raging horses, flaming structures, brinks of cliffs, waterfalls, canyons and divers heights.

Early covers are a hair more sedate. Obsolete figures face each other in rigid postures, as if copied from a sheet of paper dolls. Woodsmen, buckskinned and rifled, peer toward the wooded grandeur of mountain ranges thrusting whitened peaks against the azure purity of the skies.

But time mellows all. By the 1900s, the drawing style had softened, grown supple, of such joyous vigor that it would not be equalled until the height of the pulp magazines.

In early dime novels, the type face is as obsolete as the drawing style. The type is often incredibly tiny. The story marches in two, sometimes three, columns down the page. And page size varies madly: 4 x 6 inches, 6 x 9 inches, 9 x 13 inches. Or larger, or lesser.

Page counts are as erratic. Early novels frequently contained more than 100 pages. More usually, 30-60 pages. Less frequently, 80 pages. A few issues priced out at 25¢, the majority at 10¢ each—the price that gave the genre its name.

Around 1895 the dime novel gradually stabilized as a 5¢, color-cover, 32-page pamphlet, with legible, double-columned type, issued weekly. This is the classic format that entered the Twentieth Century. But there were innumerable variations, then and later.

The fiction, volatile in the extreme, was not to be kept in this single format. Very large amounts were published in the story papers of the time. The Sunday supplement and the Sunday school leaflets are distant cousins of the story papers, and *Grit* is their nearest living relative. In form, the story papers were short newspapers, ranging in size from tabloid to larger than those presently sold. Pages varied from 8 to 32. Selling for 5¢ they offered large quantities of fiction—a complete novel, perhaps serial parts, several short stories and ancillary matter. New and reprinted material appeared—weekly for the most part.

Like the dime novels, some story papers appeared only for the sake of disappearing. Others lasted for generations. Great names include the *New York Weekly* and *Frank Leslies' Boys' and Girls' Weekly.* The story papers all managed to consume large amounts of fiction and left behind a shining trail of stories and characters. If a character made sufficiently deep an impress on the reader, there was a good chance that he might spin off into a dime novel series. It happened to Buffalo Bill and Nick Carter. With every new character, it might happen again.

Whether the fiction was first published in dime novel or story paper, it was almost sure to be republished. And again. And again. Reprinting was big business in its own right. The market was insatiable and readers' memories gratifyingly short. At one time or another, most dime novel series reached into their own past and republished earlier stories, cannily tricking them out in new covers and titles.

Reprints appeared not only as dime novels, but, as commonly, in the form of fat little paper-backed, pocket-sized books. These measured about 5 x 7 inches and contained 200-300 pages. Usually two or three dime novels were reprinted in such books. Or sometimes four were squeezed in, not necessarily in their issued sequence, nor always in the same form. Often some smirking editorial fiend butchered them to impose a narrative continuity otherwise lacking. The chapters are almost always numbered consecutively, no matter how many dime novels are compressed between the covers.

The reprints make up a separate field in themselves. Their history is almost maliciously confused. They were, themselves, reprinted and re-reprinted, sometimes with new titles, sometimes with the contents scrambled from earlier scramblings. New novels were interwoven at unspecified points, together with popular English novels on which (we may suspect) no royalties were paid.

Once launched, a reprint series could persist over extraordinary lengths of time. One of the most successful, the Magnet (later, the New Magnet) Library, appeared continuously from 1897 to 1933, and consists of some 1369 volumes, some reprinted to the third reiteration. Later cover illustrations and paper quality are markedly inferior to the original covers.

But what did it matter? In a way remarkable to us now, the reprints literally spanned the generations. Each new generation seized them avidly, defects and all. Each generation read them. Preserved them. Even borrowed them from lending libraries, the sons relishing what their fathers had cherished.

Well, no wonder.

The dime novel was a vigorous art form, with an extremely long publishing history. From 1860 to 1927 dime novels were merchandised by four or five major publishers and a mazy swarm of minor ones. At the height of their power, for about 50 years, the fiction gushed out in a roaring howling rip-snorting exuberance, a foaming tumble of series, titles, characters, reprints, transient, fascinating, sparkling in bright scarlet and purple prose.

The first dime novel, published in the summer of 1860, was "Malaeska, the Indian Wife of the White Hunter." One hundred and twenty-eight pages long, in salmon-colored covers, it reprinted a serial written by Ann S. Stephens for *The Ladies' Companion* in 1839. In its 10¢ format, "Malaeska" sold 65,000 copies in a few months. Obviously there existed a huge market for sensational fiction—and, at that point, the dime novel era began.

Thereafter came a freshet of novels featuring fabulous frontiersmen, wondrous woodsmen, riders of the plains, mountain men, and similar adventurers along the skirts of civilization—all offered to assuage the public's raging thirst for frontier adventure.

Hardly was the frontier story established than the dime novel began thrusting into all sorts of areas, all sorts of subjects. It was a whirling shimmer of fiction, transient as butterfly breath: war stories, stories of the sea and forest;

reprints of whatever the English publishers had found profitable. Stories of hounded damsels. Stories of pirates, murderous and black-hearted but shot through with veins of improbable sentimentality.

Stories of rudimentary science fiction appeared, a curious blend of engineering and fantasy, somehow inserted into the Western scene. This subject soon expanded into tales of adventure where the pot of gold spilled all over the heroes in the last chapter.

And there were detectives, legion upon legion of detectives, stalking their prey. And outlaws, hordes of them, ravishing society. And poor ragged friendless boys, endlessly rising by hard work, devotion, moral superiority and luck. And athletes performing feats unusual.

Newsstand racks filled and emptied with the exploits of boy inventors/explorers/adventurers; or, for your sentimental moments, love between two worthy young people, oppressed as they were by machinations of black sinisterosity.

So the stories flowed. Legions of them. Myriads. Adventures in ranked thousands, composed and sold, read and laid aside. Massed libraries of stories, accumulating, the old gradually dissolving into memory.

Illustrated story papers, dime novels, reprint libraries— the format didn't matter much.

It was the stories that counted.

The splendid stories.

The extraordinary adventures of peril and glory.

Of menace.

Savage menace.

Danger and daring.

Of valor extreme, against all odds.

Death traps, poisons, hypnotic spells.

Disguise.

Yes, even disguise.

Foreign scenes, exploits with cool head and superhuman strength.

Weekly.

Available each week for twenty years. Twenty-one years.

Twenty-four years of continuous publication. Issue No. 1294.

Marvels.

Decades of action. Generations of passion and struggle. Whole towering ranges of paper, immensely accruing. Till the early stories vanished in the dim green translucence of decades past, glimmering, remote.

Titles vanished. Series vanished, lost even to the reprints. But the primary themes remained. Subject areas were staked out that the coming pulp magazines would fill in all their specialized hundreds.

The heroes endured, too. Some by name; others only by the kind of hero that they represented and how they went about their business.

In dime novel pages the pulp fiction of the next forty years lay implicit. Most major pulp themes were pre-figured here and many of those attitudes and assumptions which energized the 1930s pulp series character world. These endured, channels through which the river of fiction poured steadily toward the magazines of the future.

3–

Illusion that it all happened is a staple fiction device.

Nick Carter's biographer visits Mexico and soon Nick, himself, is lowered into the mouth of a volcano there. Walter Gibson sees an interesting alignment of buildings from his 1935 hotel window and immediately The Shadow climbs among them. Philip Marlowe walks the same Los Angeles streets that Raymond Chandler observed in detail.

Familiar backgrounds and realistic detail sugar your acceptance of all that other melodrama. Narrative reality is also enhanced by the introduction of real people into the fiction. The dime novels were particularly addicted to this practice. Inspector Byrnes (New York City Police) figures in many Nick Carter adventures. Such individuals as Anna Held, Grover Cleveland and the Crown Prince of Sweden appear, momentarily, in stories of Frank Merriwell.[1] The Jesse James novels bristle with familiar western badmen. And that splendid institution, the Buffalo Bill series, introduces famous Indians and scouts and gunfighters and puts them busily to work.

So reality heightens to fiction. Colonel William Frederic Cody, more resplendently known as Buffalo Bill, is an historical figure transfigured. Down under the legend was a living man who did shoot buffalo, did ride in wild west shows, did contribute a silver dollar each Sunday to the collection plate, and did squabble for years with his wife among the foothills of divorce. Above this routine stuff soars the true reality—the towering glittering figure of Buffalo Bill, dime novel hero.

The stories began in 1869. That year the *New York Weekly* published "Buffalo Bill, King of the Border Men," by E.Z.C. Judson. Thus the long biography began: almost fifty years of weekly chapters, spread through *Buffalo Bill Stories, Buffalo Bill Border Stories, New Buffalo Bill Weekly,* and other series, original and reprint, great and small, American and English (for he was wildly popular in England also).

When the dime novels eventually yielded to the pulps, Buffalo Bill made the great cross-over. Three of his final adventures (themselves reprints) transferred to *Western Story Magazine* in 1919. And so Bill became a pulp hero in addition to his other accomplishments.

It's an imposing record. He was an imposing personality.

Cody's magnificent personal appearance is still well known. Long brunette hair sweeps his shoulders. The mustache is assertive, the imperial vigorous. He wears fringed buckskins and thigh-length black boots. On dime novel covers, he also wears tight white pants tucked into the boot tops and a broad-brimmed white hat, the symbol of integrity and worth.

The general impression given in the novels is that he stands about 270 feet tall. More accurately, he is tall, manly, of fine physique, broad shouldered, and with a strong handsome face. Cool self-sufficiency glows from him. Intense competence. On a frontier swarming with harsh selfpermissiveness, he possesses the "courtly manner of a well-bred gentleman."

The characteristics are familiar. We stand shuffling our feet in the presence of the Legend Become Flesh. Not surprisingly, his word is bond. Once given, it is kept without regard for personal conscience, a characteristic shared by such other unlikely personalities as Fu Manchu and Richard Wentworth, the Spider. It is part of the hero canon: Adherence to a personal code unswayed by the irrelevances of situation, untarnished by expediency.

Personal integrity is accompanied by cheerful fatalism. "I have always lived prepared to die," he says. He was certainly willing to thrust into situations which would be lethal to a lesser being. Part of the fun is to watch him slip gracefully from the snap of death, week after week. Hordes of Indians whoop in vain. Badmen curse in dismay. From fiendish ambushes, caves with trap doors in the floor, from raging torrents, dynamite blasts, from prairie flames, Cody extracts himself (and others) deftly, with grace. The reader need suspend disbelief but a fraction of a second and the trick is done. Adroit.

As adroit is his marksmanship. This is simply fabulous. What he sees he hits. For some years, he decimated the redskin with dedicated zeal. But about 1900, humanitarian instincts began slipping in. He began crippling more than he killed. Still he was lethal, indeed, with rifle or sidearm. Or, for that matter, bow and arrows and rocks. He mastered them all, as he rode and roped—superbly well.

Customarily he traveled with a small group of friends. Perhaps there was a trusted Indian companion or Pawnee Bill. They were occasionally joined by Will Bill Hickok or a comic German-accented companion who spiced the excitement with levity. The emphasis is on close companionship. Cody saves them. They save him. An agreeable arrangement.

So the years passed. Scouting, guiding, Indian fighting. Cleansing the West of outlaw bands. It was an enjoyable life, although not particularly well paid. In one novel, it is noted that Cody seems to lack the ability to gain fortune that is shown by lesser men. Maybe so. But he owns a ranch in Wyoming and other residences scattered across the wilds— unpretentious cabins decorated with paintings, musical instruments, books, the obligatory mounted heads and skins. The furnishings emphasize the gap between his personal and public lives. The cultural artifacts are a shorthand for the superior moral plane on which Cody, as folk hero, stands, and, therefore, his innate superiority to the rough world outside the cabin.

Such retreats—and all the shorthand surrounding them— are common in the dime novels and almost mandatory in the later pulps. By the 1930s every single-character magazine hero possessed a Fortress of Solitude, a penthouse, or Rectory, or blackened sanctum, filled with items of high culture and higher morality. It was one of the conventions.

Moral planes and possessions to one side, the area in which Cody really excels is personal pre-eminence. He is recognizable at a glance, unless disguised. He excels in all manner of physical skills. His feats are unparalleled. Friends admire. Enemies respect. He embodies all those elements admired by his time: honesty, self-reliance, integrity— Emerson's grand nouns. To these we may add coolness and force of personality.

"As long as I can meet bad Indians and renegade men in open fight," says Cody, "my hand is always against them, but I don't take part in their formal and cold-blooded murder. Frankly, I don't like lynch law."

A careful bit of discrimination. The fight, if lethal, is to be fair. The opportunities are even in serious matters of death combat. No aces are hidden. The odds are weighed only in favor of the morally superior.

Under all this runs a quiet ruthlessness, concealed by other bright virtues. Remember, Cody has killed thousands of buffalo, hundreds of Indians, and renegades without number. His nobility of character is starched by a gun-metal unsentimentality. If a character needs to be shot and demands to get shot, he is shot.

This is one of the conventions of the western action story form. Death is equated with excitement, the peril of death with suspense. However, all these killings take place in a Never-world where normal rules are suspended. What is acceptable on the frontier is not permitted in the big city. For as the reader well knows, the city operates by rules, and these do not encourage the casual gunning down that elates the westerner's day. This distinction held true in the dime novels as it later held true in the pulps. If you wish to watch the bodies fall, go West. Not until the 1930s and the single-character pulps did this convention change.

With the Buffalo Bill stories, the frontier adventure

fantasy reached its full blooming. Even then other forms of western adventure were forming in the dime novel. Soon Indian fighting would fade, as would casual ramblings through the continental immensity, remote from the disciplines of civilization. These chaotic pleasures were gradually replaced by the ranch/cowboy story. And there followed one hundred thousand tales of how the brawling west was tamed, cartridge by cartridge.

At this point, two dime novels series are of interest. Both are representative of the shift in emphasis, and both contain themes that would be heavily exploited in the coming pulp magazines.

The first of these series is the *Wild West Weekly*, a publication whose run, from beginning to end, rivaled that of the *Argosy*. The *Wild West Weekly* began as a dime novel in 1902 and ran for 1294 issues (half of them reprints) through August 5, 1927. At that time, Street & Smith converted the publication to the more renowned pulp magazine of the same title. This continued down the decades to 1943, with characters differing substantially from those featured in the dime novel.

In 1902 the central figure was Young Wild West, a hero as flamboyant as Buffalo Bill and deriving directly from him. The immediate difference is that his stories were carefully tailored for an audience of boys. The adventures are light, vigorous, continuously interesting; some gripping thing happens every chapter: a fight, a capture, an escape, an interval of comedy. All nicely varied to avoid the monotone of event often typical of the dime novel.

Young Wild West and his partners are just a little more than the common run of folks.

Thus a character in the story remarks, and so they are. Young Wild West (called "Wild" by his friends) is a "handsome, athletic boy of 20," of medium height, broad-shouldered and straight as an arrow. He was found as a baby hidden in the brush near a burned cabin, and was raised by an Army officer named West, who gave him the rest of the name that jangles so oddly on our sophisticated ears.

He is a most extraordinary boy. In addition to having all

Buffalo Bill Stories, Nov. 5, 1910, #495. As the series matured, the threats became steadily more fantastic. But it was save and be saved to the end, out among the cactus and Indians.

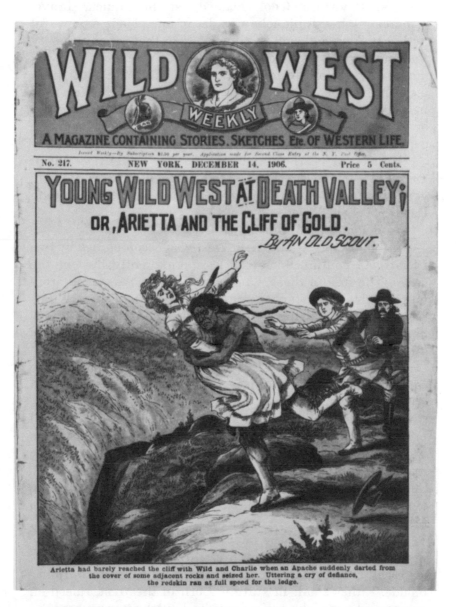

Wild West Weekly, Dec. 14, 1906, #217. Again the heroine is stolen away, a cover situation as popular as the hero facing doom.

the usual virtues (cool headed, strong, quick, brave, resourceful), he is uniquely a leader of men. He is a powerful authority figure, glowing white-hot with that inner intensity that makes men pleased to follow him. At one time he was mayor of the town, Weston, in the Black Hills. While still in his teens, he earned a fortune taking gold from the Hills. With this, he bought the Champion Ranch and, from that base, embarked on a long series of adventures all over the West, inspiring consternation in the evil wherever he went.

He wore a pearl-colored sombrero, a "well-fitted suit of buckskin" trimmed with red silk fringe, and is known, variously, as the Prince of the Saddle and The Champion Deadshot of the West.

So much for you, Buffalo Bill.

In his travels Young Wild West was accompanied by two friends who continued, more or less permanently, through the series. The first of these, Cheyenne Charlie, was a big, iron-muscled, black-mustached man in his thirties. He is Wild's right-hand man at the ranch and during their more serious business of adventuring. Charlie is close to hero caliber himself and does things right, almost always, a figure of unusual competence. He is married to Anna, who remains back at the ranch, unless she is needed to be captured or to carry a critically urgent message.

Wild's second friend, Jim Dart, is about eighteen. A special protege of Young Wild West, Jim can rideropeshoot well and is learning to do it better. He provides a figure with which the reader can identify. Back at the ranch, his sweetheart waits. She is named Eloise Gardner and has the misfortune of being over-shadowed in the stories by Wild's sweetheart, Arietta Murdock.

Arietta is one of the character high points of the dime novels. She is a delight, constantly threatening to take over the series by sheer vigor. She is described as being a charming blonde, rather small in stature. Born in the West, raised on horses and guns, she can outride and outshoot most men.

There is nothing fragile about "Et." She is entirely competent, and no trial of nerve shakes her. While she requires saving from assorted menaces rather frequently, she also does more than her share of saving. She is clearly in the mainstream of competent women who would illuminate major pulp magazine series thirty years later.

Comic relief is provided by miscellaneous regional and ethnic types—the Yankee, the tenderfoot, the Do-Good Easterner. And the Chinese. Wild has a Chinese servant, Hop Wah, who snatches the story and runs, given half a chance. No one else in the series has any negative characteristics whatsoever, apparently because Hop Wah has been assigned them all. He is a liar, gambler, whisky drinker, a slick conniver, and a sleight-of-hand artist. He is entirely and utterly devoted to Wild's best interests. Perhaps fortunately.

In the Young Wild West series, then, a core group of adventurers operates from a fixed base from which they journey out to enjoy the perils of the Post-Civil War frontier. The group revolves about the personality of the hero, a wonderful boy. He is supported by an older man (a sort of father-surrogate) who is subordinate to the hero and admires him deeply. A second supportive figure is that of a younger man who provides a vehicle by which the young reader can identify himself with the action.

The three adventurers device, with all its inner psychological appeal, is about as old as spoken narrative. At its heart, you can usually identify that interesting role reversal of the son acting in the father's capacity of authority, and the older male acting as an admiring subordinate. Popular literature employs this device extensively, and its presence will be noted throughout the pulp magazines.

Young Wild West's dime novel is sparkling, heady stuff, an extended tissue of captures and escapes and deadly perils barely evaded. In this world, dragons hide everywhere.

The hero, captured by Indians and being burned at the stake, escapes through the swirling smoke.

The hero, trapped by Indians, is saved by a hermit who lives underground beneath a mechanical rock.

The hero, menaced by prairie fire, saves Arietta, himself, and their horses through superhuman exertions.

That Wild so easily survives the deadly dangers heaped upon him by formula fiction is hardly surprising. He stands invulnerable on the high plateaus of moral excellence. Against

Wild West Weekly, Nov. 26, 1927. The dime novel becomes a western pulp and Young Wild West transmuted to Billy West, admirable cowboy. The magazine, highly popular, continued into the 1940s.

Rough Rider Weekly, April 6, 1907, #155. Inspired by Teddy Roosevelt's Rough Riders, Ted Strong and his crew of boys adventured all over a simplified West.

his armor of militant goodness, the frontier's savagery strikes in vain.

The effective word here is "militant." Wild is firm and just and even helpful. But he will not be imposed upon, not one fraction of an inch.

The border tough who spits his chew on Wild's boot is directed to pick up the chew and put it back in his mouth. And does so, much cowed.

The saloon bully is punched down promptly, or shot, or crisply backed off.

The schemer with his mouthful of lies is immediately called to account and forced to retract his words in public.

There is no hesitation, no counting of odds. The hero, supremely confident, issues his challenge at once. He will not be cowed.

These simple personal glories were sensibly dimmed in 1927, with the coming of the *Wild West Weekly* pulp magazine. In the pulp, he is identified as Billy West, a brawny young man. Or perhaps Billy West is Wild's son. It is hard to tell, but Billy lacks the flamboyance, the more-than-human glitter of that great original.

It is the difference between two literary forms. The Young Wild West dime novels bound from one action to the next, uttering great cries. The *Wild West Weekly* pulp magazine stories pursue a milder course. These are filled with bursts of detail, some very realistic. But although the hero performs deeds of valor, they lack the joyous craziness of the dime novel.

Billy West is the "courageous young owner of the Circle J Ranch." Fond of adventure, experienced in mining and in the cattle business, he is an expert rider, a brilliant shot, and an exceptional wrestler. He has dark eyes and hair and has an air of quiet authority "which proclaimed him the leader." He rides a magnificent chestnut stallion named Danger.

Billy's two intimate companions are Joe Scott and Buck Foster. Joe, a tanned young cattleman (cowboy is meant) with blue eyes and red-brown hair, is a cheerfully reckless type who has to be admonished to keep him from throwing his life away. Buck is older. Once a government scout, he is also an ex-miner and a full-time right-hand man at Billy's ranch. He is iron-gray and has long, drooping mustaches, plus a hand-gun that is fast and accurate.

So the trio image rides on, new faces replacing old. But the figures are familiar and the relationships have not changed.

Long before Billy West's 1927 adventures, the dime novels had established the operating cattle ranch as the base from which the bright young hero sallied forth against the forces of ill. The *Young Rough Riders Weekly*, 1904-1907, was generally focused around the Moon Valley Ranch in South Dakota. Ted Strong, whose series it was, appeared as The King of the Wild West—causing the uninformed to wonder if he were another Buffalo Bill or Young Wild West or what.

The series does contain a little Cody, a great huge dose of YWW, and an equally large charge of boys' book. Almost a lethal dose.

Ted Strong, a brawny young man, formerly a sergeant in the Teddy Roosevelt's Rough Riders, has inherited a cattle ranch in the Black Hills of South Dakota. He is a top-notch rider, roper, shooter, general athlete, capable of the usual astounding physical feats. His dark hair is worn short, and he customarily wears the Rough Riders uniform of khaki, boots, large-brimmed hat and neckerchief.

He is accompanied through the series by nine young boys, loosely joined in a semi-military outfit called the Young Rough Riders. Like characters in many boys' books, each is a single personal trait associated with a name. Thus Thaddeus Perkins (Beanpole) is slim, thin and thinks he's sick. Carl Schwartz loves to eat. Ben Tremont is gigantic but indolent and good natured. All have a distinguishing tag; all play noticeable, if not large, roles in the action. They make up a competent strike force under Ted's leadership and that of his chief lieutenant, Bud Morgan.

Morgan is older (as you may have surmised) and wears his yellow hair long. Tough, reliable, he is Ted's closest pard and, when not shooting rustlers from their horses or punching them in the head, entertains with tall tales of the Pecos.

In issue No. 74, the action is transferred to the Moon Valley Ranch in the Dakotas, where Ted receives a lifelong grazing lease. For the balance of the series (to issue No. 175), Moon Valley is the base for the stories, although there are numerous trips and adventures away.[2]

In issue No. 102, Stella Fosdick appears. Stella is the series' answer to Arietta of the *Wild West Weekly*. Like Arietta, she is a compelling character who energizes the series by pure charm.

She is a little, dainty girl, with blond hair flowing over her shoulders. She wears a white Stetson, a little jacket, red skirt, gun and leggings. She is the best shot of any girl in the country. Texas-born, an orphan, she goes everywhere with the Young Rough Riders—whether they wish for her company or not. To preserve appearances, she hauls along her aunt, Mrs. Graham, who must have grown terribly tired of jouncing through the wilderness, hot on the trail of crisis.

The stories involve a little bit of everything: rustlers, crooked lawyers, Indians good and bad, round-ups, baseball games, even a pair of adventures with Nick Carter. Ted takes some amazing punishment. In one story he is hypnotized into a state of suspended animation and almost dies. No sooner is he freed from the trance and given something to eat than he's off on the hard trail again, saving the girl from Indians, crushing complicated schemes right and left, solving the mystery of the secret door in the butte, and foiling the murderous dwarf. And that's only one story. It was wonderfully crazy fun.

As Ted Strong attended, rather casually, to his business of raising cattle for profit, another major branch of the dime novels pinched out. It happened in 1903, when *Jesse James Stories* ended, terminating appearances which had begun about 1881. The James Boys, Jesse or Frank or both together, appeared under many titles: *Five Cent Wide Awake Library, Old Cap Collier Library, Log Cabin Library, New York Detective Library, James Boys Weekly*, and others. The stories were primarily published by the houses of Tousey and Street & Smith, and were written by an extraordinary number of authors.[3]

The diversity of publishers, titles and authors indicates that consistency is not a major feature of the James Boys' saga. It is difficult to know where you stand with them, for the outlaws are apt to be high-minded gentlemen in one paragraph and sneering, murdering fiends in the next:

"Curse them! A million curses on their heads!" bellowed the terrible bandit. "I'll beat them yet! They'll never get Jesse James by their cursed devil tricks."

or:

Jesse started forward in his chair, a dull glow of color showing beneath his tan. For a moment it seemed as if he would hide himself from the searching gaze of the child. "... I'm afraid I am a very bad man. So bad that I am ashamed to have a sweet, innocent little child like you seen talking with me."

or:

"I'm going to leave a crimson trail across the state of old Missouri that they will talk about after I'm dead."

It is all melodrama. Blood pouring from wounds. Foaming horses. Frenzied men screaming in the night. Pistol smoke. Pursuit. The detective sprawls, shot dead. The traitor falls limp, shot dead. The Nightrider slumps, shot dead. Volleys of gun fire slam the posse. The seamed old face of mother James defying the pursuers. Bags of loot. Crammed in fresh cartridges. Trapped, he was trapped. Frank's cold cruel nature. You go north with the Youngers and we'll meet at.... Black night dense as pitch among the graves.

Backwoods Missouri, Mississippi swamps. Little towns in border states. Traitors weave plots and die in the outraged thunder of the single-six. Hunted they fled through the night. "There's a bullet in my arm but I'm dead game." A torrent of blood gushed forth. Screaming he slumped.... Still another volley emptied more saddles.... Horses exhausted, they struggled on. The detective on your trail is named....

"Curse you," snarled Jesse James, his bronzed handsome face livid with rage. "I shall have my revenge."

"Jesse James don't rob from the poor. He sees justice done."

Pick the issue and take your choice. He was a Robin Hood,

Jesse James Stories, August 9, 1902 #66. Jesse was either a saint or a devil. No one seemed sure, including the writers of his violent exploits.

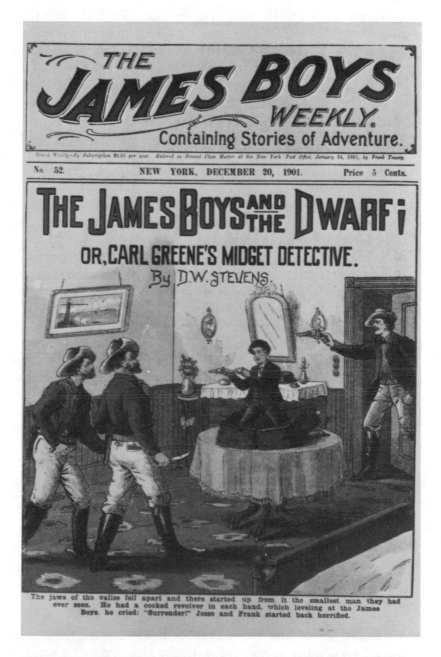

The James Boys Weekly, December 20, 1901, #52. The romantic criminal hero may be surprised by the detectives hounding him, but they will not down him for long.

a depraved killer. He honored women and little children, slaughtered detectives and sheriffs and posses and such. He was astute, noble, base, conniving, malevolent, shrewd. He was a gentleman of compassion and nobility, hounded by detectives into life beyond the law. He was a fiend, all blackened and slobbered with the pitch of Hell.

Under all this tra-la shows, in dim gray outline, the figure of reality—that tough backwoodsman, formerly of Quantrill's Raiders, who applied techniques of Civil War guerilla fighting to the problems of looting banks and railroad trains, and wherever else the cash was stacked. It is recorded that Jesse James was capable of rude generosities. He was also capable of shooting an unarmed, unoffending bank clerk through the head for no observable reason.[4]

That is part of history. And the history that is known is about as ragged and uneven and uncritical as are the events of any known life. But history does not make great heroes or great fiends. That is the consequence of the myth-making process.

The dime novels picked up Frank and Jesse James while the outlaws still bounded about uncaught. They made good copy and sold issues. The fiction garbed them—usually—in the fine old clothing of the romantic rebel, the man who strikes against the constraints of society, his emotions mountain peaks, purple and immense.

If Jesse is sometimes a gun-bearing Robin Hood, sometimes a rustic Ghengis Khan, he is always cast as the romantic rebel—although romance is a pallid way to describe the violence filling the dime novel pages. He is pursued. He is trapped. He escapes in a blaze of guns. He defies society. He will not be chained by stifling rules....

Well, it's all a part of the Romantic Rebel tradition. And if you aren't certain whether to admire or hate Jesse, just lean back and let the wild action roll.[5]

5–

If the reader has ambiguous emotions toward the James Boys, he has no problem at all with Frank Merriwell. From the beginning, Frank stood for stonewall excellence. He neither drank nor smoked nor looked with lust. He was in constant training, remaining at the peak of athletic condition through the years.

He began as a manly young man in knee pants and cap, defying a bully in the first nine lines of his existence. He ended as a superlative young man whose name entered the language and whose feats still echo through the mythology of sports.

The Merriwell adventures, written by William G(ilbert) Patten, began in the 1896 *Tip Top Weekly*. They continued through the 968 issues before the dime novel (ultimately called the *New Tip Top Weekly*) changed into a pulp magazine. That transformation occurred in 1915, with the publication of the *Tip Top Semi-Monthly* (eight issues only) which was followed by the *Wide Awake Magazine*.

Over the next several years, both Frank and Dick were essentially replaced by the newcomer, Frank Merriwell, Junior (although rarely identified as Junior). His appearances can be found in *Sports Story Magazine* (1927-1928), *Fame and Fortune Magazine* (1928-1929), and *Top Notch* (1929-1930.)[6]

More than a thousand Merriwell stories were written and the bulk of these were reprinted in fat little paperbacked books. The sheer volume of the fiction argues that Frank achieved a popularity to which Jesse James only aspired. It does not seem that action alone kept the Merriwell series in print. Perhaps it was the ease with which readers could identify with Frank. Or perhaps it was because no other dime-novel character was as dedicated to decency and fair play as Frank Merriwell was. In spite of these prissy qualities, he was a thoroughly nice person.

His face was frank, open and winning, and a merry light usually dwelt in his eyes.

The development of his chest and arms was phenomenal. Even more markedly developed was his sense of moral cleanliness. You may note that he walked these high plains for hard, pragmatic reasons. If you did not drink or smoke, and kept yourself in fine physical shape, you stood every chance of excelling in sports and, by inference, in life. In the Merriwell stories:

There is less emphasis on material success... and much on leadership by example, playing the game and doing the right thing.[7]

There is more to the Merriwell story than an endless succession of ball games. To summarize his career briefly, we meet him first at Fardale, a fine prep school and military academy. After numerous adventures there, he goes on to Yale, where he excels in everything he touches. He has the gift of success. During his Junior year, his guardian loses Frank's inheritance, forcing him to leave college. Going to work for a railroad (and excelling in that, too), he eventually recoups his fortunes. Then he returns to Yale for a glorious finish. Now begins a long series of adventures that are set in all corners of the world. At one time or another, he was:

> ambushed in Peru
> tied to a log in a sawmill which the great big saw....
> pushed off a cliff
> swept into the sea by gigantic waves
> buried to the neck in Patagonia
> lowered into quicksand up to the neck
> buried by an avalanche
> seized by Mexican bandits
> left to die in a flaming barn
> attacked by a tiger in India
> hurled from the battlement of a castle
> trapped in a ring of wolves
> arrested twenty-five times, although always vindicated
> attacked by a mad dog, which he fought off with a pocket
knife

It was a strenuous life rarely dull. In surviving so many perils, he developed a number of useful skills. He became an accomplished ventriloquist and hypnotizer. He was familiar with cattle raising and mining, could operate a locomotive and repair automobiles. He spoke Spanish fluently. A self-made millionaire, he formed the Merriwell Company with his brother, Dick, to handle their Western mining interests and, possibly, also give them time to operate their ranch.

Dick, an expert electrical engineer, was not quite the flaming leader that Frank was. Still he enjoyed most of the

Merriwell attainments and served as lead series hero whenever Frank was out of the country or otherwise occupied.

Eventually Frank married his incredibly patient sweetheart, Inza Burrage. Their son, Frank Merriwell Junior, continued his father's extraordinary exploits on the sports field. Their daughter got herself into trouble in a novel, *Mister Frank Merriwell,* written in 1941.[8]

Foreign adventures to one side, Frank is chiefly remembered as the athlete incomparable. His name is legend for his feats on the team—any team—at Yale. It was his bat that hammered out the winning run in the final inning of play. His kick that settled the football game.

And because of his abilities, how many times was he kidnapped by the unscrupulous to keep him out of the big game? How many times did he escape, appearing at the last moment to lead the team to victory before an hysterical crowd?

His dedication is magnificent. But he is not one to play to the limelight. While he is a brilliant star, the team is first in his mind; he performs for Yale, for the team, not for personal glory.

"If I knew my worst enemy would make a valuable man for the team I'd put aside personal feelings and recommend him. On the other hand, I don't propose to let an enemy stab me behind my back or cut me down before my face if I can help it."[9]

That is the same admirable tough-mindedness we have seen in Young Wild West. Do your best—be decent—but let no man impose on you.

The Merriwell influence was extremely powerful and would burn through generations of sports pulps, the immediate and natural heirs of his tradition. The moral tone, the emphasis on peak physical condition and the studied avoidance of vice (variously defined) would surface in later years in all sorts of unlikely places, the 1933 *Doc Savage* magazine being one of the more prominent.

While Merriwell focused such traits, they were by no means unique to him. Such larger-than-life figures as Young Sleuth and Nick Carter showed similar characteristics, although they worked in a different world and to different goals. Like the boy heroes of Horatio Alger, they reflected the

Tip Top Weekly, Nov. 3, 1906, #551. Brothers Frank and Dick Merriwell provided the youth of America with clean-cut heroes on and off the field of play.

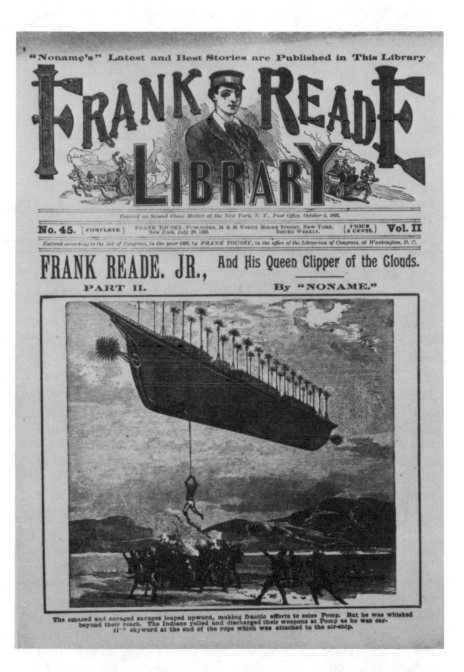

"Noname's" Latest and Best Stories are Published in This Library

FRANK READE LIBRARY

Entered as Second Class Matter at the New York, N. Y., Post Office, October 5, 1892.

No. 45. {COMPLETE}   FRANK TOUSEY, PUBLISHER, 34 & 36 NORTH MOORE STREET, NEW YORK.   {PRICE 5 CENTS.}   Vol. II
New York, July 29, 1893.   ISSUED WEEKLY.

Entered according to the Act of Congress, in the year 1893, by FRANK TOUSEY, in the office of the Librarian of Congress, at Washington, D. C.

FRANK READE. JR., And His Queen Clipper of the Clouds.

PART II.   By "NONAME."

The amazed and enraged savages leaped upward, making frantic efforts to seize Pomp. But he was whisked beyond their reach. The Indians yelled and discharged their weapons at Pomp as he was carried skyward at the end of the rope which was attached to the air-ship.

Frank Reade Library, July 29, 1893, #45. Astounding inventions, scaled up from the technology of the time, and gifted boys adventuring for joy and gold, were staples of this dime novel series.

spirit of the times. The moulds differed; the metal was fundamentally the same.

6–

As yet there were no rocket ships or interstellar travel. No blasters, matter transmitters, or brave men in pearl-gray suits. Man's tracks did not disturb Mars nor did his ionized exhaust trouble Sirus. Indeed the Time Traveler had not yet appeared, like condensing vapor, within his astonishing workshop.

It was a quiet scene, in these days before the science fantasy story. But even these remote days were touched by strangeness. Stand here, for instance, on this undulating prairie, drenched in sunlight. Around you the Indians freeze rigid and their eyes glint with terror.

For they watch the approach of a monster man.

He is fifteen feet tall and glitters in the sun. From his hat vents a cloud of smoke. From his nose, a white jet spurts, brazenly bellowing. Behind him, jounces a four-wheeled wagon and in it sits a small horrible someone guiding the giant with reins.

The terror approaches, legs rising and falling. He utters terrible sounds. With that the Indians leave, their dignity impaired by haste.

So, in 1865, the giant Steam Man of the Prairies unsettled the Indians and enthralled readers of *Irwin's American Novels*. What the Indians had seen was a choice example of applied technology—a wood-fired steam engine, shaped like a man, with steam pistons thrusting legs that stomped on and on to ever more adventures.

Over succeeding years, other stories would describe such related marvels as a steam horse and a steam team. Later steam would give way to electricity, and so the world would wonder at the electric boat, electric tricycle, electric man and electric horse. All these appeared in the *Frank Reade Library*, written under the house name of "Noname."[10]

One whole branch of present science fiction is given over to the wonderful device. As long ago as the dime novels, that subject received a great deal of attention. It ran straight through the years into the Hugo Gernsback publications and, from there, spread out through pulp magazine science fiction and adventure to the single character pulps.

Along the way, that development cross-fed into French and English science fiction and, incidentally, into the adventure romance popularized by H. Rider Haggard. Behind the apparently single form of an *Argosy All-Story* fantasy serial lies an interesting complex of influences and precursor elements, thoroughly internationalized, and cross-linked as complexly as a genetic helix.[11]

For our purposes, the beginning of the science fiction device story was in the science and adventure fiction published by the story papers and dime novels. The bulk of this material seems to have been directed toward boys—or, we may suspect, adults reading at their most comfortable educational level. The stories directly reflect the intense interest in the mechanism, the wonderful gadget, that has preoccupied so many Americans.

These adventure stories are characterized by vigorous movement to and fro. The action is episodic, the narrative climaxing in terrific peril at least once a chapter.

The stories are placed in whatever area of the world that was currently gripping readers' imaginations. In the middle 1800s, that was the frontier. At the end of the century, it was the Poles, Tibet, Russia. The emphasis is on the science-fiction gadget as a means of advanced transportation. The Steam Man merely reflected the national fascination with steam boats and locomotives. Within ten years, the submarine and the airship would thrust to the fore. These were to the 1870s as the spaceship was to the 1940s—a means for an extended ride into the unknown, to the Poles, to the bottom of the sea, to lost lands and forgotten civilizations.

The devices described are the mechanisms of the time, their performance considerably improved and their size hugely scaled up. Thus the balloons of the Civil War are imaginatively expanded to immense, cigar-shaped airships powered by wonderful electrical engines or gases of equally wonderful lifting power. The submarines—another Civil War innovation—are transformed from the death traps of reality to vast vessels, akin to submerged railroad cars or ships.

These machines that swim and fly so placidly about the

world are almost always the invention of a bright young genius. They may still be teen-age boys, but they are so mechanically creative that they dazzle their older companions. Their skills, augmented to noble heights, derive from the trades of the period; they are electricians, machinists, engineers. Or they are, even more broadly, inventors—a splendid designation that permits expertise in any field, with a minimum of hampering detail.

For these young minds pour devices to travel someplace quickly. And, once there, to explore, beat off the villains, and get extremely rich.

Thus Frank Reade Jr. uses his Electric Air Canoe to search for the Valley of Diamonds. Uses his Electric Van to hunt wild animals in the jungles of India, or to fly for six weeks over the Andes.

Extraordinary diving suits are donned to search for treasure, 12,500 feet under the sea.

Gigantic airships sweep the clouds; these flying machines are designed as clipper ships without masts, remarkably buoyed up.

Electric and steam vehicles snort across every terrain.

Five years after the Steam Man, in 1870, Jules Verne published *20,000 Leagues Under the Sea*. He followed that success with a series of novels about trips around the Moon, attempts to tilt the Earth's axis, and an 80-day trip around the world. At that time, all these qualified as science fiction. Verne broke new ground, although he was certainly not the creator of this new literary field. The dime novels, as in much else, were there ahead of him.

The dime novels were also contemporary with him. No sooner had Captain Nemo and his submarine caught the public eye than the dime novels and story papers went mad for trips into the sea, under the sea, across the bottom of the sea. Later, when efforts began to reach the Poles, crowds of dime novel heroes got there first. So transient is fame that their names are now forgotten. But they reached the Poles as they flew non-stop across the oceans as they penetrated the frontiers, as they did so many splendid things with their splendid shining mechnisms.

One particular thing they did was to discover lost

civilizations.

The lost civilization has long been a literary device used to pierce the present with thorns of scorn or to hold up a vision of future excellence against our shabby now. During the middle and late 1800s in England, a very large number of very obscure books was published recounting wonderful worlds or cities or such that ought to have been. The emphasis was usually satirical, when it was not political.

It remained for H. Rider Haggard, in 1885, to combine such disparate threads as Plato's lost Atlantis, the Troy excavations and a fresh interest in the lives of defunct civilizations. Haggard is the first master of the romantic journey to lost civilizations. The world read, seized its pen and began creating lost worlds of its own. For the next seventy-five years, others elaborated on Haggard's contribution. But his was the first coherent statement of this theme in language you could read without falling asleep.

Haggard wrote exceptionally well, much of the time. His better stories glitter with observed detail, selected with an artist's precision. His characters are pricky personalities, complex, sensitive and sharply aware of the shifting dynamics in personal relationships. Even his stock characters had blood in them and interesting twists of mind that focused them crisply among the racing paragraphs. Haggard's themes and situations have since been worked by thousands of dime novelists, boys' book writers and pulp hacks, each unique in his own way, and many of them interesting. But all of them reflect Haggard's original splendor.

What this means specifically to the dime novels is that Frank Reade Jr., and all those traveling others, leaped into their Steam Clouds and Electric Propellers, and went whizzing off to peril among the lost race of Umamnguhama. At the turn of the century, it was the fashion to do so. Even Nick Carter got into it, and Nick was as level-headed an urban type as ever got on paper.

In the course of a far-afield investigation, Nick finds a lost city, over Mt. Everest way. The city is sited in a glorious valley surrounded by impassible heights.... You know the location. In the city lives a blond-haired, blond-skinned race, with black eyes and narrow habits of mind. They are willfully mute and refuse to allow anyone to leave their city.

These people are masters of science—vibration science. By applying the Law of Vibrations, they can tune in your personal frequency and so you die. They communicate with one another by specific vibrations. The entire city, in fact, is tuned to a master tone and vibrates wildly when that tone is sounded.

Not only are these people vibration kings, but they play around on the fringes of magic. It's described as advanced science, which is ridiculous. They draw electricity from the air and they also swoop about in aircraft constructed of filmy material, transparent as thin fog. Magic.

It's interesting that this story compresses into 20,000 words a lost race adventure, aviation, mystery, pseudo science, electricity and a rudimentary love interest. It's hard to see what else could have been squeezed in.

Well, the adventure is dated 1907 and Nick survived it wonderfully. Just as he survived an earlier experience (1906) with a tribe of Indians who lived in a cave of solid gold. Or as he survived a chilling experience with a race of Amazons.... But we digress.

Whatever form it takes, the romantic adventure is a bold excursion into fantasy. It begins in the hard reality of the known and moves through multiple dangers down the long trail. At some point along that trail, the transition is made to fantasy. And suddenly there rise up strange walls gripped by jungle, home of lost races, barbaric, sinister or sophisticated. Out there somewhere.

It is the frontier story in another form. More polished, perhaps, informed by archeology and the study of comparative religions. But the frontier still. By the time Haggard had published *King Solomon's Mines* and *She*, the American Far West was virtually closed. Greenland and Persia gave up their secrets. The Poles were known. The examined world stood on every side. It was a relief, then, to learn that off somewhere, remote and secret, amazing peoples still pursued their ancient habits amid magic and the sound of forgotten language.

They waited for you at the end of bitter traveling. You came to them on foot. You flew to them in airships or balloons. You chartered sailing vessels to Zanzibar and trekked inland, or you rode in machines that gnawed down into the earth. By time machine or space warp, rocket ships or thought transference, you left your familiar present and traveled earnestly until, under the Green Star, in Perelandra, in Zamora or Opar, you found whatever you sought.

Whether you wanted it or not.

7-

From the Gay Nineties to the Jazz Age is not much of a leap across time, a trifle of thirty years. But the interval roared with change and wrenched at souls. For many it was a grim and demoralizing time, when all values crumbled in the blast of event. What began in the waltz rhythms of The Good Old Summertime transformed, with the new century's irritating inability to remain stable, into the syncopating prancing of *Fidgety Feet*. It was science that did it, and new inventions, and those French ideas the boys brought back from the war. It was the income tax and votes for women. It was Teddie Roosevelt's fault. It was a consequence of big trusts, the war, the fault of ragtime, the fault of jazz, the dilution of traditional values, booze, the horseless carriage and union agitators. It was the Twentieth Century, the lovely deadly Twentieth Century spreading out its alluring nets.

From the Gay Nineties to the Jazz Age, the Nick Carter stories extend, an unlikely enough bridge, built in weekly increments. For about thirty years, the series reflected the social and historical boiling around it. It is all there—the trends of the times, follies, fashions, slang, beliefs and enthusiasms. They all got into the Nick Carter series. It was endlessly accommodating and endlessly fluid. And the series survived, where equally notable series, fixed tightly in their own success, petrified and died.

By his extended survival, Nick Carter exerted influence on the stories of coming generations beyond what could have been guessed. Nick stands as the first modern American detective. His name endures, if little else. He is of more than routine interest and so we will turn to Nick Carter and his world—the first white fire of the coming new fiction.

Chapter III—Nick

1–

The *Nick Carter Weekly* No. 234, June 22, 1901, is a flat, squarish 8 1/2 x 10 3/4-inch- pamphlet of 32 pages. The unillustrated text is double column on brown paper smelling of attics.

No. 234 is titled "Nick Carter's Night Off" and this is followed by the conventional, slangy, second title: "or, Hot Work With A Volunteer Assistant." The price was Five Cents.

The masthead, a scarlet strip two inches deep, extends across the top of the cover. The words "Nick Carter Weekly" appear in yellow on the scarlet. To the left of the title, a 1 3/4-inch-diameter circle encloses a profile of Nick, himself, brows knit, jaw solid.

Below the masthead is a 7-½-inch square colored illustration upon which the titles are superimposed. The illustration depicts a moment of action: Nick, Chick and Patsy (our lead detective and his two aides), all gripping pistols, race toward three men forcing a woman into a horse-drawn cab. Foliage at the rear of the action half conceals the walls of a huge brick structure that dominates the background, darkly menacing.

This picture is a doorway to a world long lost. The beset lady wears a waterfall of skirts and her head is concealed in an aggressively flowered bonnet. Her attackers wear derbies or slouch hats. The cab driver sports a top hat. All men— detectives and criminals alike—wear suit coats of longish cut.

The scene of action—a secluded street corner late at night—is illuminated by a blazing gas light on a tall standard mounted at the edge of a broad concrete sidewalk. Toward this spot the detectives race, crossing over the double trolley tracks in the center of the street. These tracks straddle a sewer service grating which contains sixteen squares of purplish glass set in a metal frame.

The wealth of exact detail is typical of the dime novels. No matter how spurious the adventure, or how faked the location of the story, it is all embellished with homey details, exactly observed, that strike your heart.

Finger through the pages. Up flash crisp images from that distant world. Tall grass bends along a railroad track. The barroom's wooden table has been hacked by knives. An automobile jolts splashing along a rural road. A telegraph messenger extends his yellow envelope. Tarry ropes coil on a freighter's deck. Empty barrels heap beside a stable—and flies buzz in the sluggish heat, and wisps of yellow straw litter the brown dirt outside.

These casual descriptions catch the look and feel of the times and lend the story singular excitement for modern eyes.

Across the covers and through the streets parades the technology of the period, incessantly at change. Horses and horse-drawn vehicles give way to electric trolley cars. Improbably shaped automobiles don tops and mass and thicken. Balloons yield to airplanes, and bold penetrations of the sky are pictured, hundreds of feet above the ground.

Moving pictures appear and camera crews crank in New York City streets, filming melodrama within the melodrama. Typewriters (the machine) come into use, and a new profession of Typewriter (the typist) is created. The first telephones are installed and the voice of Central is heard and stories turn on how telephone wires are strung, how induction may accidentally tap unshielded lines, how criminals tap private calls, how calls are traced, how the Exchange handles its daily business....

Here rage automobile chases, 40-50-60 mph through tiny towns closed down by night and along grass-choked rural roads. Here stand department stores, proud with walnut counters and glass-faced shelves, and the change whizzing through pneumatic tubing between the lordly clerk and the business office on the mezzanine.

Enter a grand New York City hotel, all crystal and polished wood. Or step into a 1909 tenement, a shambles of poverty, rats and a basement of slobbering black mud where the river has seeped in. Or move invisible through a 1904 home of wealth, feeling slight suffocation at the Victorian opulence.

All of it presented in circumstantial detail, vignettes of the vanished world, sharp, fresh, once more alive.

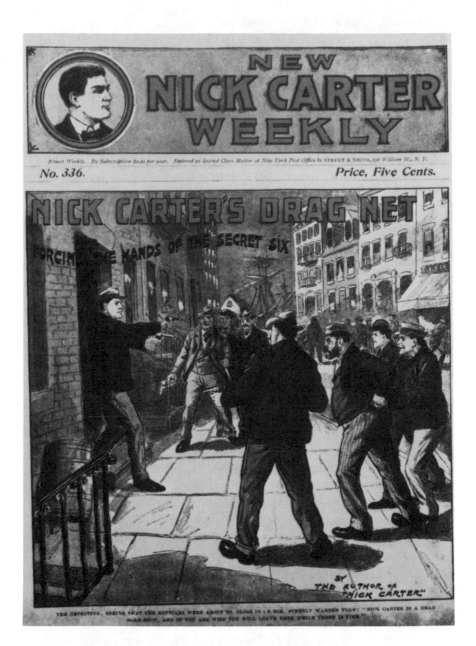

New Nick Carter Weekly, June 6, 1903, #336. Trained from boyhood to be the perfect detective, Nick Carter found peril on every block of the city.

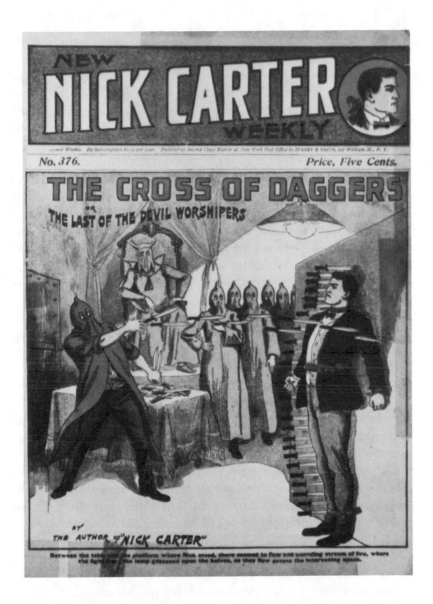

New Nick Carter Weekly, March 12, 1904, #376. Hooded friends have Nick at a temporary disadvantage. It is, however, nothing really serious.

2-

Nick Carter, that excellent man, was not the first of the dime-novel detectives. Nor did his name shine as whitely then as now. In the late 1880s, he was one of many detectives, each jostling for public attention, each disguised to the ultimate inch.

Time has had its way with these. Of them all, only Nick Carter became a byword. Today, almost everybody knows that Nick Carter was a superlative detective—just as almost no one has read his adventures. His name has gone into the language, his fiction into thin air.

When Nick first set up practice in 1886, the detective and mystery story had silently established itself in hard-bound novel and magazine short story, in dime novels, story papers and various bulky memoirs to which the 1800s were unreasonably addicted. Already some key titles had been published—not many compared to the torrent that developed during the Twenties, but enough to give form and direction to the infant genre.

Immature forms of the story of detection can be traced back to antiquity. In her "Introduction" to the *Omnibus of Crime* Dorothy L. Sayers cites examples from *The Apocryphal Scriptures* in which reasoning from observed facts illuminates a concealed situation. In *The Queen's Quorum*, Ellery Queen follows much of Miss Sayers' lead through the prehistory of the mystery story. Both commentators trace the evolution of the mystery story through European folk tales to modern times, and, having bared the deep permanent roots, then diverge happily.

There is a touch of scholar's play in these examinations. It is possible to continue indefinitely singling out literary fragments as the precursors of forms to come. It is an interesting and usually harmless occupation which leaves the boys and girls little time to get into trouble or into television. Primarily it establishes that crime is, was and shall be a basic fictional theme universally enjoyed and written about.

It isn't necesary for us to root out the mystery story's

humble origins. It is enough to point out that the modern form of mystery fiction began coalescing in the early 1800s. By then sufficient public interest had formed to make books on the subject popular. E.F. Bleiler has traced some of these early volumes in his "Introduction" to *Richmond: Scenes in the Life of a Bow Street Runner* (1827).[1] This three-volume work of fiction was presented as fact—one of the more successful literary techniques of the period. Through the 1800s formal law enforcement agencies continued to develop, and, as they did so, an articulate assortment of detectives and police dignitaries showered out their memoirs. In these, tiny scraps of fact floated in a dense syrup of fiction—as the 1828-1829 *Memoires* of Vidocq, the convict who became head of the French Surete; as the 1852 *The Recollections of a Policeman* by "Waters" (William Russel); or as the numerous books by Alan Pinkerton, head of the Pinkerton National Detective Agency, beginning with *The Expressman and the Detective* (1874).

The gaudy sensationalism of Pinkerton's accounts, a pound of tinsel on an half-ounce tree, hit precisely the tone that rang through the dime novels. Movement, action, raging emotion against a quasi-realistic backdrop. Then, too, the Pinkertons were not adverse to publicity and decades of newspaper headlines burnt into the public consciousness that detectives were out there, chasing about, gripped by bright adventure. The dime novels would not long ignore such promising material, and they did not.

The mystery story had, by then, entered formal fiction. In April 1841, Edgar Allan Poe published "The Murders in the Rue Morgue," in *Graham's Magazine,* creating the modern detective short story, with C. Auguste Dupin flashing brightly against the dullness of his friend, the narrator. Soon after that, the formal detective/mystery novel appeared.

Until all early dime novels have been reviewed, it is pure guess as to when the first true detective novel was published. Charles Burdett's *The Gambler* has been mentioned for this honor. So has Wilkie Collins' *The Woman in White* (1860) and *The Moonstone* (1868), the latter novel introducing the police sergeant Cuff. During the period Emile Gaboriau published *L'Affair Lerouge* (1866), featuring Monsieur Lecoq, member of the French police, whose ability at disguise contributed still another convention to the dime novels.

At this point, you can hear the mills of the gods begin grinding.

In 1872 the *New York Fireside Companion*, a story paper, published the first Old Sleuth story. Six years later, in 1878, Anna Katharine Green's *The Leavenworth Case* became immensely popular; she was the first of a now familiar phenomenon, a best-selling woman mystery novelist with dozens of titles to her credit.

The Jesse James dime novels began in 1881, followed by the 1882 *The Golden Argosy*, then a boys' story paper. The first periodical to feature regular detective stories was the *Old Cap Collier Library*. Beginning in 1883 the *Library* was a long series of dime novels, some featuring Cap Collier, a lot more purporting to have been written by him, the whole presenting a fantastic collection of detectives, astute and hyperactive. Only a few months later the *New York Detective Library* appeared.

Old King Brady was introduced in 1885 and became extremely popular. Nick Carter's initial appearance was in 1886, and, the following year, the first Sherlock Holmes story was published in *Beeton's Christmas Annual*.

Holmes decisively imprinted great chunks of subsequent mystery fiction. Immediate spin-offs were Sexton Blake in 1893 (a direct copy of Holmes published in the English equivalent of the dime novels), and, on a slightly more lofty plane, Martin Hewitt, who appeared in *The Strand* in the mid-1890s.

Nick Carter, then, was one wave in a foaming sea. Influential as he became he was a child of his times, shaped by many invisible pressures, among them those exerted by Vidocq, Pinkerton and those many competing characters in the dime novels.

3–

The Nick Carter series began, as so many did, in a story paper—*Street & Smith's New York Weekly*, September 18, 1886. Titled "The Old Detective's Pupil; or, The Mysterious Crime of Madison Square," it was the first part of a serial which continued through December 11, 1886. The author was identified only as "The Author of 'The American Marquis; or, A

Detective for Vengeance'."

That helped little, for that author, Milton Quarterly, was a pseudonym, behind which stood John Russell Coryell, cousin of Street & Smith president Ormand G. Smith.

Coryell had lived a life of dime novel romance. He had served as Vice Consul in Shanghai when twenty years old, adventured around Manchuria, worked as a newspaperman in Santa Barbara, California, and finally removed to New York City. There he supported his family by writing children's stories, with only moderate success. His luck turned on the day that he visited Cousin Ormond Smith and submitted a detective serial that drew a strong audience response.

Ormond Smith: Do you think you can do the trick twice?
Coryell: Twice! I can do it every time I try it.[2]

Or so the conversation is reported. Two additional Nick Carter serials in the *New York Weekly* followed "The Old Detective's Pupil." These were "A Wall Street Haul; or, A Bold Stroke for a Fortune" (March 12-June 18, 1887); and "Fighting Against Millions; or The Detectives in the Jewel Caves of Kurm" (September 29, 1888-January 19, 1889). With that, Coryell left Nick Carter and soon took up writing serials under the byline of Bertha M. Clay, a highly popular authoress who had died and left thousands of readers famished for romantic fiction.

Response to the Nick Carter serials had been sufficiently strong to keep the character alive in Ormond Smith's mind. In 1891 he had lunch with George Smith (of Street & Smith) and Frederic Van Rensselaer Dey, who had contributed fiction to the *New York Weekly*. Dey was asked:

if he could write a weekly series of stories (each about 33,000 words long) about one character. Dey said he could and was asked to prove it by writing the first ten stories in ten weeks.... Within three weeks he had written the first four stories.

At this point he was told that the length would be 20,000 words and not 33,000, so he cut the first ones and wrote an additional six. He beat his deadline of ten weeks by about three. All were written in longhand with a short-handled stub gold pen.[3]

Those stories became the initial issues of the *Nick Carter Library*, a 282 publication series that ended December 1896. In addition, Dey provided eight serials for the *New York Weekly* that ran during 1892 and 1893, and may have contributed to the dozens of Nick Carter short stories that appeared in the *Weekly* over the next several years. By this time, the pressure of work was so intense that Dey was sub-contracting the stories to other writers, including certain of the weekly novelettes in the *Library*.

The final issue of the *Library* was dated December 26, 1896. On January 2, 1897, the first issue of the *New Nick Carter Library* appeared. The title underwent various changes becoming the *New Nick Carter Weekly*, then the *Nick Carter Weekly* (Nos. 43 through 320), then back to the *New Nick Carter Weekly* (Nos. 321 through 819). With the September 12, 1912, issue, the publication changed its name for the last time to *Nick Carter Stories*. This continued through issue 160, dated October 2, 1915. At that point the dime novel shivered mightily and converted itself to the *Detective Story Magazine* (Nick Carter, Editor), under which name it swept grandly down the generations.[4]

Nick, himself, vanished from *Detective Story* with the August 1918 issue, reappearing, much later, in a scattering of stories published during 1924-1927. Thereafter, silence fell, until his revival as the lead figure of the 1933-1936 *Nick Carter Magazine* pulp.

It is an extraordinarily long series. An extraordinary number of writers contributed to it, with the predictable result that discrepancies litter the pages.

Still, taken from one end to the other, you get a fairly coherent biography of Nick Carter, Detective. Necessarily, you must ignore a substantial number of reprinted adventures inserted into the series, which raise hob with its time sequence; and you must glide over an equally substantial number of Old Cap Colliers and Sexton Blake stories that were rewritten as Nick Carters and slipped into the mainstream.

Even when these are set aside, an enormous mass of material remains. Through it moves a complex and changing cast of friends and criminals. Nick's assistants mature. Wives appear. Nick's professional reputation grows. He accepts

Presidential assignments. His tangible assets increase, until he is a self-made millionaire. Around him, America moves from gas light to electric light, from horses to automobiles, from rural to urban. The pages quiver with social change.

An official portrait of Nick appears in an insert to the *New Nick Carter Weekly*, No. 710 (August 6, 1910). The picture, deeply influenced by Charles Dana Gibson's drawing style, is of a clean-cut man, 30-ish, with a firm jaw, long straight nose, strongly delineated features. On earlier dime novel covers, the drawing emphasized his solid jaw and eyes that could be hard enough to bore through steel plates.

On these covers, Nick wears a distinctive blue-gray suit, white vest, stiff collar and bow tie. Usually he also wears a white hat with a rather wide brim.

We are told that he looked exactly like Sandow, the celebrated strong man of the early 1900s. That comparison does us little enough good today. Enough to say that Nick was about 5'4" in height (quite short for a hero) and was astoundingly muscular, having as much strength in one arm as most men have in their entire bodies. For that reason, he was nicknamed "The Little Giant." An early story remarks:

...he can lift a horse with ease, and that, too, while a heavy man is seated in the saddle. Remember that he can place four packs of playing cards together, and tear them in halves between his thumb and fingers.

According to Nick Carter, himself, he was the product of long and intensive training, under his father's guidance:

To my father, who was a detective before me, is due the credit for whatever ability I possess. He began, as soon as I was old enough to understand, to train me for the profession I have followed.

The boy received comprehensive athletic training. A deliberate effort was made to coordinate growth of the mind and body. Emphasis was placed on languages, learned on the spot, together with local customs. Art and sculpture were studied to develop Nick's memory for form and mass; he was crammed with physiology, physiognomy; vocal culture.... "The list is endless, but this will give you an idea of the thoroughness

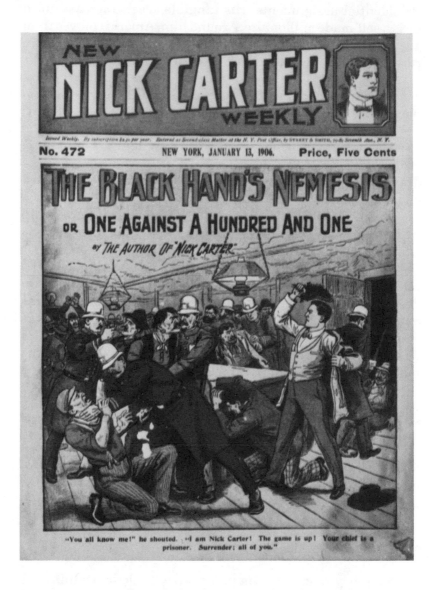

New Nick Carter Weekly, Jan. 13, 1906, #472. Disguise was part of the detective's art and the villain's plot. Nick could turn up anywhere, looking like anybody, as demonstrated above.

New Nick Carter Weekly, Aug. 6, 1910, #710. This formal portrait of the great detective was provided on a special insert reprinting several letters to and from Nick Carter. Conclusive proof that he was a real individual, if any cynic doubted.

of that tuition which began when I was a child, and which has never been discontinued."[5]

His father's rule (Nick continues) was "Keep your body, your clothing, and your conscience clean." Echoes of Frank Merriwell. Echoes of the whole period—the high moral tone, the measuring against solid standards of conduct that have gone all funny and shabby now (causing momentary embarrassment in the reader as if he has rediscovered some valued thing from his boyhood and observes how very worn the treasure has become and how much he has changed since his fingers last touched it).

Some twenty-three years later, Street & Smith resurrected that 1910 rule for use in the *Nick Carter Magazine*, further demonstrating that one publishing house, at least, kept in touch with its own past.

Viewed against the series characters to come, Nick's other personal qualities are of interest. We are told that his "word is his bond; that he never breaks a promise once given," a characteristic that is standard for the fictional hero. We are also told that Nick neither drank nor smoked—which is incorrect and the editors knew it. Nick often enjoyed an evening glass of wine and was always ready to sit down and smoke a cigar with a friend. (If you are attempting to stop smoking, avoid the Nick Carter series, for the scent of cigars rises splendid from the pages.)

What all this elaborate background building seeks to convey is that Nick Carter is real:

He is not a fictitious person who finds the solution of difficult problems in the air, or in the hollow of a hypodermic needle, as at least one well-known fiction character finds....

Take that, Sherlock Holmes.

Nick Carter gets out upon the street and does things with brain and brawn; with vigor and muscle,.. and one aim for the right and for righting wrongs.

Yes, entirely real; who would doubt it for a moment.

4–

All his meticulous training ends when Nick's father, Sim Carter, is murdered.[6] From this time on, Nick throws himself passionately against crime and begins netting thieves, swindlers, counterfeiters at a great rate. One early case takes him to a ranch in Nevada, where a 14-year old boy named Chickering Valentine is working as a ranch hand. Impressed with the boy, Nick takes him back to New York City, eventually adopts him—and so arrives Chick Carter, the right-hand man of the series.

Shrewd, intuitive, Chick grows to resemble Nick, a likeness that can be made exact by clever makeup. Frequently Chick will move through an entire story disguised as Nick, while Nick, disguised as Chick or Everyman, is out chasing down the ungodly. It is wonderful.

Early in the series, Chick marries Bertha Mortimer. She is murdered either before or after the ceremony or something awful happens to her. Anyhow, she promptly vanishes from the series. Much later, Chick marries again, causing considerable hard feelings between himself and Nick. For Nick is certain that the bride-to-be, Leila Loring, is nothing but a smirking criminal. But even Nick Carter can be wrong. Leila proves honest and both men are reconciled in one of the most clumsily contrived stories in the history of American literature.

Spiritually unaffected by these problems, Chick continues to grow in excellence. He is well able to operate on his own and, if Nick saves him from death every third chapter, then Chick always returns the favor. In spite of the demands of a detective's life, Chick was also able to edit the *New Nick Carter Weekly*—his by-line appeared just below the title on the first page.

By 1891, a respectable number of people had grouped themselves around Nick. He had married early in the series, although Ethel (whose name was later changed to Edith through writer error) played no major role in the continuous action. Nick's valet and butler, Peter, old but reliable, had appeared. And Patrick Murphy stepped grandly upon the scene.

The "Patrick" speedily changed to "Patsy," and the "Murphy" got accidentally switched to "Garvin." But whatever the name, Patsy remained the same competent young Irishman and third banana through the entire series. He came on stage as a young bootblack, summoned to help Nick—whose partiality for enrolling the aid of street gamins was second only to that of Sherlock Holmes. Bouncing impulsive Irish Patsy more than held his own in the fast Carter company; he was a capable sleuth and a vigorous scrapper, and, like all members of the establishment, could conduct investigations on his own.

On one of these jaunts, he met, wooed and married Adeline de Mendoze. It was a three-day courtship that worked into a succesful marriage. Unlike Chick's wives, Adelina remained visible during the rest of the series, pulling her own weight and saving everyone's neck. She was "a young goddess whose face and eyes are pure and innocent as a child's." But there was piercing intelligence behind that sweet expression, and a trace of Spanish temper, too.

During the early novels, Nick appears almost constantly in disguise. Heaven knows why. Only a few intimates know his true face. Whenever he appears on a case, the real Nick Carter is submerged in false whiskers and greasepaint. One favorite disguise was that of Old Thunderbolt—Thomas Bolt—the countryman detective, as freakish an individual as the most jaded taste could desire:

In appearance, he was the very last person that a client...would be likely to select as a shrewd detective.

A mass of shaggy and unkempt gray hairs covered his head and a long chin beard of the same hue half concealed the high collar and stock which he wore.

His coat was so long that it swept the floor around the chair in which he was sitting, and he wore... checkered pants.

On the floor... was a broad-brimmed slouch black hat and on the other side was a carpetbag of the "daown-east" pattern.

This remarkable vision has his own peculiar way with clients:

Old Thunderbolt: "Come in, can't yew."

Client: "Thank you."
OT: "Get out! What fer?"
Client: "Are you Old Thunderbolt?"
OT: "Sometimes, when I hev fits; ordinarily I'm only plain T. Bolt."
Client: "You are a detective."
OT: "Wall, some think so, an', ag'in, some don't."[7]

The dialogue must have convulsed them, up there in the hayloft. It has faded a little for modern eyes.

Eventually Nick dropped the Thunderbolt characterization and slowly reduced his use of constant disguise. His true face felt the sun. He had not entirely reformed, however, for he used the countryman disguise at least once a year, calling himself Joshia Juniper, the archetypical hayseed, complete with chin whiskers and comical accent.

Disguise plays a vast role in the dime novels, and particularly in Nick Carter's series. Customarily Nick and associates travel with "several simple disguises" in their pockets—a change of hair, an assortment of mustaches and face wrinkles, putty for the teeth, reversible clothing. At a moment's notice, they can slip into a convenient doorway and come out miraculously altered.

With slightly more effort, all of them could make up as another person, duplicating not only the face but the voice, habits, physical carriage and nervous tics. No one could tell the imposter from the real man, entirely disregarding Dashiell Hammett's biting little remark that "False hair looks like false hair."

Disguise was one of the conventions of the times. It was a means to an end, and no one inquired too closely into details. Disguise was a narrative device to get the hero smack into the marrow of the action. He didn't have to fumble around outside the door, but got inside at the table. If the pace slowed, he could always be detected, after which a few bright pages of violence could be written. And so disguise has its own great function to perform, Mr. Hammett notwithstanding.

More than disguises could be found in Nick's pockets. Or sleeves. Up each sleeve rested a neat little gun attached to a spring-kind of arrangement. Only thrust out his arms in a peculiar way and immediately he gripped a pair of cocked pistols. These were often supplemented by two revolvers concealed elsewhere on his person.

Less dramatic than the guns was the tiny case of tools that Nick carried in his pocket:

> Little steel tools of the finest temper, and of the greatest strength possible in implements of their size. There were awls of different sizes; saws which would cut through ordinary steel; chisels which would cut iron without turning the edges; nippers; pinchers; a tiny blowpipe....[8]

The tool kit turned out to be essential equipment, not only for Nick Carter, but for the dozens of series heroes after him. Similar kits became standard equipment throughout the pulps and may be found in current paperbacks. Once again the tool kit is a device used by the writer to speed up the action. Why should the reader wait while the hero slips silently around the house, pushing in vain at doors and windows that remain forever stuck. From the beginning of locks, every major series character carried skeleton keys. Nick Carter used pick-locks, as did a few other characters during the 1930s; all the rest had keys, skeleton, special or merely marvelous. With these, the heroes broke and entered blandly in the name of justice. Certainly illegal. But with only 20,000 words and three major climaxes to the narrative, how else could you keep the action moving along.

Meanwhile, back at the Nick Carter adventures, the cast of characters has been methodically increasing. Nellie and Warwick Carter, two new assistants, arrive for brief appearances. And now, Ida Jones, cool, self-possessed, strong-willed, has talked herself into employment with the Carters. The splendid Ida stays with the series for years, performing with dependable brilliance. She is crisp, brisk, full of good sense, and rather reminds you of a limeade made with carbonated water. Then suddenly she does not appear for several years. After which she returns, excellent as ever. Remarkably enough, the characters never notice that she was gone or has come back.

For a bunch of internationally applauded detectives, they don't notice the strangest things. They don't (for example) notice that during one of Chick's marriages, he got a son, and that son is abruptly old enough to be in the detective business himself. Trim Carter is his name. He might have been adopted. It's all a deep mystery. Anyway, Trim is suddenly in business, although barely a teenager. He has thirty-two adventures, then vanishes. At that point, Nick retires.

Well, hardly retires, since the *Nick Carter Weekly* is just gathering momentum. For the record, however, Nick says he's retired and has given up being a detective to run a detective school for boys.

There's no use grinding your teeth and sneering. That's what happened. Otherwise you are forced to assume muddled cross-currents in the Street & Smith editorial department.

The detective school permits the introduction of a variety of fine young boys: Bob Ferret, Jack Burton, Buff Hutchinson, et al. They were bright, immensely energetic, and, needless to say, at the peak of physical perfection. If Frank Merriwell didn't look out, they might lure away some of his readers.

About this time, Roxy the Flowergirl appears, a strong figure in this story series. About fifteen, she was:

...exceptionally neat in her dress, patched and skimped though it was, and her bright, saucy face showed that hard knocks with the world had made a keen little business woman of her.

Roxy is the Orphan Annie of 1898. She is the sole support of a ferocious drunken uncle and she has been trained in circus skills. Very useful these are, too. Her first appearance in the series is on a collapsing scaffold. From this mild challenge she plunged resolutely into all manner of menaces and dangers, a tough little sprite who consistently exceeded the boys.

Eventually Nick gets back into the detective business and the detective school evaporates like last month's rain. But new faces are constantly added to the series. Perhaps the most important of these is Ten-Ichi, son of the Mikado, who comes to the United States to study the detective business. Speaking perfect English, Ten-Ichi can disguise himself to simulate any nationality and fake almost any dialect. Being Japanese, he is automatically a jui-jitsu expert—almost as able as Nick. Without comment, he adapts to the rather peculiar life the

Carters live and becomes a valued member of the establishment.

In one case the criminals trap him, strap him to a couch and open one of his arteries, apparently to save the cost of a cartridge. Before much royal blood is lost, he is saved by June Lamartaine, the woman he marries in 1905. What the public thought of that mixed marriage isn't recorded—although June was one of those French girls, and you know what they're like. As in the fine tradition of wives associated with the series, June promptly vanishes from sight.

Over the years, Ten-Ichi also appears less often. Finally he, too, vanishes. No harm was done; in the Nick Carter series, there were always more people than stories for them to appear in.

Other faces are added. Danny Maloney becomes Nick's chauffeur. Peter, the butler, retires (probably) and is replaced by Joseph, an older, gray-haired, faithful fellow. Pedro the Bloodhound is introduced—this happens just after Sexton Blake, over in Baker Street, London, got himself a bloodhound named Pedro. Then Conroy Conners of the U.S. Secret Service enters the action and provides a link with Washington, D.C. Conners works closely with Nick on a number of counterfeiting and piracy cases. Then a couple more street boys are brought in the series—Philip Pommery, who meets Nick in Moscow, of all places; and Pop-Eye, whose eyes do and who is very small and aggressive.

While this stream of faces, old and new, rushes through the adventures, Nick's wife, Ethel, is murdered. Nick will remain unmarried for the rest of the series, although it is believed that an unrecorded marriage occurred off scene to account for the other Nick Carters, 20-30 years hence. In 1907, he does carry off Carma, the Amazon Queen of a lost race, to New York, with the evident intention of proposing to her en route. We leave them on shipboard. When the next novel opens, Nick is back in New York and not a single, solitary thing is ever afterward heard of Carma, love or marriage.

If there are a bewildering rush of assistants, wives, butlers and street boys through the series, there is an equally bewildering number of villains. Of both sexes. The prince of these was Jack Quartz, Nick Carter's Professor Moriarty.[9] Dr.

Quartz was a suave magnetic homicidal maniac who enjoyed nothing more than a leisurely vivisection of a beautiful woman. An accomplished hypnotizer and poisoner, Quartz trafficked in bizarre methods of murder. In one of his better efforts, he furnished a boxcar as a luxurious room, and placed at its center a table, around which a company of corpses sat at cards.

As Nick had his detective school, so Quartz had his crime school. There he instructed willing pupils in the art of murder by untraceable poisons and deadly gases. Eventually Quartz got captured and hung. Then he got resurrected. Then he got killed again. Then he came back again. Or perhaps it was his brother. After Nick polished him off for the last time, Quartz stayed gone until 1927. Returned once more (the series appeared in *Detective Story Magazine*). Finally was jailed and didn't return—although he would have if the series had continued.

Not only did Quartz enjoy slicing up beautiful girls, he enjoyed having them assist his fiendish plots. One otherwise successful aide, Zanoni, the Woman Wizard, botched things by falling in love with Nick and reforming. Up to that point, she had enjoyed a richly successful career with Quartz during which they committed every known crime twice or more.

Such exceptional women as Zanoni fill the Nick Carter series. There are scores of them, utterly beautiful, utterly murderous, their warm little hands scented with the poisons of Araby. As a group they are almost inhumanly intelligent. Ruthless, clever, quick, they stalk the pages sneering defiance at the great detective, evading justice issue after issue.

Dazaar, the Arch Fiend, The Criminal Queen, the Beautiful Sorceress. Zelma the Female Fiend. Madge Morley, The Dangerous Woman. Scylla, The Sea Robber. Black Madge and Gipsy Madge and all those Madges. The Bird of Paradise, Mirabird Thurber. The Princess Possess (crazy all her life). Diana, the Arch-Demon. Cora Dalney, the strongest individual in the entire world. It is an inspiring sorority.

The male criminals are equally interesting. Some appeared a number of times—Quartz, of course, and Burton Quintard and Dan Derrington. Others had briefer, if equally colorful, runs. There was Codman the Poisoner, full of original ideas. Ordway the Unaccountable Crook. The Dalney Brothers, all far stronger than Nick; they collected people's skeletons while the people were still around them. And there were Praxatel of the Iron Arm. Hans Pretzel, the 300-pound killer....

Through the Nick Carter stories these terribles flow, a mazy stream of them. No softies here. Most are powerful men, able to battle Nick on almost equal terms. Not one of them is easy. They delight in complexity. They murder at random. If they have any goal, it is to acquire every available dollar, every diamond, every scrap of loose stock.

To bring them down, Nick must exert every possible erg of skill. During the almost equal battle, he loses about as frequently as he wins. Routinely Nick is trapped. Routinely he plunges through trapdoors, is locked in rooms filled with gas, is tied hand and foot in black caverns, is struck mercilessly on the head. He is left to die in flaming rooms shot stabbed blown up lassoed drugged poisoned.

But a clean body-mind-conscience can overcome all things. There is always a way out. Nick is wonderfully adroit, and Chick, Ida, Patsy eternally hover in the background, eager to save him before the horrible end.

The adventures sprawl across the world. No one can accuse Nick Carter of sticking to a single scene. A case may lead from New York City to Canada to Chicago to California. Today Nick experiences the San Francisco earthquake. Tomorrow he faces bandits in the Old West. Next week brings cases in England, Russia and Japan. Never linger in one place: New Orleans, Cleveland. Above all, don't bore the reader. The Atlantic seaboard. A Pacific isle. Vary the scene. A lost race in South America. Pace the stories. East Side crooks and piracy out from Long Island and so it goes. Nick may live in New York City, deeply tied to its legal, financial and public offices, but he feels easy anywhere.

> Nick Carter loved danger... he enjoyed the exercise of his mental and physical qualities... brought into play in pitting himself against it.[10]

As many a series character was wont to do after him, Nick was given to walking, lightly disguised, into hardcase barrooms, massed with thugs who would cut his throat for exercise. Less frequently he introduced himself into conclaves of murderous businessmen, all tricked out in robes and hoods, each identified only by a number. Familiar scenes these and customary perils.

Nick's investigative techniques were as formal as his action scenes were informal. For most of his career, he worked arm in arm with the New York City police. They rewarded his support by letting him carry off any piece of evidence that struck his fancy. Quite cheerfully, they would release a prisoner or defer an arrest at his request. Later in the series, things became less friendly. But at first every cop knew Nick Carter. His was the first name requested when the police blundered into a problem too baffling for the Force to handle— say, twice a day.

A few years after Sherlock Holmes got into high gear, Nick showed an unfortunate habit of evolving long long long long chains of reasoning, working from insignificant clues through spurious analogies to the correct conclusion. He dropped this habit after a few years.

His initial investigations remained miracles of detailed observation into which no logic-chopping intruded. Called to the scene of some unaccountable outrage, Nick would fix himself in the doorway and begin to scrutinize the room before him inch by inch. That is to be accepted as literal fact. He would examine the area wall to wall in inch-wide strips, straight across the room and back. Reviewed the walls and ceiling the same way. Saw everything. Reflected on everything. Then he entered the room to collect all that evidence that good Officer Mulvaney had overlooked. Nick's preliminary survey of a room is exhausting; afterward, your eyes ache and you want to lie down.

5–

In 1915, the *Nick Carter Stories* terminated after printing Part I of a 4-part serial. The remaining bulk of the serial appeared in Street & Smith's brand new pulp magazine, *Detective Story*. Through mid-1916, only three other short stories featured Nick, these being modestly signed Sergeant

Ryan (George C. Jenks in this case).

For the next several years, through 1918, most Nick Carter adventures were short stories reprinted from the *New York Weekly* of the 1890s and a scattering of stories from *Ainslee's*, rewritten to Nick Carters by Sergeant Ryan. The reprints petered out in March, 1918.

For the next six years, Nick Carter lived on only in the New Magnet Library paperback reprints. A revival attempt began in *Detective Story* during 1924, with the 4-part serial, "Nick Carter's Sealed Crime," (August 23-September 13). This was followed by a trickle of short stories written by George Jenks (1924-1925), Johnston McCulley (1926-1927) and Edward L. Bacon (1927). In these, Dr. Quartz was brought back and cornered again. And Nick met that lethal lunatic, The Shadow Woman, and the Black Cat, a slick gentleman burglar.

Under this new authorship, Nick changed in obvious ways. He seemed hesitant, almost fragile. His aggressive competence had faded to a solid gentility. In the final story, he gets himself stabbed nearly dead, an indiscretion that the old Nick Carter would never have tolerated, not for a moment. His influence on events is rather dim and the best that can be said for the series is that the magazine covers' paints make him look very much like Sherlock Holmes.

So matters rested until the hot upwelling of the single-character pulps in 1933.

Interlude—The Vanishing

One day, the dime novels were gone.

It was hard to realize that it had happened. In many used magazine stores, back issues still heaped—*Tip Top Weekly. Secret Service. Work and Win. Wide Awake Library.* The finely worn names of years, all you could carry, all you could read.

How could they be gone? Heaps lay boxed in your friend's basement. In your attic, stacks of dime novels slumped across the floor, inviting you to read through the long hot afternoons, amid the smell of dust and old paper, feeling the slow crawl of sweat down your forehead.

Down at the railroad station, fat, pocket-sized New Magnet Library volumes hung for sale in their metal racks. But now you must hunt for that single copy of *Buffalo Bill Stories* concealed among those thick new magazines, *Blue Book, People's, Argosy, Adventure, Snappy Stories.*

This month *Top Notch* (15¢, 192 pages) has a football story in it about that Merriwell fellow and there's a first-rate Terhune mystery. *Popular Magazine* (15¢, 224 pages) comes out twice a month, big substantial issues full of excitement:

"Out of the Miocene" by John Charles Beecham—The mind of a modern man travels backward through the eons and lives again in his progenitor of the Miocene Age.

Slowly the new magazines arrived, packed with short fiction and serials. Some also provided interesting articles and photographs. *Blue Book* showed scenes from plays even then on Broadway. It seemed decent enough, wholesome entertainment. And these magazines you could lay down in the front room without worrying for fear that the kids might pick them up.

One day, only three or four dime novels appeared on the news stand. One day there was only one. One day they were all gone. Had been for months. You understand that The Liberty Boys are being published, that Buffalo Bill continues. But you never see them. Where? When? They just don't seem to sell them anymore.

The dime novels were gone. The single-character

publication was dead. It would not return for a decade and a half, until 1931 and *The Shadow, A Detective Magazine.*

The dime novel heritage remained. The bright clarity of that active prose flowed through the new stories in the new magazines. The techniques of the action story, the swift start, the quick movement, the sudden adventure, had melted imperceptibly into the popular fiction mainstream.

Those subjects in which the dime novels had specialized were now reflected in the general magazines. *All Story* regularly featured science-fantasy fiction. The *Detective Story Magazine, Western Story, Adventure* each appealed to specific tastes of the general readership.

The sun had not set. The sun was rising.

And the series character, hero of so many burning pages, what of him?

The dime novels had polished him to a high brilliance and had, over ten thousand issues, laid down those requirements of personal excellence and accomplishment from which he dare not deviate.

He was a marvel of accomplishment, that fellow. Generally well to do (often a millionaire) he towered before the world, admired as much for his moral authority as his professional competence. An astounding athlete, possessed of steel-like muscles and inhumanly quick reflexes, he glowed with personal force.

Women loved him; enemies respected him; associates idolized him. He was a genius of disguise, a master of weapons and science. Equipped with the artifices of the latest technology, he indulged in adventure however remote it might be.

He was free, but it was a peculiar freedom, shaded by subtle overtones in gray. In some manner, the continuing series hero had become the embodiment of justice. He served society without much reference to the laws by which that society was bound. His Duty lay outside the law. It was pre-requisite that he react directly to those great abstracts of goodness, truth, honor. As the accredited agent of society, he was bound by these, rather as the Avenging Angel is bound by Heavenly Law and cares not a whit for local ordnances forbidding the possession of a flaming sword.[1]

Strange prices were charged for this unique position. Eternally, the hero was condemned to purity. He must rigorously control himself, indulge in no vice or emotional excess. He could hardly be permitted a cigar and a glass of wine. His sexual purity was such that it was doom for the woman who coveted him. If he married, his wife faced untimely death. If he acknowledged a sweetheart, perils clustered about her.

In consequence, the hero maintained no significant relationship with a woman. His companions were almost entirely male, frequently of almost equal competence. But not quite. Even his opponents, dark geniuses that they were, could not match him, quite.

A curious position, this having no equals.

These hero figures, these immensely magnified dreams, plant their feet on granite. They represent a society in which there are, yet, stable values—untarnishable and fixed. From these values, the dime novel hero drew his authority.

As the 1900s wore into the 1920s, this splendid simplicity began to tarnish. The stable values showed a shocking tendency to crumble at the edges, and the moral base from which the hero launched his exploits cracked across its face, a phenomena explored in detail by the later *Black Mask* writers.

Back in the Good Old Days (say, around 1910), the moral base was accepted. Get on with the story and stop those crooks from stealing that sweet girl's inheritance. Bring forth the substantial hero.

But while Nick Carter and Frank Merriwell toiled, something dreadful had happened to one branch of the popular series character line. An American dime novel writer had moved to England and while writing there....

So it is to England that we now turn to trace out a new step in the development of the pulp magazine series characters.

IV—Rogues and Bent Heroes

1-

Your life has become a tissue of delicate horror. Last year, your world was precisely solid, firm as a gold coin in the fingers. This year it has all gone wrong, terribly wrong. You feel the gold coin crumble to dust and the contours of your life shimmer with imprecision. Horror enough.

A title is yours and a towering fortune, based solidly on South African diamond mines and nurtured by your financial genius. Your name, Sir Charles Vandrift, is honored. You have married respectably; your brother-in-law, Seymour Wentworth, is also your personal secretary. Although he attends efficiently enough to your daily problems, he is an ignominious toady, likely wetting his fingers in your wealth.

One day you will expose him, as you expose other cheats and frauds. It is a hobby you love, your constant practice. Just as it is your practice to turn a stroke of business whenever, wherever possible. Bluntly, to profit, when you can, from the simpering imbeciles of the world. If they part with their properties, jewels, mines for less than value, then they are fools. Anyone can learn the market value—even such puppy-eyed dolts as these.

This is business. Then why must Clay intrude? The swindling thief, Colonel Clay, the trickster, the cackling rogue, Cuthbert Clay, the monster of many faces.

Far too many faces. You can look directly at him and not see the disguise. Every business dealing is soiled by the possibility of his presence. Once he appeared as a Mexican seer and fooled you completely. Then he was a shy, stumbling curate from the North country with an imitation pearl necklace he wished to sell (not realizing that it was real; although when you bought it, the thing was false enough). After that he appeared as a Scottish fellow and after that, a German scholar, and each time, the face, the voice, the mannerisms were real, accurate, exact. Of the man beneath the disguise, there was no trace. He is transient as morning, evanescent.

Who is Colonel Clay? He is real as earth and out there he glides among the faces of the world. He could be any one of them. Yes, there's the horror. As the waiter at your table, he may pour your wine. His eyes may look from the face of the detective you hire for protection. The world swarms with people. And which of them is Clay?

It is horror, horror. Out there, among these unfamiliar faces at your hotel, he may be patiently planning another stroke against your fortune. He games with you. He writes mocking letters. Your strokes of business he transforms to strokes of humiliation. He is the chameleon man, gulping down your fortune bite by calculated bite. That mocking, brazen, unaccountable thief, Colonel Cuthbert Clay.

The adventures of Colonel Clay appeared in a series of twelve connected short stories written by Grant Allen and published in *The Strand Magazine* from June 1896 through May 1897. The stories were later collected in the book, *An African Millionaire* (1897).[1]

Colonel Clay arrived in public print about ten years after Nick Carter and nine years after Sherlock Holmes. The Colonel represents an early wave of that tide of series criminal heroes which, for the next thirty years, boiled through the popular fiction magazines. Of all these varied talents, Clay was the most specialized. His single victim was Sir Charles Vandrift, the African Millionaire, whose acquisitive greed and shoddy business practices left him—and his fortune—vulnerable to Clay's elaborate plots.

The twelve stories are written in the first person by the secretary, Seymore Wentworth. They are sequential and concentrated into the period of about a year. During that time, Sir Charles and party move grandly across Europe and the United States, shedding the stately glory of the wealthy. During this long tour, Sir Charles is persistently victimized by that swindler, Colonel Clay. Like an invisible man, Clay hovers close to the party, watching, planning, scheming. For every coup he wears a different face. Each time, the scheme is different and almost always gouges loose another substantial strip of Sir Charles' wealth. It is a pleasure to watch such an artist at work.

Colonel Clay is certainly an artist. He is self-created, from the name, which is a pseudonym, to the face, which is concealed by a curious mixture of gutta-percha (a plastic rubberish compound) and india rubber. When applied to a face and carefully tinted, that face is altered beyond recognition. To the changed face is coupled acting skill and audacity. No wonder that fortune melts away.

Two women aid Col. Clay. Unorthodox as always, he loves both but has neglected to marry either. One of these, Cesarine, is maid to Sir Charles' sister and serves the Colonel by lurking within. White Heather, the second woman, helps the Colonel on the outside, often herself disguised, luring Sir Charles repeatedly into the web.

A perfect ability at disguise, amiable consorts, and a dim opponent will not protect a criminal forever. He reckons without those iron editorial laws decreeing that the most delightful rogue is obligated to suffer for his crimes. So it happens to Colonel Clay. In the eleventh story, having just completed his final raid upon Sir Charles, the incredible happens. Clay is detected. It is by accident, not plan. He was accidentally photographed and the camera exposed the disguise materials on his face. Arrested and brought to trial in the final story, he conducts his own defense. But the evidence is too overwhelming. He is sentenced to fourteen years hard labor, a not inconsiderable price to pay for skimping on legal fees.

Sir Charles does not escape unblemished, however. His relentless criminality is thoroughly exposed in public, as is the more feeble cheating of Seymore Wentworth. By the end of the chapter, you assume that both these men, revealed for slippery rascals, will spend their remaining days taking tea alone, disdained by Society. Which is the convention in fiction, if not the practice in reality.

The Colonel's two ladies, grieving wetly about his punishment, are untouched by the Law. They prepare to spend fourteen years together, drying each other's tears, waiting for husband to complete his sentence.

2–

Fiction in which the hero is a criminal contains innate contradictions. A successful criminal hero menaces the reader's welfare. It is difficult to sustain admiration for an individual who might, at any moment, strip your pockets and rap you on the head—even if he is only a surrogate for your urge to be rich without work.

Perhaps for this reason, criminal heroes rarely overstepped certain carefully established limits. They selected as their victims the Sir Charleses of the world, people who deserved to be robbed. For, after all, it is no crime to pluck evil doers. And if some of your stolen proceeds buy a warm coat for Little Sal the Matchgirl, trembling amid snowflakes at Broad and High, then the crime is fully excused. The ethical position is shaky but it is a venerable one, well understood by Robin Hood and the Greenwood Boys.

Criminality, however, can't be encouraged. If it were, the reading public might rise and descend upon wealth and privilege, uttering weird cries. Best to divert the thought. Thus the convention that the criminal hero must lose either the final play, or his ill-got gains, or both. In this present age of sin, the criminal is more apt to write a book; but at the turn of the century, the rules were more austere.

Since final success is forbidden the criminal hero, delight in his activities is the main bait used in catching the reader. And when the reader tires of qualified successes, the series folds.

For these reasons, the world of a criminal hero is unstable, and, in a series of any length, this instability generally displays itself in changes to the basic concept. The hero at series' end rarely resembles himself at the beginning. The greater the author/audience ambivalence toward the hero, the more strikingly he alters, and the more rapidly.

Even as the character of the individual hero changes, so styles in popular criminal heroes change. The fad for gentlemen burglars, which filled so many cubic yards of early magazine fiction, received more variations than a theme by Bach. But the gentleman burglar was only one fad among many. There were others.

There were safecrackers, con men, and yeggs with golden hearts. There were master criminals, some with gangs and some operating alone, Chinese fiends, and buccaneers who robbed other criminals. There were cute crooks, and misunderstood saviors incorrectly assumed to be social menaces; and clever crooks redeemed by love.

If we are obsessed by the urge to classify, we may separate these multitudes into two groups, like loaves and fish. One group will include the Rogues—those willing criminals, inventive and interesting, whose charm excuses almost everything but a personal interest in our affairs. The other group, Bent Heroes, are hardly criminals at all; perhaps they once were, but the love of a good woman has transformed them. Now they are occupied in making restitution for the past and purifying themselves for the married raptures to come.

Justice Figures represent a variant of the Bent Hero. A Justice Figure has voluntarily stepped outside the Law to correct injustices that the Law and its representatives are unable to deal with. Seeking neither personal gain nor revolution, he is an agent of stability, a free-lance law enforcement agent, like a white corpuscle with a gun.

Unrecorded hundreds of all these characters exist, stuffing each category to bursting. Only a few of these can be recalled in the iron confines of these chapters. In this orchard, we can pick only what the hands will hold. There are, however, certain figures whose creation triggered series of other characters dipped from the same vat. Additional characters, less forceful of personality, are also of interest—even though a fickle public has long forgotten them. Each contributed his own special flash of light that would, later, magnified, reappear in the dazzle of the pulp magazines.

In their day, all enjoyed a popularity now accorded only to the newest television face. They were read hugely. They got into moving pictures. They impressed themselves on the public mind and were carried forward in time, as themselves or as types.

Most are gone now. But their influence lingers like tracks in sandstone, indicating that something wonderous passed this way, long ago.

3–

Mr. A.J. Raffles was a thief.
What? you cry. Ridiculous! That distinguished man, that

well set-up fellow, enthralling the flower of English society with his presence. His conversation gleams; his personality radiates. Gad, sir, look how he wears his clothing.

If you are Lady Y____, your powdered bosom glowing agreeably under Mr. Raffles' eyes, what reason have you to think his glance appraises the diamonds, rather than the charms beneath. If you are Lord N____, by Gad, sir, AJ is of the best family, a sportsman, sir, perhaps the finest cricketer in England, stake my life on that man, sir, private means, you know, gold fields, I fancy.

How else should a gentleman burglar appear?

Mr. A.J. Raffles was a thief. A society thief, when possible. A gentleman burglar at all times, with the implication that when "burglar" is qualified by "gentleman," his unfortunate choice of profession is excused.

Raffles preferred the rare and valuable: the art treasure from the museum, the set of *Thrill Book* from the manor house. But he would also carry off your YMCA swimming medal, if that's all he could find.

None of this was called stealing. Not in the Raffles adventures. Evading plain fact with the blandest of smiles, the author treats these thefts not as crimes but as thrilling adventures.

It was an evasion appreciated by the times. Nothing so tickled the sensibilities of the early 1900s as a nice gentleman crook. The fiction is swamped with these characters—particularly after Raffles' appearance. For the most part, gentlemen crooks were fine fellows. Between forays, they conducted themselves above reproach, acceptable at any formal reception.

And if they elected to become reformed gentlemen crooks, then the heart of every reader gushed sucrose. The attitude is perfectly presented in a ghastly little play by Barrie—"Nevertheless" is the name—in which a burglar, creeping in by night, encounters a darling sweet little golden-haired child. They get to giggling over the pronunciation of "Nevertheless," and he gives up being a burglar and dedicates himself to a decent, wholesome life. You wonder what Al Capone would have made of this.

Whether transformed or unrepentant, the gentleman crook

stands colossal in the popular fiction of the time. His personality booms down the decades. Fiction—particularly dime novel fiction—had featured gentlemen crooks before. But in Raffles, the concept was crystallized, sharp, vivid, influential. He was one of the great originals. After him innumerable variations appeared, all based on the theme of Raffles.

The Raffles stories first appeared around 1898. They were written by Ernest William Hornung (1866-1921), a prolific creator of crime, mystery, and adventure fiction. He was a cricket authority and the brother-in-law of Conan Doyle, to whom the first collection of Raffles' adventures is dedicated.

That book, *The Amateur Cracksman* (1899), was followed by *Raffles* (1901) and *A Thief In the Night* (1905). A single novel, *Mr. Justice Raffles,* appeared in 1909.

During the early 1930s, the English story paper, *The Thriller,* revived Raffles with the permission of the Hornung estate.[2] A series was commissioned from Philip Atkey, writing as Barry Perowne. To meet *Thriller* editorial requirements, Raffles was updated to a contemporary adventurer, much altered from his original character. Still later, additional stories appeared in the American pulp magazines *Thrilling Detective* (at least during 1936-1937) and *Black Book Detective* (1938). In 1939, the *Thriller* series terminated, a casualty of the Hitler War, and Raffles vanished again for more than a decade.

During the 1950s, Atkey began another Raffles series for *Ellery Queen's Mystery Magazine.* In these stories, Raffles returned to his original period. Again his character was modified, deemphasizing his ruthless coldness and emphasizing his impulses toward social justice. During the following twenty-five years, these stories appeared in *Ellery Queen's* and *The Saint Mystery Magazine.* Collections of them appeared in 1974 as *Raffles Revisited* and in 1976 as *Raffles of the Albany.* A further collection of short stories, these by David Fletcher, was released in 1977 under the title, *Raffles.*[3]

The long endurance of this character is surely a consequence of Mr. Atkey's skill. But the character is intrinsically strong. There he stands among his unsuspected associates, tall and broad-shouldered, smoke rising in an unshaken line from his Sullivan cigarette.

The stories describe him as rather more handsome than is shown by the book illustrations. These picture him as older, with a craggy sort of face. He is cricket mad, terrifyingly informed about that arcane game, one of the world's great players. Presence shines from him; he dominates any group. He is full of cold effrontery, delighting to walk a single hair across a volcano's maw. He is, in short, splendid.

So why a thief?

Once in a moment of desperate need, he stole. It was exciting. It was profitable. Oh, it's wrong, surely. But the challenge, the thrill. How enticing it all sounds.

Particularly to Bunny Manders. He is that nice young gentleman, smiling, genteel, of superior breeding, standing modestly behind Raffles, on his right side.

Bunny is also a thief. He is a young man gone wrong: Good family, slovenly life, debts, verge of suicide and disgrace. Raffles saves him. He devotes his life to Raffles, revels uneasily in a life of crime, becomes a jail bird, becomes a journalist, narrates the adventures in the first person.

So we see Raffles from Bunny's point of view—which means through a fog of rose and violet hero worship. Raffles is enshrined, the supreme, the ultimate, his figure gilded by Bunny's admiration. His most trivial exploits are presented with gurgles and slobbers of ecstasy.   The difficulty with Bunny is that he is the stupidest character in the literature of Western Civilization. Beside him, Bertie Wooster towers as a pillar of intellectual force. Now Bunny is brave enough, although creeping along other people's halls by night makes him nervous. The stories he writes have a charming swing and density. And he is devoted to Raffles. Lord, yes, he is devoted. "My devoted rabbit," Raffles remarks, watching Mr. Manders pant audibly.

In spite of these admirable traits, Bunny seems to have selected the wrong profession. Perhaps Raffles thinks so too; he is careful to keep Bunny thoroughly uninformed of plans and projects. This is necessary. Whatever is in Bunny's head is on Bunny's face. And as for self-possession or foresight, he has none.

Nor has he luck. He could make a cement floor squeak. If there is a time to be silent, Bunny blurts. If it is time to flee, he bolts into the thorn bush. You can hardly imagine a more unsuitable assistant to a professional housebreaker.

In the first story of the series, Bunny is saved from disgrace by Raffles, who steals what is needed to protect the Manders honor. After this exploit, one fascinating crime follows the other. They culminate in Bunny's arrest and Raffles' disappearance and probable death.

But no. He is not dead at all. When the police close his file, Raffles escapes to Italy. There he falls deeply in love with the most beautiful girl in the world. But she gets murdered and his hair turns gray. Back he goes to England, to Bunny (stunned to see him), and to various small adventures. Eventually both men slip from England to the Boer War, where, on active service, their identities are disclosed by a noxious spy. The Boers shoot Bunny in the leg, permanently crippling him. In the same action, Raffles may or may not be shot (also by the Boers) and dies (or perhaps not) after lingering paragraphs while he tends the wounded Bunny under fire. The story, "On the Knees of the Gods," may be found in the collection, *Raffles*; it is one single gigantic wave of syrup, a dose of bathos so intense that the numbed reader finds himself slapping the book shut blindly, crying "Brave fellow. Well done."

Or perhaps you miss the point entirely and conclude that Raffles has discovered how to evade the Boers and the English army and get off to safety, with or without the wounded Bunny.

You can have it both ways. In the next book, they are both back in England. Bunny says that he is relating earlier adventures. Maybe he is. Maybe it's all a big cover-up to project AJ. But the series continues.

Hornung isn't the first author to discover that his character won't die.

These stories are interesting in spite of their layers of snobbery, the icy underside of Raffles, the archaic posturing, the awful adoration of Mr. Manders. If you are able to disregard these unpleasant qualities, you are captured by the slick competence of Raffles, the remarkable man.

An interesting by-product of the series is that the adventures tend to de-criminalize crime:

That was the year there were so many burglaries in the Thames Valley.... It

was said that the thieves used bicycles in every case.... They were sometimes
on foot to my knowledge, and we took a great interest in the series, or rather
sequence of successful crimes. Raffles would often get his devoted (landlady) to
read him the local accounts.... We even rode out by night ourselves, to see if we
could not get on the tracks of the thieves, and never did we fail to find hot coffee
on the hob for our return...the misty nights might have been made for the
thieves. But their success was not as consistent, and never so enormous, as
people said, especially the sufferers, who lost more valuables than they had
ever been known to possess. (from *Raffles*, "The Wrong House")

This is, we may suppose, what is known as "delicious"
irony; the thieves in question being Raffles and Bunny, riding
bicycles over the region. Note particularly the final lines
where, by a curious inversion, those who had been burglared
and then inflated their losses are made, deftly enough, to
appear greater criminals than the thieves, themselves.

This sleight-of-hand is played throughout the series:
Robbery is all just a delightful joke. Perhaps it is against the
law. But the Law is such an Ass, don't you agree. And those
robbed—it gives savor to their tedious lives. Pitiful dull things,
those householders. It's God's blessing to offer them a whiff of
burglary to break the clotted tallow of their days.

So Raffles has made crime respectable—at least fictional
crime. It's all fun and thrills. Of course, the police chase you
and you often have to lay low. But how you do fool everyone.
High sport.

4-

It was high sport, too, for Romney Pringle, another face
among the thickets of English crime. Pringle is that
specialist's specialist—an urban buccaneer. He lives by
robbing other criminals—by theft, swindles, misdirection, and
occasional violence, the small change of magazine adventure.

Since his profession seems to require it, Pringle is learned
at disguise. He is no Colonel Clay, altering face and
appearance, burying himself in a new personality. Less
elaborate arrangements do as well. Wigs conceal his blond
hair. He glues on a false mustache or adjusts spurious
sideburns. A mysterious liquid darkens his eyebrows and fair
skin. From his right cheek, he scrubs a small, portwine
birthmark—this birthmark he wears constantly, when not

otherwise disguised.

Other changes are as easy. Normally tall, slim, straight-backed, and dressed with elegance and taste, he varies these characteristics at will. Then out into London's tangle to extract a cash penance from the dragons hunting there.

—Learning of a mail swindle, he insinuates himself into the office for several days, cleans it out, robs its mail, and arranges that it be raided by Scotland Yard after he departs.

—Posing as a C.I.D. man, he enlists a Lord's help to rob a blackmailer.

—Interferes in a plot to have a wealthy man declared insane, and, by forgery, cleans out most of the villain's savings.

—Trails a diamond thief to Holland, where he not only steals the diamond star, but the money for which it has been sold.

It is Pringle's fancy to pose as a literary agent, although his mail is bare of manuscripts. Just as his rooms at 33 Furnival's Inn, London, are barren of visitors. His life is unsoftened by friends, loving ladies, associates of any kind. He is a solitary hunter. His audacious mind seems untarnished by a need for others.

That isolation may be the result of his predatory life. Or perhaps human contact is too strong a wind to let among the artifices of his life. Whatever the reason, he lives alone, hunts alone, celebrates his triumphs alone.

Romney Pringle appeared in only thirteen stories (so far identified). Most were published in *Cassell's Magazine* in two groups, June through November 1902 and June through November 1903. A single story also appeared in the May 1903 issue of the *Windsor Magazine*.[4]

These stories, signed Clifford Ashden, were written by R. Austin Freeman and Dr. John Jones Pitcairn. Freeman, a civil servant and doctor, would soon create Dr. Thorndyke, the first scientific detective; Pitcairn was Medical Officer of Holloway Prison and collaborated with Freeman on the later *Cassell's* series, "From A Surgeon's Diary" (December 1904 through May 1905).[5]

The Pringle stories were collected into two books: *The*

Adventures of Romney Pringle (1902) and *The Further Adventures of Romney Pringle* (1970). The adventures are loosely sequential. The series is framed—that is, presented to the reader by a third party. In the Preface to the series, we learn that a retired gentleman, Mr. Romney, has died at his home in Sandwich. He had lived there for some years, quietly bicycling around the country, puttering with his gem collection. After his death—he died alone—a group of manuscript stories were discovered and these, the Romney Pringle adventures, are published with no definite statement as to whether they are biography or fiction.

So this charming little series, ambiguous from the first page, moves from guile through stratagem to deceit. The prose is simple, the adventure direct, but there is hardly a fact in the series you feel would bear weight.

Romney Pringle is much less well known than Raffles. The *Cassell's* series ended, *The Adventures* went out of print, and Mr. Pringle entered his long retirement. That grand old line of Buccaneers, so well represented by Pringle, continued undiminished; in English fiction, it would include such names as Edgar Wallace's Twister and Brigand and Leslie Charteris' The Saint. In American fiction, it would include many of Johnston McCulley's series characters in the 1920s *Detective Story Magazine* (The Avenging Twins, the Crimson Clown, The Man In Purple), as well as Erle Stanley Gardner's Lester Leith series from the 1930s. Gentlemen rogues all, cheerfully wringing a living from criminal purses. Charming people to know—providing that you are poor and honest.

5-

If Raffles and Pringle made stealing a gentleman's sport, then Arsene Lupin made thievery a delightful jest.

(Lupin) worked at his profession for a living, but also for his amusement. He gave the impression of a dramatist who thoroughly enjoys his own plays and who stands in the wings laughing heartily at the comic dialogue...which he himself has invented.[6]

Laughter rings all through the Lupin stories. The police are sober, hard-working fellows, sweating at performance of their duty, constantly tweaked and cozened and mocked. The other characters of the stories, solid citizens all, watch uncomprehendingly the peculiar doings about them. Everywhere rings the friendly laughter of Lupin. His hands are filled with plot misdirections. His head whirls out silver and gold schemes to separate the undeserving from their money.

All this began in 1907, in France and in French, by Maurice LeBlanc. Lupin first appeared in the United States in the book, *The Exploits of Arsene Lupin. The Popular Magazine* serialized his adventure, "The Hollow Needle" (5 parts, end of March to end of May, 1910), and he continued on through various collections of short stories and novels to 1933.

The stories are more or less loosely connected, with enough continuity in them that you can tell about where you are in Lupin's career whatever you read. He begins as a wonderfully merry thief, as interested in the situations he creates and manipulates, as in his casual robberies and swindles. With Lupin, it is never the gross fact of theft, but the deftness with which it is staged, the light amusement he takes in foreseeing everything, being aware of everything, and maneuvering— ever so artistically—those around him.

His likeness? How can I trace it? (So says the narrator of the first short story, the confidante to whom Lupin told enough for his adventures to be recorded.) I have seen Arsene Lupin a score of times, and each time a different being has stood before me...or rather the same being under twenty distorted images reflected by as many mirrors, each image having its special eyes, its particular facial outline, its own gestures, profile, and character.

The science of Colonel Clay seems to have reached France. We are told that Lupin has unparalleled skill at make-up and possesses the useful ability for "changing even the proportions of his face and altering the relations of his features one to the other."

Under these circumstances, you can understand why few of Lupin's descriptions get down to specifics. He is around middle height and of rather slender build. His wrists are lean but capable of terrible power (which should surprise no reader).

His eyes are

> ...at once innocent and satirical, grave and smiling, eyes through which you could certainly not penetrate their owner's baffling individuality, but which nevertheless looked at you with an expression of absolute frankness and sincerity.[7]

Unlike most other great criminal heroes, Lupin begins his literary career by getting arrested. Ganimard did it, the famous French detective who chased Lupin relentlessly before the book began, and through it, and later. This initial arrest is Ganimard's main success. More usually he is toyed with, baffled, and put upon. Always with a good-natured affection, for there is no malice in Lupin.

To begin at the beginning, Lupin is sent to prison and plays hob from there. Escapes and plays hob outside. Twice he tangles with that extraordinary English detective, Homlock Shears. These adventures end in draws and off Lupin goes to years of successful criminality. So deft is he, so sparkling, that he can be forgiven anything.

He collects around him a small army of subordinates, mostly unidentified. By a masterly stroke, he becomes Chief of Detectives (under the name M. Lenormand). For four years, he directs the police search for himself. Still later, he fakes his death and enlists in the Foreign Legion, serving out his time in glory as an informal general directing a vast military campaign. The Legion knows nothing of this. The Legion thinks him dead.

Eventually, Lupin resurrects himself and, heaped with honors, returns to France. There he is identified by the police. Since he is legally dead, they end up (very reluctantly) allowing him to help them unravel a case of serial murder. Not only does he do this, but he is able to turn over to the French government a vast chunk of North Africa. This he acquired while acting as an informal general; having conquered a vast segment of that region, he had established a civilized government headed by himself, as Sultan of Mauretania.

As Sultan, he gracefully yields his private domain to France—and how are you going to jail a national benefactor who performs on that scale? From that point, he essentially retires from crime. Using the name Don Luis Perenna, he marries Florence Lavasseur and takes up residence in the village of Saint-Maclou. There he raises flowers (including many lupins), advises the French police, now and then extends personal assistance to "victims of oppression." In later stories, he acts as a detective, although with not quite the blue-white glitter of his days as France's greatest criminal.

It is a remarkably mild ending—a benefactor of society, a confidante of the police, no longer even the necessity for disguise. (Which is fortunate. If there is one thing a wife hates it is to have her husband fussing in front of the mirror, puttying his nose and applying false eyebrows.)

But then Lupin was essentially a humorist. You could hardly find violence in him, although he possessed the usual proficiency with arms characteristic of a series hero. In his Foreign Legion days, he once held off a swarm of Arabs all by himself, 75 of them down in 75 shots.

Altogether, Lupin is a charming individual of astonishing influence. His image shimmers down through the next decade, both directly in moving pictures and indirectly through the characters he influenced. His example brightens innumerable pages of coming fiction which might otherwise have reflected a different fire.

6-

Arsene Lupin has the distinction of being not only thief, genius, practical joker, adventurer, and detective, but one of the earliest examples of that popular character type, the bent hero.

The bent hero is a more socially acceptable form of the criminal hero. If a character is a thief, you must endlessly excuse his behavior. Nor does the thief enjoy any real status—not, at least, until he is elected to political office. Popular fiction requires that the criminal pay for his crimes. By the end of the series, the iron bars clamp around him, as happened to Colonel Clay and Bunny Manders; or he ends his life in solitude; or he performs an outstanding social service, dying among the Boers or turning over chunks of Africa to the government.

The bent hero, however, makes his peace with the reader

by the less simple process of reformation and restitution.

Reformation comes in a variety of ways. Lupin drifts into reform, marries, and becomes a force for good. This is not the usual way. More typically, the bent hero reforms because he has been transformed by a woman's love. Once panged by her eyes, he finds himself unworthy of her. The soiled texture of his life revulses him. He turns away, flinging the past from him and, for the balance of the series, performs a self-imposed penance, his face pallid but serene. Often he attempts to pay back his thefts. At the least, he performs such services to society as will sponge his conscience back to white.

It is customary that his past returns to nibble darkly at him. Constantly he is impelled to do good by committing new crimes. And at no time can he clasp that lovely innocent lady in his arms and propose. For there is always one more act of restitution. And then one more, to the limits of the reader's patience.

At once, the bent hero became a popular favorite. In his adventures could be found all the excitement of the criminal hero with all the greed left out. Suddenly you could crack safes, swindle, lie, and tie people up, and still remain among the blessed. All in a rush, the magazines reeled with bent heroes and their accomplishments were everywhere, for more than twenty years.

Towering among these figures stands one of the great originals, the pure essence of the bent hero, Hamilton Cleek, The Man of Forty Faces.

Cleek's story begins long long ago, in the 1890s, when T. W. Hanshew and family moved from the United States to England. Hanshew was a man of numerous names, among them Old Cap Collier. For Hanshew was a practicing dime novelist and saw his wares published by such monolithic names as Street & Smith, Tousey, and Munro.

As his first literary production in England, Mr. Hanshew wrote *The World's Finger: An Improbable Story,* publishing this as a hardbound novel in 1901. In this book was introduced Mr. Maverick Narkom, a name whose singular improbability brightens modern eyes. Narkom was Superintendent of Scotland Yard. He would become a familiar figure in the long series of short stories and books to come.

A familiar figure, but not a leading one. The position of command was assumed by a rather enigmatic figure named Hamilton Cleek—an assumed name; his real one is never stated. Cleek is a reformed thief and unofficial genius of Scotland Yard.

Way long ago at the beginning of history, he was:

> The biggest and boldest criminal the police had ever had to cope with, the almost supernatural genius of crime...who, for sheer deviltry, for diabolical ingenuity and for colossal impudence...had not met his match in all the universe.
> Who or what he really was...no man knew.... In his many encounters with the police he had assumed the speech, the characteristics, and, indeed, the factial attributes of (various nationalities)...with an ease and a perfection that...had gained for him the sobriquet of "Forty Faces" among the police, and of "The Vanishing Cracksman" (from) newspaperdom.[8]

It is Cleek's practice to advise the police when and where he is to strike next. They have twelve hours to prepare. They are never successful. The morning after each exploit, the fuming Narkom receives a small item from the theft, always contained in a small pink box tied with rose ribbon, and a card:

"With the Compliments of The Man Who Calls Himself Hamilton Cleek."

What all the cleverness of Scotland Yard fails to do is accomplished by the—um, er—bright witchery of a woman's eyes, so to speak. Cleek gets a look at Miss Ailsa Lorne during one of his merry robberies. Instantly his conscience grows fangs. Regret, regret. He offers to return the stolen jewels, give up his life of crime. He must make himself worthy of her. If only Scotland Yard will agree, and so he writes to Narkom:

> I have lived a life of crime from my very boyhood because I couldn't help it, because it appealed to me, because I glory in risks and revel in dangers.

Cleek proposes that he become a detective, working directly with Narkom:

> *Cleek:* "...let us work hand in hand, for a common cause and for the public good. Will you, Mr. Narkom? Will you?
> *Narkom:* "Will I? Won't I? Jove! What a detective you'll make. Bully boy! Bully boy!"

Then, for the first time, Cleek reveals himself. He is

...faultlessly dressed, faultlessly mannered, with the slim-loined form, the slim-walled nose, and the clear-cut features of the born aristocrat....

He is around 30, as clear-eyed and clean shaven as the young executive in a Rolls Royce ad. "There was something about him, in look, in speech, in bearing, that mutely stood sponsor for the thing called 'birth'."

Now that the physical prototype for 7,000 lithe young pulp magazine heroes has been established, we learn why the police could never lay hands on him.

His features seemed to writhe and knot and assume in as many moments a dozen different aspects. "I've had the knack of doing that (he tells Narkom) since the hour I could breathe."

It is a singular gift, since apparently the bone and cartilage of his face go flexible as putty. He explains this talent, in another place, by remarking that his mother, while pregnant, amused herself by playing with a rubber-faced toy. The genetic impact was obviously severe. As a matter of course, Cleek also used disguise materials deftly, but his flexible face saved lots of bother.[9]

Thus amazingly equipped by Nature, and by the Law approved, Mr. Hamilton Cleek began a fourteen-year career. The complexities of his bibliography are many. First came short stories in the magazines, followed by books, followed by rewrites of books, and British and American editions with varying titles and contents. Eleven books are known, plus a long series of short stories in the *Short Stories* magazine, 1913-1920. At least one serial, "The Riddle of the Night," was published in *All-Story Weekly* (5-parts, July 17 through August 14, 1915). The first book, *The Man of Forty Faces,* was published in England in 1910; the last, *The House of the Seven Keys,* in 1925.[10]

Since Hanshew died in 1914, other hands obviously carried on the Cleek adventures. (For only rarely does a successful series character lapse because his original author leaves.) In this case, it appears that the series was continued by

Hanshew's wife and daughter, Hazel, working at least partially from his notes.

The scene was England and the adventures were bound in hard covers. But Cleek springs from the good rich soil of the American dime novels. True, the stories are longer, and so are the sentences. The pages are spread with Good Old Boy sentiment as strong as ripe cheese. But the characters' attitudes and the situations in which they find themselves are straight out of the thrill-a-page weeklies. Hanshew was fascinated by odd crimes and odder clues and his stories are dense with devices and singular ideas:

—A horrible flopping red horror shloggs dark manor corridors.

—Murder in a locked room, although no wound or murder weapon can be discovered.

—A mysterious purple inscription is found on a dead man's hand.

—Poison gleams on the skeleton's finger bone.

—At the murder scene are found gigantic, claw-like tracks.

—A man disappears from a glass room directly under the eyes of observers.

—The story action is haunted by Apaches, fresh from France, dreadful menaces, scowling for vengence.

Apaches infest the popular literature of the time. But nowhere are they more troublesome than in Cleek's adventures. They represent unfinished business from his past. Back when he was The Vanishing Cracksman, while still in Paris, he became decidedly friendly with Margot, Queen of the Apaches. She was a little French doll with a "graceful, willowy figure" and an "enchanting, if rather too highly tinted face, with almond eyes and a fluff of shining hair." Even at this distance in time, one feels her appeal.

When he reforms, however, Cleek dumps them all— Apaches, Margot, and, as it turns out, his peace of mind. Forever afterward, Margot, simmering with the hatred of a scorned woman, glides on his trail, eager to administer a dagger, a bullet, or a heart-felt curse. Let him escape one trap, and she plans another, her tinted face glowing with demonaic fury. He pretends to be dead and buried. But even that ruse fails. When last seen, Margot and her French toughs still haunt the shadows out there.

By contrast, Cleek's own true love, Ailsa Lorne, seems a pallid little wisp. She is a slight, fair girl, gloriously beautiful. As the series opens, she is twenty, an orphan, penniless, who directs the household of her uncle, Sir Horace Wyvern. It takes innumerable pages before Ailsa decides that she loves Cleek. For one thing, his gift of distorting his face repels her. For another, he is so awfully determined that he must be worthy of her that, in her presence, he is hardly more tangible than a ghost.

Cleek has resolved not to press his suit until he has made financial restitution to all the victims of the "Cracksman." And so the years roll by. He does not seem to have married Ailsa, a girl of singular patience, even by 1925. Beyond that date, we have no authority to speak.

It is through Ailsa that Cleek acquires his faithful boy assistant, Dollops. (There is no cure for these names; they are the ones Hanshew wished on his people.) She walks home in an evening fog and Dollops tries to rob her. Cleek stops him. Boy's first attempt at crime—starving—ragged—thin—red-headed—Cockney—nineteen. Certainly he tried to be honest. But there was no work. He is a brand to be saved from the burning.

Dollops turns into one of the most devoted assistants fiction ever described. Even Bunny didn't sleep curled up outside Raffles' door. Dollops turns out to be clever, quick-witted, constantly hungry (in the fine old dime novel technique of putting a name to a stack of traits). He brings a feeble trace of humor to the series and seems to have borrowed from the Katzenjammer Kids the trick of strewing glued papers to discourage pursuit.[11] (These stick to your feet and hands and you fall down and are annoyed. "Ach, dos dodghasted kids!")

Superintendent Narkom is above such horseplay. But not by much. If he had some dignity in *The World's Finger*, he rapidly loses it in the Cleek stories. Although he is Cleek's best friend and official contact, he is portrayed as a small, round-faced, chubby idiot with little fat legs. Unable to grasp the simplest clue, he meanders through the action entirely at sea, unable to grasp the meaning of all these complicated goings-on.

"Cinnamon!" he cries in exasperation. "By all that's wonderful! By Jove!" Or, simply, "Gad!" In addition to being a boob, he is also a collector's-grade snob. In the early novels, he scoots around London in a bright red Rolls Royce. In a later effort to tighten security, the color of the Rolls is changed to bright blue. Narkom is particularly given to clasping Cleek's hand and gasping spats of admiration and early 20th Century drivel about man-to-man friendship. He is married, has a daughter, and his wife chaperones Cleek and Ailsa to assure the continued purity of the text.

In spite of these infantile characters, demeaned to heighten the hero's gleam, the stories are interesting. Although often slow. Although often worked for the device. Although driven by dated melodrama. In spite of all, an imp glitter touches each. Credit for some of this goes to Mr. Hanshew, the rest to Cleek.

Aside from his extraordinary face, Cleek has one or two other physical designators. He displays a queer little smile that darts up one side of his face. He walks with a swinging, soldierly stride—at least when out of character. His voice is smooth and even.

Like most detectives, he concentrates powerfully. When in the clutch of thought, his lower lip pushes far out, his eyes focus on his feet, and his thumbs twiddle slowly round and round. Immediately afterward, the essential elements of the mystery are penetrated. It is now time for action.

And now does he gather Mr. Narkom into his confidence? Not by the shadow of Sherlock Holmes. No self-respecting detective ever reveals what the solution is by the middle of the story. Instead, he calls for flour dredgers or tin pepper pots. "Ayupee," he remarks, "the Javanese method of procedure." Or, "If there's soap on the window sill, I know the man." Or, "Five lacs of rupees...By George, I've got it."

Poor Narkom gapes, bemused. But Cleek's got it. Always.

Once the foul plot is crushed, the handcuffs clicked, and Cleek's disguise removed, then it's off to the countryside. No hero loved nature more. Flowers sent him trembling with passion; a branch of apple-blossoms charges him with poetry. His leisure is spent lolling with Nature, finding sermons in birds and concertos in brooks.

All this rouses terrible despair in Mr. Narkom. Cleek's adoration of nature means that he is seldom to be reached when the Yard is faced by still another incomprehensible mystery. So Narkom is often reduced to advertising in the agony columns for Cleek to come back. In his office, he peers intently at visitors, murmuring (in a self-depreciating way) "Er—you mightn't be... Um. Gad! That is...." In vain he waits for someone to whistle the opening notes to "God Save the King," Cleek's identifier, whatever face he is wearing.

Admittedly, Narkom is at a disadvantage. He has seen Cleek's true face only twice. How then to find the invisible? But Cleek never stays lost.

For quite some time, Cleek has maintained a little establishment under the name (and face) of Captain Burbage. Eventually the Apaches blew up a large piece of the house, sadly jarring the landlady. Perhaps, with such relentless enemies, Cleek was wise to limit his friends.

(And how do you find a faceless man? Just shadow that bright blue Rolls Royce or trail that skinny boy eating his way along the street.)

A curious kind of life, you say—like a dime novel.

Indeed, it's even more curious, when you consider what he has given up. For Mr. Hamilton Cleek, the nameless, the faceless, is of royal blood. Yes, by golly. In reality, he is the titled King of Maurevania, "dear land of desolated hopes, dear grave of murdered joys."

The background history is complex. His mother, Queen Karma, got exiled and died in poverty. Her son (Cleek) vanished; one daughter died; the other disappeared into Persia. Nothing more is heard of the royal family for years. Then the Maurevanians discover that Cleek, their rightful king, is alive. At once they flash to frenzy that he return.

And eventually he visits his country once more.

Bands. Guardsmen. Scarlet carpets. Cheering: "Vivat Maximilian! Vivat le roi!"

Throngs kneeling. Throngs in ecstacy.

And what does Cleek do?

What any decent hero does: Refuses it all. For if he is King, he can't marry Ailsa. It's as simple as that. If he becomes King, he may have Ailsa only as his "morganatic wife," an evasive way of saying "mistress." You can guess the emotions of a 1914 hero when hearing that suggestion.

Cleek: "Kings after all are only men—and a man's first duty is to the one woman of his heart.... My only kingdom is here—in this dear woman's arms. Walk with me, Ailsa—walk with me always...."

It would take almost 25 years for reality to catch up with fiction. Meanwhile, Cleek and Ailsa, burnt shining white by renunciation, exit arm in arm. Glory, glory, glory. It's a shame they never got married.

7–

Cleek's world exists at about the same level of reality as a 1910 operetta. The characters exist for the story; the story exists for the scenes; and these exist for the puzzle and the special efforts. Once the hidden situation is exposed, the content evaporates. What remains is only that spurious affection that the characters express one to the other, with exclamation points and intense moos.

You read the Cleek stories while keeping your eyes half closed. They are dime novels at heart—dime novels magnified, intensively scrubbed, polished, curled, and told to sit up straight, like a gentleman. That the stories succeed so well is a tribute both to Hanshew and the vitality of the form.

With Cleek, the bent hero took on characteristic shape and form. But other ways of handling this character type were possible.

At about the same time that the Cleek stories appeared in England, O. Henry had published a single short story about another interesting criminal, Jimmy Valentine. Jimmy might have lived and died in that single story. Instead, he became the subject of an extremely popular play, *Alias Jimmy Valentine,* (1910), and so impressed the public that his name is still associated with gentleman safe-crackers.

Jimmy's story, "A Retrieved Reformation," was included in the 1909 *Roads of Destiny*. It has barely aged. Its tone is crisp, cool American, pleasantly sardonic. Every sentence shines as brightly as Mr. Valentine's specially tempered steel burglar tools. Where Hanshew is fuzzy and extravagant, O. Henry is precise and restrained. They are writers of two different schools and the difference shows.

In summary, Mr. Jimmy Valentine, professional safe-cracker, is released from prison. (Influence has had its way with the governor.) Reclaiming his burglar tools, Jimmy takes up business again—which is opening safes and removing their contents. The Valentine touch is unmistakable and detective Ben Price is soon on the trail. By this time, Valentine has arrived in Elmore, Arkansas, intending to give the bank his professional attention. Instead he meets Annabel Adams, falls in love with her, gives up his criminal career, and becomes Ralph D. Spencer, shoe store owner.

A few days before their wedding, Annabel's sister's daughter, Agatha, gets herself accidentally locked in the bank vault with the time lock set. Forced to action, Jimmy drills her free before she suffocates, although he realizes that this will reveal his past. Once Agatha is released, he strides out of the bank, coldly controlled, iron faced, to find detective Ben Price waiting for him. But Price refuses to recognize him as Jimmy Valentine and turns away, leaving Jimmy unarrested, to make what explanations he can and to continue his reformation.

The major bent hero characteristics are firmly in place: the skillful criminal reforms for love, then uses his professional abilities in the service of others. Moreover he is such a personable, quick-witted, humorous young man, such a nice boy to be a cracksman. Valentine's adventure added further glamour to the belief that the cracksman—the box man, the safe mechanic—was of the aristocracy of crime.

How familiar the scene. The cracksman crouches before the iron door, his fingers sanded, his ear intent, coaxing out the hidden numbers. It is not thieving, not really. It is, actually, a demonstration of high personal skill. And, besides, those wealthy robber barons who hoard up riches in their complacent safes deserve to be robbed.

Through the 'Teens and 'Twenties slipped a horde of night

workers, listening to the tumblers fall. Even after the scene was worn to the back cords, and the cracksman replaced by more faddish types, the identical situation was continued in the 1930s pulp magazines. By then, it was the avenging hero who manipulated the dial. For the sake of justice. All major magazine heroes possessed the cracksman's skill. Their fingers never faltered, nor were they forced to the ignominy of Valentine's drills and punches.

Of those celebrated cracksmen to follow Valentine, two tower above the rest. Both are young, resolute, clever. Both, renouncing their ignoble ways for a woman's love, traveled spiny roads in their return to a decent, Republican style of life.

These gentlemen were, respectively, Michael Lanyard, the Lone Wolf, created by Louis Joseph Vance; and Jimmie Dale, the Gray Seal, by Frank Packard. Both exerted profound influence on the course of pulp magazine fiction. The Lone Wolf appeared a hair before Dale—Vance had him in a book by 1914, the year that Dale first reached the magazines. In respect to this fragile seniority, we will first turn to the Lone Wolf.

8–

Eight books of Michael Lanyard's adventures were published from 1914 to 1934. It is unfortunate that he is primarily known for a series of gosh-awful moving pictures which, as that medium was prone to do with the bent hero, altered most of the facts and vulgarized most of the substance.

The fiction is something else again. Lanyard stands in sharp focus, a hero with a clear and immediate intelligence. In a medium where lead characters performed unfettered by thought, Lanyard's mind glitters and leaps. Straight through the rind of melodrama he cuts, impatient of posturing, slashing direct to reality.

He faces four masked criminals, beautifully tailored and professing to represent the leadership of an international cartel of crime. Snorting cheerfully, Lanyard punctures the romance with the iced facts of their identities and professional incompetence.

Facing the psychological necessity for reform, he reforms. He will make restitution to the extent possible; because of this, he is to remain poor throughout the series. A trial period of testing his will to reform is self-assigned. His own internal tensions and pressures are understood and allowed for. Not a vestige of purple emotion shows. All this, you understand, in a period when a fictional character showed emotion by beating himself on the short ribs and howling until the ceiling cracked.

The first novel, *The Lone Wolf,* was published in *Munsey's Magazine*, early in 1914. The scene is 1913 Paris and the story is modern in feeling, lacking only modern despair. True, the novel is filled with devices once remarkable, now obsolete: gas lights flicker, hotels have no running water in rooms, pilots of pursuit aircraft are armed with rifles, since the machine gun interrupter gear has not yet been invented. But these matters merely emphasize the period, enhancing the story without smothering it.

The narrative moves along with a minimum of character posturing, an innovation that can hardly be appreciated unless you are steeped in 1914 popular fiction. The personality of the Lone Wolf is presented in some detail, warts and all, with emotional deeps that are at once understandable and unfaked.

Certain elements in the early Lone Wolf history seem to contain echoes of the Cleek adventures. Apaches abound and the underworld slinks through sordid Parisian alleys, muttering, plotting, knifing. It is believed, however, that both Cleek and Lanyard benefited considerably from the *Memoirs of Vidocq* (1828-1829), a semi-fictional account of an ex-criminal and France's first chief of police, a bent hero in his own right, whose example was not lost on Arsene Lupin, either.

Michael Lanyard's origins are as obscure as his literary connections. He became a criminal willingly and willingly rejected that profession to prove himself worthy of a woman. Like Cleek, Lanyard decides to make restitution for his crimes. And, in the pattern of The Vanishing Cracksman, Lanyard receives the indulgence of Scotland Yard. At least, they don't arrest him, and eventually he enters the British Secret Service.

Beyond these similarities are more fundamental differences. It is as if Vance were holding up the Cleek story, turning it in one ironic hand, saying: "This point, this, and this—these are sugar dreams. Here's how they really would be. Disguise? No flexible face, please. Instead, two days' whiskers, old clothing, a menial job. That disguise will work fairly well. No more. You can hardly expect more."

These are the keys to the mind of the Lone Wolf: Rationality, self-disciplined competence, objectivity; intelligence and perception of the highest order. All coupled with the ability to assess alternatives and take almost instantaneous action.

Our lead character, born about 1888, is brought to France when five years old, permitted to raise himself in a carefully obscure hotel. He becomes a petty thief. Under the tutorage of Bourke, a talented Irish criminal, the boy is rechristened Michael Lanyard (his French name is Marcel Troyon). He is taken to America, learns the language, customs, social graces of that foreign land. And also receives the technical training appropriate for a first-class cracksman. He also learns Bourke's philosophy: Study the objective; strike fast; be friendless.

In his young manhood, Lanyard is tall, leanly built, but with exceptional strength. His hair, heavy and dark, is worn rather long. Dark eyes glitter in a face of "extraordinary pallor." The description is that of an aggressive poet. From childhood, he has learned the techniques of close-in fighting. He has mastered *la savate,* as well as the Apache version of jiu-jitsu.

To these accomplishments is added fluency in French, German, English, and American—both the formal drawing room languages and the street argots of each. Lanyard is typical of most educated men in being self-educated. He attended French public school irregularly and seems to have dropped out early. But he was a compulsive, persistent reader in a variety of fields.

Under Bourke's tutelege, Lanyard's education became more technical. He showed unusual aptitude for mathematics, skill in mechanics, and became "a connoisseur of armour-plate and explosives in their more pacific applications." To these specialities was added detailed knowledge of precious stones and an understanding of paintings so deeply knowledgeable that in Paris, the city of art, his cover as wealthy young art connoisseur was unchallenged.

Although staying only irregularly in Paris—professional

activities in England and America kept him absent for long periods—he maintained a small apartment, rented under an assumed name. The rooms are furnished and on the sixth floor, with a window conveniently overlooking the roof. He has, in addition, free use of the studio of Solon the painter (more often drunk than painting) from which there are numerous concealed avenues of escape.

Lanyard is very careful to provide himself with alternate escape routes. He prepares with the assumption that all plans will fail. His precautions are laid in depth. As a last resort, he maintains an automobile powered by a high-performance engine. This machine is garaged in a rented stable off the Rue des Acacias, and he personally maintains it. His cover story is that he is the chauffeur for a crazy Englishman who keeps traveling—thus explaining why the automobile is so infrequently used.

Lanyard's professional work is conducted as carefully as is his planning for disaster. Each job is scouted in detail. Entrances and exits are marked. Household schedules are learned and the personalities understood of the people in the house. As a result, his crimes glide smoothly along, with a minimum of danger. At work, he wears a black velvet half mask, dark clothing. Usually he carries a gun, although he does not like to use weapons and rigorously refrains from shooting, even in self defense.

Thus Mr. Lanyard, as seen from the outside: intelligent, controlled, precise, a coolly careful mind whose main sign of tension is shown in his inordinate love of gambling. But only at the tables; he does not gamble with his liberty.

As is clear, the figure described is the bent hero, this time tinted French-English. As is obligatory, he falls in love and determines that the Lone Wolf shall walk no more. The girl who catches his heart, Lucy Shannon, is an operative in the British Secret Service. As a welcome surprise, she is not unusually pretty. Rather small, brown eyed, in her early twenties, she is self-composed and quite self-sufficient. Unlike other 1914 heroines (always excepting the wonderful women of the dime novels), she is neither a fainter, a ninny, nor an innocent. Her face suggests the possibility of thought; her actions confirm it. How pleasing it is to read a story in which the heroine is more than a decoration and plot device.

Because of Lucy, Lanyard resolves to give up Lone Wolfing. While he hints broadly enough to her of his affection, he will make no open declaration. Not yet. First, he must prove to himself (not her) that he can reform and support himself for a year by means other than the contents of people's safes.

In making this resolution he plunges characteristically into an analysis of his own emotions. These are particularly interesting. In almost the whole of pulp magazine literature, no hero is allowed to be sufficiently articulate to describe his inner perceptions. Occasionally, you learn that he is angry or pleased, or that he likes yak butter or can play the clarinet. But it is seldom that a lead character dips deeper than his own skin—as does Lanyard, when he assesses his life as the Lone Wolfe:

> I saw myself for the first time clearly, as I have been ever since I can remember—a crook, thoughtless, vain, rapacious, ruthless, skulking in the shadows and thinking myself an amazingly fine fellow because, between coups, I would play the gentleman a bit.... I thought there was something finer and thrilling and romantic in the career of a great criminal and myself a wonderful figure—an enemy of society.[12]

So much for the romance of crime.

The Lone Wolf novelettes and novels make up a long biography that extends from pre-World War I Europe to the mid-Depression United States. It separates naturally into two parts—this because Vance seems to have tired of the character and, like Conan Doyle before him, sought to terminate the series. (The dedication to *The Lone Wolf Returns* is to F. E. Verney "because he asked for more and because there won't be any more.")

The first group of stories is found in the books *The Lone Wolf* (1914), *The False Faces* (1918), *Red Masquerade* (1921), *Alias the Lone Wolf* (also 1921 but chronologically after *Masquerade),* and *The Lone Wolf Returns* (1923). To condense this history. Lanyard marries Lucy Shannon after he reforms, and they go to New York City. The machinations of the German spy, Ekstrom, forces Lanyard to flee the United States. They take up residence in Belgium, have a son and daughter (who is not mentioned until the 1931, *The Lone Wolf's Son)*. Both children and Lucy are murdered by the Germans when they invade Belgium—Herr Ekstrom instigated the killings. Lanyard pursues Ekstrom all over the continent of Europe while the war goes on, never quite catching this master spy but collecting intelligence information valuable to the Allies almost incidentally to his main quest.

He returns to New York City to fight the German spy machine there. It is a difficult crossing. His ship is torpedoed under him and he is captured by a U-boat (with a secret berth by Martha's Vinyard). The U-boat he is able to sabotage and sink. Escaping to New York City, and considerable plot complications, he is able to manipulate matters so that Ekstrom dies in a hail of his associates' bullets. While Lanyard set the situation up, he never pulled a trigger. In 1918, only western heroes shot people.

The False Faces (serialized in the *Saturday Evening Post)* introduces Detective Crane of the New York Police Department. Crane is far too intelligent to be a Watson and far too flexible to be the stodgy dumbkin of the movies. He is an American archetype, long, lanky, with a thin nose and a lantern jaw. His face has a vaguely Indian cast, but, in general appearance, he looks like a beardless Uncle Sam. An unlighted cigar juts from his mouth. Crane is an utterly competent policeman. He regards Lanyard with amused respect. Over the years they become firm friends, fortunately for the novels, because Crane provides the means by which the law can officially sweep up the debris, arrest everyone needing arrest, and so clear the stage for the next volume.

Late in his career, Crane bends police regulations just a fraction too far and is asked to resign. He sets up his own investigative business, apparently on an international basis, and between actions, commutes to his home in Scarsdale. He is a fine fellow, understating everything, fooled by nothing.

The next book in the series is *Red Masquerade,* based very loosely on a moving picture titled "The Lone Wolf's Daughter" (1919). Lanyard is now working with the British Secret Service. There is this bunch of radical fiend types who plan to murder the King and assassinate the Cabinet members, and overthrow the Empire. Lanyard prevents this ambitious undertaking.

In *Alias the Lone Wolf,* he has resigned from the Secret Service to vacation in Spain, meets Eve de Montalais, widow of a French war hero, and is promptly framed for stealing her jewels by a remarkably rough gang of crooks. The effort to recover the jewels leads to Paris, multiple murder, and a wonderful automobile chase across France. As a matter of course, there follows a trip across the Atlantic in a small yacht; this Lanyard wrecks on American shoals and recovers the jewels.

Once in New York City, he runs afoul of a fat mastermind of crime. This paragon frames Lanyard by introducing a duplicate Lone Wolf. As soon as this matter is cleared up, the crooks hit Lanyard with an automobile, giving him concussion, amnesia, and a seven-month gap in his life. But he comes about handsomely: the fat man gets shot by his own henchmen (shades of Herr Ekstrom) in an ending manipulated by the Lone Wolf. And to his astonishment, Lanyard finds himself again a married man, Eve de Montalais Lanyard having arranged the ceremony about the fifth day of his concussion.

That concludes the first group of stories. The last two books, *Alias* and *Returns,* are made up of novelettes originally published in the *Cosmopolitan Magazine*, 1921 and 1923.

Until 1931, nothing more is published about the Lone Wolfe. The character is continued in an endless series of moving pictures which were as far removed from the novels as left is from right. At the beginning of the 1930s, Vance once more took up Lanyard's career, publishing *The Lone Wolf's Son* (1931), *Encore the Lone Wolf* (1933), and *The Lone Wolf's Last Prowl* (1934). These pick up the story about twelve years after *The Lone Wolf Returns.*

Eve has died, a victim of that doom which stalks any woman who marries a popular hero. Lanyard is now the New York manager of Delibes of Paris, dealers in antiques and objects-d'art. To his great astonishment, he discovers that his son, Maurice, is still alive—somehow Herr Ekstrom missed him. The boy has been roaming around Europe for something over twenty years and is a typical Lanyard—looks like his father and has become the Lone Wolf II. After a considerable amount of superficial emotion, Maurice is reclaimed from a

Life of Crime and marries an exceedingly wealthy girl.

In the final book, there is quite a lot to do, with Lanyard worrying about Maurice and Maurice worrying about Lanyard; nobody believes that a thief can reform, and the reader is kept all stirred up. Tough gangsters swagger into the action, and guns and cars go off in all directions, and reputations are saved at the last possible instant, and other satisfying ingredients. By now, Lanyard is a grandfather and the series, too, has become thin and elderly. The stories are short, their type is large. While they are still of interest, the superb earlier novels will come no more.

Which seems to be what Vance was afraid of, all along.

Louis Joseph Vance died in 1933, before publication of the *Last Prowl.* Born in 1879 in new York City, he first studied art but switched to fiction with the coming of the family-oriented pulps. His work appeared in *Munsey's Magazine, The Popular Magazine,* and then in the higher paying slick magazines, including the *Saturday Evening Post* and *Cosmopolitan.* His mystery novel, *The Brass Bowl,* became a best seller in 1907, and, over the course of an extended writing career, he published more than thirty mystery and crime novels.

Six years after Vance's death, *Detective Fiction Weekly* serialized *The Lone Wolf,* beginning with the September 9, 1939, issue. You can look all day without finding a copyright date or an indication that the novel was being reprinted. At about the same time, the Magazine Publishers group brought out a pulp titled the *Lone Wolf Detective Magazine.* This, however, had no discernible connection with either Lanyard or Vance, the magazine reprinting action detective stories featuring "Lone Wolf" detective types.[13]

In August 1965, *The Saint Mystery Magazine* printed the unpublished short story, "The White Terror." This, set in 1919, is a pleasantly complex adventure beginning on a train from Vienna to Paris. A rather deadly woman is attempting to deliver The Seven Emeralds of St. Stephen to Prince Karl, the last Hapsburg emperor of Austria and the King of Hungary. Her enemies are ferocious and the Lone Wolf is promptly drawn into the struggle. It is a charming period piece and Lanyard conducts himself with accustomed grace and efficiency.

The mechanics of the bent hero requires that the lead character sin, be redeemed, and, by dangerous and long-continued efforts, rehabilitate himself in the eyes of The Woman. Lanyard fits part of that pattern, although in other parts, he is curiously atypical. In intelligence and introspection, he has real dimension. He is informed, richly immersed in the culture around him, unique in his ability to reason out courses of action appropriate to the world of the reader, as well as the world of the fictional adventurer.

The blending of crook-hero elements in reasonably realistic settings place the early Lone Wolf novels in that select group of influences heading off down the pike toward the 1924 *Black Mask*. Obviously, the tone of the fiction is different, so don't worry yourself trying to discover Race Williams in Lanyard. The essential difference is not in the number of guns that go off, but in the stability of the society through which the Lone Wolf moves. Even through the disintegration of World War I and the giggy 1920s aftermath, the Lone Wolf's world is free of that social festering and inarticulate horror which underlies the *Black Mask* world.

These are differences enough. The great similarity lies in the disdain for inflated melodrama, the insistence on character, and the attention to the details of reality which are characteristic of the best Lone Wolf and *Black Mask* adventures. The same qualities which distinguish the writer from the action hack.

While Vance was polishing his character to a hard brilliance, another writer, Frank Packard, took up about the same elements and moved off in a different direction.

Packard is of great interest. He exerted direct influence on several of the major single-character pulp magazine series of the 1930s. Packard hit upon a highly popular mixture of materials and played them to the hilt. His work is more superficial than that of the early Vance. His characters are easier to assimilate because they are shallower, and the sense of reality that fills his work is slickly deceptive, the vivid descriptions concealing brazen sleight-of-hand. How deftly Packard evades those constraints of real life which cause the

Lone Wolf so much time and energy to overcome.

Packard's world derives from many sources. He placed on paper environments borrowed (on one hand) from Dumas, Dickens, and Crane, and (on the other), from the Nick Carter school. His pages glare with melodrama, disguise, sentimentality, agonized emotion, and triple doses of suspense. A writer of considerable facility, Packard produced a long series of novels and stories. These resonated through the pulp magazines for the next twenty years. For Packard was a master builder of semi-realistic romances. His lesson was not ignored.

Nor was his hero, Jimmie Dale, The Gray Seal.

The Monthly Story Magazine, June 1905. Second issue of another general magazine that offered both fiction and 14 pages of still photographs from popular plays. The magazine would soon become the *Blue Book,* the grande dame of the pulps.

People's Magazine, August 1906. This is the second issue of a general magazine for the entire family, offering fiction, humor, articles, and theatrical gossip.

V
Alias The Gray Seal

1–

Jimmie Dale. Born 1888. Father manufacturer of safes. Family wealthy. Lives New York City, Riverside Drive mansion.

Graduated Harvard 1909. Member St. James Club. Entered father's business full time. Informally associated with safe manufacturing and design several years prior.

Has strong, restless intelligence. Retentive memory. Unusual mechanical aptitude. Remembered in college for fondness of jokes, skill at amateur dramatics. Read S. Holmes, Dupin, Raffles, Lupin. Much amused by Jimmy Valentine. While in father's office read safe robbery reports from police/insurance companies. Felt imagination flame.

In 1911 created the character of the Gray Seal. Intent to tease police, to prank, to joke. Entered homes, stores, public buildings by night, opening safes and leaving behind a gray diamond paper seal. Took nothing. A game. The sport in the doing: I was here; I did this.

Mid-1912. Entered Marx's high fashion jewelers, Maiden Lane, New York City. Surprised by unidentified person(s). Fled. Found that in excitement, he had accidentally retained a pearl necklace.

Next morning arrived first of a long series of letters, hand-written by woman unknown. She knew all about him, all about the Gray Seal. All about crime for a joke:

She wrote: "...the cleverness, the originality of the Gray Seal as a crook lacked but one thing...a leading string to guide it into channels that were worthy of his genius."

Letter ended with ultimatium: Act at her direction or prepare for 20 years in Sing-Sing.

So it began. A life in which the joke was set aside for serious matters. A long series of break-ins and burglaries. Yet never a crime committed. It was thieving in the cause of justice, blunting the underworld's attacks on the innocent, outwitting the evil. To all the world, it was otherwise. Newspapers screamed. Police records bulged. The underworld gaped and admired. Night after night, the tall figure in black silk mask glided silently to new outrages, competent and endlessly resourceful; branding each job with gray paper diamond.

1913, his father died. Mother long dead. Dale calculated his worth, sold out interest in safe company. Turned to sedate life of rich young gentlemen. Outwardly. Idling through life in a big home on Riverside Drive. Alone except for faithful old butler, Jason: deep sentimental attachment; long ago bounced infant Jimmie on knee. Also chauffeur, Benson, faithful, clever tough, saved by Dale from assault of East Side thugs.

From Benson, from Jason, Dale's secret life hidden. Vanished irregularly from his home. Kept queer hours. Intimately familiar with worst of New York City underworld, he kept a room, third floor, tenement, called it his Sanctuary. There, disguise kit, a secret place for clothing change. Tricked up as dope addict, Larry the Bat. Recognized and accepted in the Badlands. Moved freely through underworld. Yet apart.

One day, *she* wrote:

Things are a little too warm, aren't they Jimmie: Let's let them cool a year.

And for a year, silence. Dale scoured the underworld for her. Found no trace.

Early 1914. "Dear Philanthropic Crook," she wrote. There followed exact, neat information, concise as an intelligence report. Directions to prevent another miscarriage of justice.

Again the Gray Seal walked. Again, success. His return blasted into headlines. Dale's close personal friend, Herman Carruthers, managing editor, Morning *News-Argus,* offered $25,000 for capture of Gray Seal. $60,000 other rewards were added.

From May to late August, 1914: eleven exploits. Through them, certain criminals sent to penitentiary. Underworld raged. Gray Seal a squealer. Unforgivable. "Death to the Gray Seal!" they cried. "Death to the Gray Seal." Every foray now, exposed him to gangland's vengence, police action—to revelation that Jimmie Dale was Larry the Bat was the Gray Seal.

Early July 1914: by accident, he almost caught *her* placing a letter in his car. She fled. Left behind a golden ring, the crest a bell surmounted by bishop's miter; under this, inscribed words *Sonnez le Tocsin*—SOUND THE ALARM.

The Tocsin, he said. Yes, The Tocsin.

November 1914. A bitter three-day battle with slickly malevolent ring of criminals. Purring crime geniuses in evening dress linked with shabby toughs: The Crime Club. For the first time, he meets The Tocsin face to face. Silver Mag, a broken crone.

No.

It is disguise. She is beautiful, lovely young Marie LaSalle.

Crime Club murdered her father and uncle. Introduced fake uncle. They seek her death—for $11-million family fortune. She, in hiding, seeks evidence, vengence.

Violence climaxes violences. Danger. Exploits most thrilling. Ultimately, Gray Seal penetrates heart of Crime Club. The evil perish. But he has been recognized as Larry the Bat.

"Death to the Gray Seal!" Shrieking gangland hordes pursue him to Sanctuary. Vicious gun battle. Fire destroys Sanctuary. Dale and Marie escape.

Three weeks' peace.

Marie knits up the raveled sleeve of her fortune. Then vanishes.

Six months. No word. No trace. Dale worried to pale frenzy. To re-establish his window into the underworld, creates the figure of Smarlinghue, a junkie-artist. Slowly accepted by crookdom. No trace of Marie.

Suddenly, letters again. Crime Club leaders still live. Her life at forfeit. Work, still, for Tocsin and Gray Seal.

June through August 1915. Gray Seal strikes nine times. No trace of Marie. She trying to preserve him from worst of struggle. He loves her, loves her. Is shot in leg. Is trapped. Escapes. Receives notice from Tocsin that it will soon end happily.

It does end. As current Crime Club leader writhes on floor, dosed with Club's special secret colorless odorless invincible poison—as Secret Service batters down doors of shed on old wharf—down trapdoor to boat Gray Seal and The Tocsin escape. Across river....

But on other side, happiness not yet. She must leave him, ah yet again, mine own.

There still lives the final master of Crime Club—a disguise artist—unseen—known as the Phantom.

She must disappear. No, he cannot follow her.

Gone—to a new disguise. No temporizing now. The Phantom and his brutal minions are fought in long bitter engagement through New York slums and alleys. 42 days of it. Into late October 1915. Behind panels of a hidden room, in a secret corridor, The Phantom dies, gunned by the thugs he sought to cheat. Marie reveals her new disguise as Mother Margot, ancient push-cart hag, the Phantom's right-hand assistant. Explaining why his plots kept failing.

Happiness now?

For a year. Peace broken in 1917 as President Wilson leads the nation to war. Jimmie overseas. Combat in France. Returns unharmed. Formally bethrothed to Marie in the Fall of 1919. Off to Paris she goes, that exquisite girl, to purchase her lacy trousseau.

But...in July, she chances upon plot hatched by expatriate crooks. It emmeshes Ray Thorne, close friend of Dale's. Marie secretly to New York as Mother Margot. The tocsin sounds again. Reluctantly, with foreboding, up stands the Gray Seal, alive once more.

But too late. Ray Thorne lies murdered, apparent victim of Gray Seal. To clear the GS—who has never killed—Smarlinghue lives again. Larry the Bat walks. Again death in sleazy rooms. Shadows drifting in refuse-clogged alleys. Brief bitter gun flame from darkness. Fear again and peril and dread for Marie's safety, while Dale walks those streets he never wished to revisit.

But how can a series hero quit this sordid savage melodrama?

July 25, 1920. A stinking celler room, secret under the East Side. Carruthers, concealed, hears the real murderer sneer out a confession to Larry the Bat. The case is over. Now, thank God, now, the Gray Seal can vanish forever.

Carruthers vanishes instead.

July 27th, 1920. Over the next three days, a frantic mad

blind chase. Leads are fragile. A mysterious map. A mysterious red-headed man. Mysterious gangsters, snarling, shooting, scheming. A treasure hunt at dawn. $200,000 concealed bank funds. Then Larry the Bat drives raging crooks into a sealed underground room, his pistol glittering. Carruthers watches, in grateful amazement, his benefactor, the Gray Seal. Of all people. The Gray Seal.

It is full morning: July 31, 1920.

Police come, The Gray Seal is gone.

The wedding impends, just out of sight. The series is ended. The passionate, exhausting adventures are complete.

2-

With minor interruptions, the fictional adventures of Jimmie Dale extend from early 1914 to July 31, 1920. The chronology of the published stories is longer. The first Jimmie Dale story appeared in the May 1914 issue of *People's Magazine* and ran every month through August 1915. These stories were collected in the book, *The Adventures of Jimmie Dale,* published in 1917. A second series of stories, "The Professional Adventures of Jimmie Dale," began in the November 1916 *People's* and ran, probably consecutively, though the July 1917 issue. These were collected in the 1919 hardback, *The Further Adventures of Jimmie Dale.*

After the fashion of the times, both books were presented as novels. Actually they are closely connected short stories, plus one novelette appearing at the end of the first "Adventures."

The first true novel, *Jimmie Dale and the Phantom Clue,* appeared as a serial in *People's,* beginning with the July 1921 issue, and as a hardback in 1922. A second novel was published eight years later, in 1930: *Jimmie Dale and the Blue Envelope Murder.* The magazine appearance of this story has not been traced. A final novel, *Jimmie Dale and the Missing Hour,* ran as a serial in *Detective Fiction Weekly,* March 16 - April 20, 1935; the hardback was published the same year.

The Jimmie Dale story is essentially one long piece. The adventures occur in rapid succession. Where they are separated by any appreciable time lapse, the continuity is so tight that the overall effect is sleek and seamless.

A metronome clicks inside the paragraphs. You may puzzle as to the season or wonder why it always seems to be August. But you are usually able to say what time it is, down to the nearest quarter hour.

In "The Adventures of Jimmie Dale," Part I, each of the eleven chapters is from ½ to 1 day. Between chapters occur exactly stated intervals, ranging from 1 night to a month, the average intervals being eleven days. At the beginning of each chapter appears specific continuity.

...he recalled the occasion of a week ago....
...he had outwitted Kline...two nights before...

That was how long ago? Ten days? Yes; this would be the eleventh.

Within each chapter, the time stream is sharply marked: From Chapter VIII:

Dale is reading the evening paper.
Walks into warm evening.
It was now after ten o'clock...
A minute passed—two of them.
...a clock began to strike...Eleven o'clock.
Time passed.
Ten minutes went by.
...he had been there well over half an hour...
...just time enough to have accomplished what he had come for.

He is wounded, loses consciousness. But the clock continues.

...woman brought you here five minutes ago.

The passage of time is coupled with severe deadlines, the combination developing rising dramatic tension. Most of Jimmie's exploits must be performed before a specific moment, because:

a Police raid will strike precisely at 12:00.
the mob will arive in exactly 12 minutes.
the criminal conclave convenes at 3:00 am.

Minutes are sliced thin as the credibility of a congressman. 12:01 is too late. That single minute means disaster—Jimmie will be trapped. The crooks' plans will succeed. The innocent will be destroyed. Only if that iron time limit can somehow be beaten, will roses bloom.

In Part II of the *Adventures*, the same pressure is even more intense. The novelette occuring about three months after Part One, covers 2½ days from evening (Day 1) to dawn (Day 3). The action, heaven knows, is fierce and unrelenting. To this is added the cumulative urgency of time moving toward disaster, pressure packing ever more intensely as the chapters thin to climax.

Similar structure appears in all other books. *The Further Adventures* contain 9 adventures (in 24 chapters), each about 1 day long. In two cases, one adventure continues directly from another, not a minute being lost in transition. The others are separated by intervals up to three weeks.

The Phantom Clue was published four years after *The Further Adventures*. Yet it picks up at the exact second where the earlier story stopped and continues for an additional 42 days.

The only significant gap in the series occurs during the First World War. The Gray Seal's activities do not begin until one year after the war's end. (That according to Curruthers, who was wrong by at least 4 months.) From that new start, the adventures again continue sequentially. *The Blue Envelope* runs from July 12-25; *The Missing Hour* from July 26-31. The novels, themselves were written five years apart.

Packard's technique of time accounting was later slightly adapted and used by Norvell Page in writing his 1934-1936 *Spider Magazine* pulp novels. The same ferocious deadlines loom and the clicking off of irreplaceable minutes rings as grimly as it ever did in the Jimmie Dale series.

3-

Frank Lucius Packard produced the Jimmie Dale stories almost incidentally during an extended professional life. He began writing about 1902, while managing his father's shoe-blacking plant in Stoughton, Massachusetts. For his first fiction, Packard drew from earlier experiences working on the Canadian railway system.

These stories proved extremely popular. So much so that, about 1906, he gave up plant management for fulltime writing. After his father's death, Packard sold out his interest in the shoe-blacking factory and moved to New York City. There he free-lanced until his marriage in 1910. Taking a house near Washington Square, he spent a year writing fiction under contract to a publishing house (probably Munsey).

At the year's end, he returned to Montreal, settling in a suburb. After a year of traveling the Pacific area for material, he began production of a stream of serials, short stories and novels that continued into the mid-1930s. He died in 1942. At the time of his death, he was working on another Jimmie Dale adventure.[1]

(Frank Packard) is a born story-teller with a born story-teller's instinct for vivid incident, vigorous action and dramatic or even melodramatic climax.... In his detective stories...he is concerned mainly to give his readers the indispensable thrill.... In his other stories and novels, however, Frank Packard is dominated by two themes—heroic self-sacrifice and moral regeneration.[2]

The statement trips neatly enough off the page. It is partly true. Packard was, indeed, interested in self-sacrifice and moral regeneration, themes he industriously exploited in *The Miracle Man* and subsequent novels. What concerns the devoted pulp magazine reader even more, he was fascinated by the New York City underworld and worked its characters, one way or another, into most of his fiction.

Packard began writing in the golden afternoon of the dime novel—back when every sleuth carried disguises in his pocket and the Bradys and Nick Carter plunged fearlessly through the dens and street gangs of the city. Distinct dime novel traces remain in Packard's writing. Many of the characters crossing his pages would have been equally at home in a Nick Carter 32 pager—although Packard was more consciously literary and went inside his characters far more deeply.

Crooks and crookdom, however, were a major subject in Packard's work. Like the dime novelists, he reached into the streets for his characters. His backdrops were immigrant-jammed slums, drinking dens, fetid alleys, The Old Bowery, the lower East Side, Chinatown.

At the time Packard began writing under contract, the dime novels were guttering out. Change stirred the country. It was a time of astonishing events and new beginnings.

In 1908, Model T production began. The following year, the North Pole was reached and a specatacular tong war broke loose in New York City. *Blue Book* was three years old. *Adventure* and *Short Stories* were newly founded, with *Snappy Stories* and *All-Story* only two years away.

And out into the the streets thundered the New York police, clubs in brawny hand, to smash the power of the street gangs.

The fiction of the time reflected the change. The dime novels had superimposed melodrama, all purple-eyed in fiery robes, on familiar scenes of the day, described them tersely, rushed on. Packard, working in a more literary tradition, treated similar scenes, similar character types naturalistically—realism (qualified) with strong moral overtones. He was a well-read man, versed in French and English classics. It is no wonder that shadows of Zola and Dickens, as well as Stephen Crane, inform his work.

A murky yellow flame spurted up, pitifully weak, almost as though it was ashamed of its disreputable surroundings. Dirt, disorder, squalor, the evidence of low living, testified eloquently enough...that the place was quite in keeping with its tenant.... Larry the Bat, the dope fiend.

It was a squalid place, a miserable hole, in which a single flickering yellow gas jet gave light. It was almost bare of furniture; there was nothing but a couple of cheap chairs, a rickety table—unpawnable.

...he hurried, talking in the accepted style through one corner of his mouth to hard-visaged individuals behind dirty, reeking bars that were reared on equally dirty and foul-smelling sawdust-strewn floors.

Another Dance Hall: ...there was the usual hilarious uproar, the usual close, almost fetid atmosphere that mingled the odors of stale beer and tobacco...a dozen couples swirling in the throes of the bunny hug...

This is the world of Fagin, updated to 1914. This, the underside of the *Police Gazette*. For the readers, it was a ruthless glimpse into the lower depths, American-style.

The denizens stunned. Low, vicious, debauched, they spoke an argot familiar mainly to readers of dime novels and

Detective Story Magazine, Jan. 5, 1917. The Nick Carter dime novels melted insensibly into the *Detective Story* pulp magazine, edited by and featuring stories about Nick. He stands in the background of this cover, while Sgt. Ryan interrogates a suspect.

People's. Nov. 1916. In the deeps of the underworld, among the cut-throats, Jimmie Dale, the Gray Seal, probes for information, wearing his new disguise of Smarlinghue, the junkie artist.

those who relished burlesque turns:

I don't know wot youse mean. Come across wid it.
I got de wrong dope. Some of dem words I ain't hip to.
Sure t'ing. De old geezer'll have a pile of shekels hid away.
Say, de fly cops has got tipped off.... Youse want to beat it on de jump.

De old yegg cant, laugh stuff now for a TV routine.[3] Back then, relatively new (though not to the dime novels), still unsettling. An enticing ragout of slums, argot, dope fiends, fallen women. Redemption for a few. Wonderful.

Down through the years, Packard served these ingredients in book after book: *The Miracle Man, The Wire Devils, The White Moll, Doors of the Night, The Adventures of Jimmie Dale,* et. al.

Ghosts of the dime novels move transparently through these, many of the characters and scenes familiar, though altered and freshened, almost real.

To the end, however, Packard shared the dime novel's predilection for secret passages and trap doors.

At this time, the New York City underworld—that loose collective noun—was severely fragmented. During years prior to 1900, ranging back to Civil War days, loosely organized gangs of immense size, 500 to 1200 strong, infested the city. Protected by politicians, hardly bothered by a corrupt and ineffectual police force, gangs warred openly on the streets, incoherent armies in riot.

By 1900, the situation had begun to change. Indictment thinned the ranks of Tammany, reducing the gangs' political protection. Police reorganization, around 1910, coupled with an iron-fisted policy of clubbing known criminals senseless on sight, and the arrest (or murder by friends) of major gang leaders, broke the power of the larger gangs. They were not destroyed. Instead, they splintered into hundreds of smaller units.

In size, these ranged from 10 to 50. The size was complicated by endlessly shifting alliances. The city already was a jig-saw of territorial areas, defined to the nearest telephone pole. The break-up of the larger gangs hardly changed these claims, although it intensified the struggle between opposing factions. Within this matrix, various independent groups also floated, owing no allegiance, their size and strength varying with the ferocity of the members.

Superimposed on these territorial alignments were more specialized and professional groups of criminals. Their primary business was crime—loft theft, luggage theft, dock theft, general burglary, or assault or murder. Members of the street gangs might indulge in these, if given the opportunity— but intermittently. The professional groups, relatively small, varied from 2-4 to as many as were required for a given job. Thus a single individual could be loosely associated with half a dozen sporadically active gangs, simultaneously being a slugger for his block and a recognized leader in the neighborhood territory.[4]

The complexities of these interlocking heirarchies are not really shown in Packard's novels. It is the novelist's prerogative to write with a tight focus. So, in the Jimmie Dale stories, as in later hero pulp novels, only a shade of the real situation appears. The gangs opposed by the Gray Seal customarily included from 3 to 7 members. Even the Crime Club, although described as a powerful international group, appears to have contained only about 30 or so members. We may, however, postulate legions of tough minions-at-hire glowering from the wings.

In 1876, Chief of Police Thomas Byrnes established his famous deadline:

Any crook found on Manhattan Island south of the north side of Fulton Street will be arrested on sight regardless of what he may be doing there.

While not solving the gang problem, the deadline at least sought to limit it and restrain the thugs from braining the Wall Street crowd. Practically, the deadline was subject to huge fluctuations. When the distinguished visited the city, the deadline swelled to include all of Manhattan Island. Normally, however, it lay at Fulton, which meant that the bulk of Manhattan Island lay available for promenading or fancy work with lead pipe and knuckle duster.

To those densely populated areas north of the deadline toward Times Square, Packard applied the word "badlands," a slang term from (probably) the late 1880s. The badlands included the Old Bowery, as well as the streets bordering Chinatown. The big gangs did not operate in Chinatown. But the newspapers bannered enough tong war violence (kicked off by disputes over gambling concessions), so that desperate adventure among secret passages and hatchet men was a staple of fiction from the dime novels on. Major tong wars occured in 1904, 1909, 1912, and again in 1924, all being duly reflected in whatever form popular literature was taking. It is no particular surprise, then, to find Packard placing his hero in an opium den or tracing the black passages twisting beneath Mott Street and environs.

Following the end of World War I, the character of the gangs changed radically.

Prohibition brought formal organization. The street fighters took second place to compact groups equipped by benefit of modern technology. Which is to say, the automobile and the airplane, the machine gun and grenade, the cost accountant and the lawyer. Fifty years before, the loot remained in the hands of the politicians, with lesser funds dribbling down to the thugs and their leaders. Prohibition, however, provided vast quantities of money directly to the criminal. With these funds, it was possible to buy the requisite politician or judge, or lawyer, and to make wide-spread penetration into the social fabric. The territorial gangs remained. But their political power and much of their audacity were diminished.

Packard wrote his two final novels looking back to the 1919-1920 period. In doing so, he seems to have compressed ten years of social change into a few months. The character of the Bowery had changed by then. The action had moved elsewhere. But the pre-war image of New York's underworld, on which Packard had concentrated, remained a living image in pulp fiction 15 years later. It is one of the several views of underworld haunts and activities borrowed by later authors, who somehow combined 1905 sawdust-strewed drinking dens and the "dese and dose" talk with 1928 machine guns in touring cars, and speakeasys.

The dime novels first described the scene. Packard, through his immensely popular stories and novels, brought the scenes to life. When the public thought of crooks in the New York underworld, they thought in terms of these images. And the pulp authors, having about the same degree of first-hand experience as the public, laid these images into their stories.

4–

Six feet he stood, muscular in every line of his body, like a well-trained athlete with no single ounce of superfluous fat about him—the grace and ease of power in his poise. His strong, clean-shaven face...was serious—a mood that became him well—the firm lips closed, the dark, reliant eyes a little narrowed...

His forehead is broad, his jaw as square and solid as appropriate for a firm-minded hero. His fingers are slim and sensitive enough to tease the secrets from any combination lock. Thus Jimmie Dale, the splendid young society bachelor, crackling with wealth, drifting on pink clouds of privilege. You would suspect succulent debutantes, fragrant, daringly tinted, would dangle about him thick as invitations to the VanRiches' dinner parties. But he is rather a recluse, his social life so slender that it is hardly mentioned. The mansion in which he lives apparently contains only himself, the butler, and the chauffeur. Reason tells us that off-scene lurk maids, caretakers, possibly a cook—although Jason, the butler, does most of the cooking for Dale. Considering the hours Jimmie keeps, it's a wonder he ever tastes anything hot.

Once Dale's imposing physical presence is established, we plunge directly into his triple life and its complexity of emotions.

The emotional life of few pulp magazine heroes is laid out on the page. It's rare, indeed, that you can figure out what the hero is feeling at any given moment. Perhaps the style of brief sentences, briefer paragraphs, and sweltering action keeps the writer so busy he doesn't have time to figure out what his hero is thinking, assuming that the hero's attention ever strays from violence, wealth, and the heroine's extraordinary chest. Few of the heroes feel intensely. Of these Jimmie Dale and the

later Richard Wentworth (the 1930s Spider) stands out. It is
interesting that they are shown as artists—Wentworth as a
skilled musician, Dale as a painter, both men as accomplished
actors.

Dale sketches well, oil paints competently. His is the
artistic temperament which has spread, rather than
concentrated. He shows great ability in limited fields. Likely,
his paintings are adroit, although tending to one palette and
subject matter. At acting of a limited, but demanding, role, he is
superb. As Larry the Bat or Smarlinghue, no nuance of
underworld inflection, proper to those characters, escapes his
ear. He reproduces the physical attributes and habits of a
particular underworld type with precision. It is a limited role,
flawlessly portrayed.

He shows a similar competence in the technology of safes.
Here he is thoroughly schooled, knows both the design and
manufacturing aspects and brings to the locking mechanisms
that instinctive understanding that distinguishes genius from
craftsmanship.

In this professional area, as in disguise, he is precise,
accomplished, entirely in control of his nerves.

Lord knows, he needs control. His nights are spent
crouched before someone else's safe. From outer rooms comes
the sound of stealthy approach. Someone lethal this way
comes. Behind the safe, innocence's reputation lies; it must be
secured.

Only seconds remain before the door flies open, the lights
blaze on, and...

Steady nerves, you see. Jimmie Dale almost always
succeeds, almost always in the last syllable of recorded time.

When all fails, there is always audacity:

> He nerved himself to a quick, desperate attempt, trusting to surprise and
> his own wit and agility for victory....

Which is a swell way to intercept a bullet by accident.

Mr. Dale is wounded several times—a wrist crease, a leg
wound, a head graze that knocks him cold for an hour.
Remarkably, he receives few other injuries, considering the

risks he ran. On the other hand, although he traveled
constantly armed with an automatic or an automatic revolver,
it was a rare thing when he shot someone.[5] But he never killed.
It was 1914, and American heroes never never killed anyone
deliberately. Not in family type magazines.

Toward the end of *The Adventures of Jimmie Dale,*
Chapter XIII, it seems the only way to save Marie is to kill the
villain. This precipitates an intense emotional storm:

> ...the one thing from which he shrank, the one thing that, as the Gray Seal, he
> had always feared...to kill a man deliberately...he shivered a little and his
> hand shook as he nervously drew it across his eyes....

We continue in this vein, on and off, for an entire chapter:

> ...the horror that the impulse to murder inspired...his face, deathly white,
> was full as of the vision of some shuddering, abhorrant sight...while his
> hands at his sides clenched until the skin, tight over the knuckels, was an ivory
> white. To kill a man.

And more:

> To be a murderer. To know the horror of blood forever upon one's hands...
> Mind and soul recoiled before it...

Needless to say, circumstances so work that he doesn't
have to kill the fiend, who considerately takes poison. But the
position, affirmed throughout the series, is that the hero
doesn't kill—and if he thinks about doing so, he gets the colly-
wobbles.

When sufficiently upset, Dale was willing to blast a thug in
the arm, or shoot the pistol from his hands. Even bash him on
the head even or tie him up till arms and legs tingle. Never kill
him—not even by accident during one of those glorious battles
in a totally black room.

True, that during one particularly desperate moment—he
is trapped with Marie in the third floor room and outside the
door an army of foaming crooks rage—he fires blindly through
the door panels. By luck he doesn't kill anybody. Then the
crooks fire the place and obligingly go off to the next floor
down, where they curse and threaten and snarl. Jimmie and

Marie open the door to the room and walk out and go up to the roof and escape and it was pretty thrilling up to the point the crooks decided to make it easy. But, understand, he didn't kill anybody.

Jimmie Dale wasn't very lethal. Nor were those figures following after him through the rest of the '20s. Several later bent heroes got modeled on the Jimmie Dale image. They were thinner, a little grayer, and, because they didn't feel their hero in three-dimension, all lacked the emotional intensity rushing through Packard's paragraphs.

Dale hunts for Marie: Days of searching! Days of futility! Days that brought no reward.
Dale battling adversity: Defeat. . . but he would not accept it. He ran doggedly. Again he stumbled, and again. And now he winced with pain. This hurt his side brutally. . .
He went on. His breath came hard. He swept beads of moisture away from his forehead—and then once more he reeled. . . . There wasn't much chance—one perhaps in a thousand—not that much. . . .
Dale rhetorical: Was it possible that men like those two lived, festering God's green earth!
Dale shot. . .a vivid flash, like a fork of lightning seemed to leap toward him to sting and blister and bring him agony, and the room seemed to swirl and be full of deafening, racheting reports. . . .

Norvell Page's phrasing is no historical accident.

As mentioned, Jimmy Dale used three other personalities: that of the Gray Seal, Larry the Bat, and Smarlinghue.

The Gray Seal, "the most puzzling, bewildering, delightful crook in the annals of crime," resides in a special barrel-shaped safe in an alcove in Dale's bedroom. Within the safe, behind two separate doors, may be found a wide leather belt filled with small pockets; each contains a burglar tool, made of fine blue steel, highly tempered. With the belt is a black silk mask and a thin metal case that contains gray paper seals, adhesive-backed, shaped like diamonds.

Some sort of revolver and flashlight complete the rig.

The Gray Seal does rather more telephoning to police and Carruthers than you might expect from a mystery man of crime. At first, he speaks in a deep, relatively cultured voice. Later, when the Gray Seal is firmly identified with Larry the Bat, the voice is switched to a rough "dese and dose" type.

The character of Larry the Bat—so-called (according to Packard) because the underworld saw him only at night—was established about two years after the Gray Seal began operations. In this character, Dale had direct access to the underworld. Accepted as one of them, he could move freely about collecting information. In appearance, Larry is a filthy bum, ragged, sneering, caked with dirt, a junkie to boot. To meet him, go the Sanctuary, a room on the third floor of a tenement in one of the worst slums. It is a gas-lit sewer, having the advantages of three separate exits and a cleverly concealed hiding place under the oilcloth holding disguise kit and clothing.

From the kit comes wax, applied behind the ears, in nostrils, under low lip. Stain on wrists, hands, neck, face. Black wax under fingernails. His clothing is a choice collection of rags—mis-matched shoes, mis-mated socks, a flannel shirt stiff with grease, trousers ripped and patched, worn-out, a crumpled slouch hat. Add to this, the habit of talking from the side of the mouth and a surly disposition, and—behold—Larry the Bat.

At the end of the first book, the underworld identifies Larry as The Gray Seal and the identity is temporarily discarded.[6] It will be used again, for special appearances. For everyday use, a new character is necessary. This is Smarlinghue—Smarley to acquaintances—the dope-ridden artist who whines and snarls the streets of the Badlands.

Smarlinghue lives in the new Sanctuary, a filthy hovel on the first floor of another filthy hovel. French windows open to a backyard filled with trash, a board fence with a plank that lets you through to an alley and thence to the street.

Smarlinghue, pallid, threadbare, hang-dog and constantly fondling a worn hypodermic needle, is dressed almost as badly as Larry the Bat. His clothing is worn out, doesn't fit, filthy. From sleeves of a coat, a size too small, project shirt cuffs frayed and black with soil. A crumpled felt hat is pulled down over his eyes. His face, deathly pallid under dirt, looks starved. The nostrils flare. The thin lips shake. One hand thrusts into a pocket to fondle the hypodermic (which seems to be carried loose) or a tiny supply of coins—about 7¢ total. A contemptible wreck, then, often seen sprawled in the bunk of an opium joint

or crumpled over a bar-room table, human jettison, one of the
destroyed.[7]

In the Badlands they are almost all destroyed. The
Badlands is moral as well as geographic. It includes the Lower
East Side, but it also includes a moral sump in which human
vermin coil and lash among clots of slime.

Again, Packard gives a slender slice of reality, projected so
large and brilliantly that the slice seems the whole. It isn't that
the honest, poor and clean do not live in the Badlands, but that
the lens concentrates solely upon the depraved, the lost,
bottomed out in the lowest levels of the underworld.

Down there, down among the stews and dens, the denizens
stalk, poison in their blood, their eyes mad. Their clothing, stiff
with filth, encloses fetid bodies. Things creep in their hair.
Down there they strip coat and shoes from the crumpled drunk.
In their eating places, down there, roaches swarm visibly
across the kitchen pots. They swill camphor and alcohol. They
huddle in festering rooms, smelling of urine and mildew. Down
there, they sprawl mindless across an infested cot.

Strong, persistent images, describing the moral corruption
of the underworld in terms of physical filth.[8]

Against these images is contrasted Dale's life as a rich
young bachelor—the life he seriously compromised by playing
romantically at being a mocking safecracker.

These elements are manipulated, against each other, for
maximum emotional effect.

In one passage (played for a light smile) he winces when,
as Larry the Bat, he reads a theater poster reading:

HIS
DOUBLE
LIFE!

By this time, Dale is thoroughly tired of the game. Larry
the Bat and Smarlinghue have shown him the true face of the
underworld. It is not much like that of the gentleman burglar in
evening clothing.

Now, it would likely be indiscreet (and, in a discussion of
pulp magazine heroes, possibly ludicrous) to discuss Mr. Dale's

problems in terms of "sin," "guilt" and "redemption"—high-intensity words, indeed, carrying connotations too weighty for the more modest intent of these pages.

Still, these concepts, in various guises, flash through much of Packard's work, and are carefully worked into the Jimmie Dale series, although heavily masked by action.

Recall that Dale possessed all the advantages offered by affluent parents and generous author. To indulge his personal whim, he played at burglary and, if not guilty of intentional theft, he certainly could be jailed for breaking and entering. Certainly his pranks must have cost the police an inordinate amount of work.

"To prank—to tease" are curiously self-destructive motives. To enter by night, opening safes and affixing the gray seal may entertain for a time. But to continue at this argues something interesting in the way of an obsessional neurosis—or, perhaps, a degree of undigested adolescent malice uncomfortable to consider.

Whatever concept you favor, the end result is that Dale finds himself paying open-ended penitence for folly.

The instrument of change is the Toscin. She, personally, assigns the labors that Hercules must accomplish. Under her benign guidance, he still may have fun opening safes. But now the purpose is no longer to joke, but to save lives and preserve reputations of those the underworld would destroy.

He is caught and caught fairly. In the stories, the situation is glamored over, so that Dale's continuing exploits as the Gray Seal are supposed to be a noble form of self-sacrifice. (The brave man risking reputation and life to right wrongs and aid the innocent.) But self-sacrifice is hardly the right word. Dale is intensely eager to abandon the Gray Seal's life and works. He has had enough.

—Tough.

More penance is required. Penance will be exacted to the final drop. Marie demands it first. Circumstances later. He pays all the way.

Whether or not Packard intended the situation to develop in this way is a moot point. It is reasonable to think that he deliberately planned the redemption of Jimmie Dale as the foundation for the series. Whether he also deliberately built in some of the disturbing overtones and harmonics is another matter. Probably not.

On the whole the stories work very well. The primary failure in the series—and this is characteristic of the genre—is the over-simplification of every circumstance and emotional relationship which does not bear directly on narrative movement. Associative links between wealth, politics and the underworld are not examined, for instance, nor are any of those ambiguities (ethical, moral, social or interpersonal) with which the stories are littered. That such subjects could be handled within an action narrative was repeatedly demonstrated by Talbot Mundy and Dashiell Hammett within the next few years.

If we regret what Packard did not achieve, we can applaud what he did accomplish—the first full-length presentation of the bent hero, richly embellished, against a background intensely if narrowly realized. It would influence pulp fiction for the next generation.

So the hero of the story and his several faces. Of the other people of the drama, one major and three minor, there is more to say.

5—

Elderly, ruddy-faced, wrinkled, white-haired Jason, butler of the Dale establishment, has been with the family since Jimmie was a small child. Jimmie treats him not as a servant but as a rather fragile friend to be protected at all costs.

Jason is never admitted to the secret life of the Gray Seal. What he may have suspected is another matter. It is probably the worst since, at different times, Master Jimmie returned home—

—shot and fainting on the floor.

—at 4 am to announce that the telephone was tapped. And keep away from the windows, there are lurkers....

—only to leave immediately on receipt of still another of those hateful letters written by *that* woman. Always they meant trouble, Mr. Dale away from home for days, no one knowing how to get in touch with him, while all around, a formless menace clings and threatens....

Jimmie is quite unable to break Jason of the unfortunate habit of waiting up. Perhaps the Young Master might need me. Customarily, Jason takes station in the front hall, seating himself in the big chair, and waiting out the hours. Customarily he falls asleep and must be roused up at small hours of the morning to be sent off to bed, gently admonished. On the surface it appears rather mawkish. The relationship is one of those sentimental 1900 things, and involves the usual role reversal, the older man being as child to the young hero.

But consider more than the surface. Then Jason takes on an unexpected richness. The old man regards Dale with genuine affection. Matters, he knows, are somehow brutally wrong, ever since that first envelope from the mysterious woman. Perhaps even before. He does not understand. Apprehension bites him. Waiting alone in that huge house, he paces the shining silent rooms. He is alone. He straightens a chair, removes a fallen petal. He peers intently down the silent hall toward the silent front door and listens to the night.

Benson, the chauffeur, is a brawny, out-going man, who lives at the rim of the story. Only rarely is he involved in events. Nothing is explained to him. Yet he is invaluable. For it is his job to get Dale to the scene of the action—a major function.

When you live at one location and operate in another, the simple act of getting there is a problem. Buffalo Bill rode in; others used steam tricycles or red Rolls Royces; you may drive your own vehicle. All have the same problem—what to do with the transportation once you have arrived. Its safety hangs over you like a sore conscience. While you go off to shoot the sinful, your machine huddles at the curb, target for any casual thief and stealer.

Packard solved the matter by using the chauffeur to move Dale from place to place. There was precedent for that solution. Nick Carter, in his later years, added a car and driver—Danny, a fierce fighter and demon wheelman, unrepentently Irish.

Danny arrived in 1907. So the problem of transporting the lead character was faced long ago. Those major 1930s series, The Shadow and the Spider, blandly adopted the convention. Over an active series, The Shadow rarely drove himself, but was whisked about New York in a limousine (piloted by a particularly phlegmatic chauffeur), a privately-owned taxi (Moe Shrevnitz, operator) or the police commissioner's official machine.

A similar solution is used by Richard Wentworth, the Spider, traveling furiously about town in a silver Daimler. It has a distinctive license, a turbanned Sikh at the wheel and, from time to time, it slows to allow a hunched creature in a long black cape and floppy slouch hat to emerge. Wentworth's movements are a trifle less anonymous than the Shadow's cab.

The final continuing character of the Dale stories is Herman Carruthers. At the beginning of the stories he is 26 years old, about Jimmie's age. The magazine illustrations show him to be a thin-faced, severe man. Intelligent and tough, he is a leading figure in the newspaper world and rose from reporter to managing editor of the morning *News-Argus* in a span of time so brief as to arouse rich waves of emotion in the heart of any newspaperman.

Carruthers, all intensity and enthusiasm, is given to telephoning Jimmie Dale in the tiny hours of the morning to announce the latest Gray Seal outrage. This is not suspicion. Far from it. He never suspects. It is but unchecked zeal, as he seeks to infect the languid Mr. Dale with interest in a boring subject.

At the beginning, Carruthers spoke admiringly of the Gray Seal. After that individual got accused of several murders, Carruther's admiration soured. He hued and cried for the Seal, offering prodigious rewards. His mind was changed only after startling adventure—including falling into crooks' hands and being beaten with a crutch, prior to having his toes shot off. Larry the Bat stopped these festivities after the crutch and before the shooting. Carruthers ended by shaking Larry's hand. Never did look closely at the face under the dirt.

In the stories Carruthers serves usefully as a mouthpiece for the author. Through him, Packard presents, in dialogue, masses of material concerning the early activities of the Gray Seal. Afterward Mr. C. conveniently represents social indignation. He also receives messages from the Gray Seal. Since he insists on talking Seal Seal Seal Seal to the bored Mr. Dale, the reader is allowed moments of heartwarming mirth to lighten his concern.

Marie LaSalle is the heart and blood in the story of the Gray Seal. The series rests on the bedrock of her personal problems. Her mind manipulates the Gray Seal's activities. Her efforts transform the Seal into a hero of significance and purpose.

Popular literature of the slick magazine school notoriously concerned itself with heroines of beautiful fragility, given to inconvenient swoons and personal inadequacy under stress. They seem to exist chiefly as goals toward which the hero might aspire. There is a whole school of fiction in which the heroine seems to exist only for the purpose of being abducted.

It was in the dime novels that really competent feminine characters appeared. Calamity Jane and Annie Oakley (freely romanticized from the originals) appeared as self-sufficient women holding their own in a tough country. Stella Fosdick and Arietta Murdock continued the trend in the post-1900 western dime novels. At about the same time, as the detective action story focused on the city, additional, strongly characterized, secondary feminine characters were appearing—particularly in the Nick Carter series, which was replete with competent women on both sides of the law.

Outside the pages of popular magazines, the lot of women was slowly improving or rapidly going to perdition, depending on your point of view. The society of the day fermented with woman's suffrage (to the point where Suffragettes rioted outside the White House in 1913). Every day, more women joined the nation's labor force. Brazen ones sampled cigarettes. Brave ones drove automobiles. Others, coolly self-sufficient, got illustrated by Gibson.

Popular fiction reflected much of this. But even in relatively enlightened pages, it's surprising to find an intelligence as competent as that of Marie LaSalle.

Her description is less detailed than we would like. Her eyes are brown, her voice soft and rather silvery. She is small, slender, about 22 years old, heir to millions and millions.

Since her teens, Marie has lived in an environment characterized by violence, savagery and filth. She has been in it, not of it, like a diamond immersed in engine oil. The bulk of this time she has spent in disguise.

A hag! And one as disreputable in appearance as...Larry the Bat....
A woman, old bedraggled, ragged, was thrusting a bunch of cheap pencils imploringly toward him....

Her characterizations are built around the figure of a disheveled crone, lined, bent, ragged, perhaps padded beneath the shawls and scarfs. Lank gray hair dangles about her face. As Silver Mag, she carries a bag of dimes and quarters to pass to wives and children of men serving jail time.

Mag is eventually linked with Larry the Bat/the Gray Seal, which makes the disguise worthless. She adopts a similar get-up as Mother Margot, push cart peddler:

...the thread-bare black shawl pulled hoodlike over her head and clasped tightly around her throat—the gray wisps of hair that straggled over her eyes—the heavy-lensed spectacles—the pinched face that was none too clean.

She speaks a rich version of the Bowery accent:

"Wot's safer dan dis de way it is now? I wanter get home. Youse ought to go down to an antique dump an' buy yerself a suit of armour, an' walk around in dat. Youse'd look fine.... De pip, dat's wot I'm contractin' from youse." (*Jimmy Dale and the Phantom Clue*, Chapter V.)

In these disguises, she prowls the Badlands, slowly working out the links to the Crime Club. While doing so, she is constantly discovering plots and plans, all malignant, generally devised to suck in some poor innocent and ruin him utterly.

At this point, out comes the writing paper. In long-hand she sets down the details:

"Dear Philanthropic Crook..."

...marshalling the information as precisely as an intelligence report. At this time, go here. Do this, enter here, move to there. You will find safe in.... Remove whatever. Accurate, solid information, which the Gray Seal thoughtfully commits to memory, then tears the communication into fine bits. Marie's main difficulty is to get the information to him on time. The US Postal Service, providing 4 to 5 deliveries a day, and half-day service on letters mailed within town (this was 1914, remember, and the service was real, not fiction), is a great help in smashing crooked plots. Still, you have to reckon with a certain time lapse. The Gray Seal is always pressed for time. Rarely does the Tocsin assign him a job that is not painfully time tight.

After two years of this, the relationship is marred by their falling in love.

Well, it was only to be expected.

No sooner do the tender flowers of a dainty maiden's faithful true selfless love rise in glowing richness from the perfumed sweetness of her own dear heart, bless her, than she must start protecting him from violence. This gives him mice. Each time, she breaks silence—but only after matters have become so desperate that Satan laughs in the streets.

Toward the end of the series, they get engaged. As usual, the wedding doesn't occur in the text. But it is so close—and the Gray Seal's activities stop so abruptly—that we must assume they finally beat the jinx separating series characters. It's a shame that we have no record of their adventures after the ceremony. They have enjoyed such outre experiences together (their courtship was almost totally in the darkness), that it's hardly possible marriage could repress their instincts for trouble.

As the constant reader may have noticed, in popular fiction, intelligence is usually equated with a certain starkness of personality, a gleaming like oiled metal, lacking internal warmth.

Not so with Marie. She manages to be one of the cleverest and warmest people in the pulps. Her head can organize and plan with implacable accuracy without impeding a warm range of emotions. If she can think, she can also love and despair. She is full of sly humor. She teases and laughs and makes up her mind with steely resolution.

She handles Jimmie with the precision of Glenn Gould playing Bach. His few weaknesses are known to her. He is an improviser, rather than a planner; under the spur of emergency, he reasons accurately, if intuitively. So they neatly complement each other. With her lucid perception, she understands precisely how their talents best blend. A most clever girl. She knows where to give way to his judgment—even when this relegates her to distasteful inaction on the sidelines.

For a little while.

Her appearances in the novels are severely limited. She enters rather briefly twice, three times in each. You are never in doubt of her worth, yet she never intrudes.

Greatest miracle of all, she never has to be rescued because she is never captured. It is an all-time high for the feminine lead.

An accomplished woman. As mentioned.

6-

Jimmie Dale was one of the earliest of the true pulp heroes. Tarzan and John Carter arrived before, by a narrow margin. Fu Manchu had just arrived. The Four (more precisely, Three) Just Men had long ago demonstrated the concept of personalized justice.

Sherlock Holmes still appeared in *The Strand*, burning that indelible personality ever deeper into the fabric of fiction. Although contemporary with Tarzan and Hopalong Cassidy, he was of an earlier world. A new world was forming now, seemingly thousands of years removed from the intellectual problems at Baker Street.

The final Sherlock Holmes collection, *His Last Bow,* appeared in 1917, three years before the first issue of *Black Mask*, and the year that saw book publication of *The Adventures of Jimmie Dale*. This is, on the whole, symbolic of Dale's place in popular magazine literature. He bridges two eras, closing the world that Holmes and Carter knew, opening the way to the violent series characters of the 1930s.[9]

The evolution was not preordained. It was not even clearly marked. Numerous other characters appeared whose presence, to various degrees, would influence the development of popular series fiction. Still, Packard's Jimmie Dale clearly established the figure of the bent hero who operates amid criminal violence. Certain of Packard's technical solutions, designed to maintain credibility of narrative, became accepted as the obvious way to do things. Thus:

The wealthy young bachelor has the time to perform his exploits and does not have to worry about making a living.

Nor does he have to explain anything to his wife.

He moves equally well at all levels of society.

His freedom of movement is based on the automobile and, since he is driven close to the scene of action by a chauffeur, he is not anchored to the machine.

His penetrations of the underworld are aided by his ability at disguise.

He is armed and uses weapons for defense.

He maintains a secret base where he transforms himself.

A small but faithful group of friends supports him.

A strong feminine character plays in counterpoint to him.

The stories focus on his direct struggles with the underworld.

One or more of these elements appear in the stories concerning those other characters discussed in earlier chapters. The advantage of hindsight is that we can see how all these focused in the Jimmie Dale stories and observe how similar concentrations of similar elements appeared in the pulp magazines of the 1930s.

The assessment of the 1920s on Packard's work throws a curious forward light on coming fiction. An article in *The Bookman*, like a specialty Chinese dish, both sweet and sour, touches a few of those matters which led informed literary opinion to disdain the dime novels and, later, reject the pulps:

... as in all tales of this character, it is borne upon the reflective reader that both police and criminals are wooden Indians to allow even a prodigy of ingenuity and invulnerability (i.e., Mr. Dale) to repeat the same exploits with such frequency and impunity. But detective stories are not built for reflection. They are our modern fairy tales for adults, intended to engross, divert, and thrill....
... Packard's heroes are all... flawlessly and wonderfully strong, self-reliant, and humanly attractive... they never, on their errant path, forfeit your interest and good will by consummating anything really mean or injurious to the deserving. In brief, they are the proper heroes of romance.[10]

Try substituting such a name as Matt Helm or Ed Noon for Jimmie Dale and observe how little has changed in fifty-five years.

Although it was not yet observable in 1920, Packard had codified an overall format. This, proving workable, was

adapted during the next fifteen years of pulp fiction as one of
the primary mainstream elements. Not the only one. But a
major strand.

7–

Not all bent heroes were reformed cracksmen dedicated to
foiling criminal plots. As we have seen, the cracksmen, as a
group, bloomed brightly for twenty years before fading to
brown petals. By the late 1920s, the subject was tired, and the
cracksman found himself elbowed aside by two different
varieties of hero—the buccaneer and the justice figure.

The buccaneer, that adventurous fellow, earned his living
preying on high-toned crooks. Mingling social sensitivity and
advanced Robin-Hooding, he did particularly well in England.
Our finest examples—including the notable Simon Templar—
appear in London, laughing through coup after coup. We will
meet the buccaneers in a later chapter.

The justice figure achieved horrific popularity during the
early 1930s. By then The Shadow had demonstrated the way
and other pulp magazines began intense exploitation of the
type. By 1933 justice figures tumbled from every crack, an
enthralling rush of individuals with secret identities and a
habit of dispensing death as the universal medication.

Justice figures habitually performed when the Law stood
helpless before major crime figures of more than usual
subtlety. These were punished mercilessly from the night, a
contemporary Angel's Sword falling on the Unjust.

As a frequent by-product of these well-intentioned efforts,
the justice figures discovered themselves considered murderers
by ungrateful police and got hounded and treated badly. On a
few occasions, their services proved so desirable that the police
eagerly cooperated with that unknown carrying those
unilateral guns. In consequence The Shadow and The
Phantom Detective rendered no accounting for their heaps of
corpses. But the Spider was always a wanted man by all sides.

If the 1930s were blessed by a surplus of these heroes, the
1920s were undersupplied. Other than the celebrated Just Men,
major justice figures did not seem to flower during the 'Teens
and 'Twenties. To some extent this observation depends on

how you define justice figure, for armies of heroes slaughtered armies of villains. But not as a matter of considered policy. The fiction of the 'Teens was hyper-sensitive about showing a lead character who was either sexy or systematically murderous. In the 'Twenties most leading popular series figures would rather give up liberty than press a trigger in their own defense. (You must understand that Bulldog Drummond and the Black Mask Boys are exempt from this easy generalization.)

Given these circumstances, it is surprising to find the first major representatives of the lethal heroes appearing as early as 1905. On that date, Edgar Wallace published *The Four Just Men* and on that date, the road opened to the single-character pulp magazines, about twenty-five years away.

In 1905 the dime novel stood in its Golden Autumn. Sherlock Holmes and Raffles contested for space in the English magazines. In Paris, Cleek twisted his face over newspapers detailing Lupin's new exploits. Cracksmen swarmed by night and no jewel was safe. Haggard's heroes located ever more remote civilizations and, far off in wonderland, Buffalo Bill drew trigger against those pesky Indians.

Into this sylvan scene comes deliberate murder. The first of the great death givers have stepped on stage.

On Research

When you speak of those who comment on popular fiction, speak gently. They are childish in their enthusiasms, these commentators. They scratch endlessly in that gray-lighted immensity of forgotten novels, sniffing at the track of the past.

Bits of brown paper cling to their clothing. Their eyes are huge. Soiled papers bulge their pockets, notes scribbled in the stacks. For they have had valuable insights and scrawled these down, so that the thoughts might not escape, not one— although how easily blunted these are when transmuted from thought to the written word.

Speak gently of these commentators. Their thoughts are not of this present. Their bodies consume dinners and feel the sun and even drive automobiles on public highways. But their minds, all interlocked with speculations on the past, balance the merits of books no one cares to read. In doing so, they achieve a sort of dusty happiness. Their candle dwindles. But little they notice that shrinking light. There is still another Nick Carter to read, another Cleek to consider, another cracksman to emplace in the shabby mosaic of their thought. They honor the forgotten. They search earnestly, stumbling from volume to volume, seeking to understand what is of dubious importance. Accident guides their minds as much as design.

Drop a nickle in their cup and hurry by. For Heaven's sake, hurry! That one wants to tell you about Jimmie Dale.

A pitiful case. See what reading does to you!

VI—*The Death Givers*

1-

October 7, 1899, London. Thomas Cutler murdered. He was a sweatshop operator, with a particularly unsavory reputation concerning his treatment of women employees.

February 28, 1900, Liege. Jacques Ellerman. Shot dead. He was an embezzler of public funds.

October 1900, Seattle, Kentucky. Judge Anderson strangled in his room. He directed feud murders of seven members of an opposing clan.

October 30, 1900, New York. Patrick Welch, hung in the woods. He was a grafter, embezzler of public funds.

March 4, 1901, Paris. Madame Despard, smothered. A white slaver

March 4, 1902, Paris. Monsieur Gabriel Lanfin, shot dead.

Between March 1902 and August 1904, ten others killed.

By action of the Four Just Men.

2-

To certain men, two warnings were given. These arrived in the mail, thin-textured envelopes of a greenish-gray paper containing a terse note:

You have done this, and this, and this. If, by [a given date], you have not ceased this activity, we shall have no other course but to kill you.

FOUR JUST MEN

The language was formal, the information specific.

If the first warning were ignored, the second warning confirmed the deadline for compliance; in the event of non-compliance, the note also included a clear statement of that most intensely interesting date—the day of the addressee's death.

No appeal.

Sixteen murders in five years.

3-

The Four Just Men they called themselves. By that name they were known to police around the world. By that name they were known internationally to a public not sure whether they were devils or something more.

Their activities caused widespread consternation. They struck mercilessly. At times they seemed to strike at random, their reason for singling out a victim not always known. In some instances even the public might agree that a given death improved the world. In other cases, a roar of protest rose.

If the newspapers were outraged and the public shouted in fury, the Four Just Men remained aloof, undisturbed. Their course was clear. It had been clear since they had agreed to merge their lives into this single enterprise:

... they waged war against the great world-criminals; they pitted their strength, their cunning, and their wonderful intellects against the most powerful organizations of the underworld, against past masters of villainous arts, and brains equally agile.[1]

An ambitious undertaking. And in addition to those masters of crime, whose activities created what amounted to a state within a state, there were lesser criminals whose activities drew the Just Men's attention:

There were men, free of the law, who worked misery on their fellows; dreadful human ghouls fattening on the bodies and souls of the innocent and helpless; great magnates calling the law to their aid or pushing it aside as circumstances demanded.... There had grown into being, systems which defied correction; corporations beyond chastisement; individuals protected by cunningly drawn legislation, and others who knew to an inch the scope of toleration.[2]

The small habitual criminal, prey of the police, did not usually concern the Just Men. It was not necessary that they perform functions the police were admirably designed to handle. Only in special cases, where the police were helpless and justice failed, did the Just Men appear. Selectivity was essential. Nor was it necessary to reach all criminals. For the death of one was the admonition to many.

A simple idea, basically. Fear keeps the evil man in check.

The discipline was terror of death from the unknown.

Perhaps the concept might work, although history suggests otherwise.

Thus, behind the laws and police systems of England hovered a spectre, a self-appointed group, implacable, invisible. Their faces were unknown. Their descriptions were unrecorded. Nor were their nationalities known. That they existed was certain. But they existed almost as an abstract principle, an unbodied menace to whom no appeal could be made.

In Europe, England, America, their lives were forfeit. If once their identities were known, the police of the world would unite against them—no matter how warmly individual officers might agree with the Just Men's selection of victims.

This is the identical position to be explored, at length, in the pulp magazines of the 1930s, whose heroes, incorruptible agents for justice, were frequently wanted men, under general indictment for murder, although wholly dedicated to the benefit of the state that condemned them.

That prerogative most zealously guarded by government (apart from the power to tax) is the power to establish and administer law. No state is so antique, or so newly emerged, that it does not luxuriate in rules by which its people are to flourish, perhaps in joy.

Among Western nations, the power to execute erring citizens is tightly controlled. The way to the death chamber is hedged by procedures, and clusters of lawyers peer from behind each. Even those murderous dictatorships of the 1930s formalized their slaughters by legal ritual. They murdered in quantity. But each death was enabled by legal citation: authorized, approved and with viable references.

The law itself is not uniform, as a wall poured from plastic is uniform. More nearly, the law resembles a fence of scrap lumber: some parts are beautifully joined, sleek and firm and sound; other parts are scrappy, indeed, all knotholes and voids. Some planks wobble visibly. Others, rotten beneath the paint, easily twist aside or crumble when struck. Equal justice before the law is a noble concept; only equal administration of justice is a difficult practice.

The inequalities of the law are notorious (said the leader of the Just Men) and I recognize the impossibility as society is constituted, of amending the law so that crimes such as we have dealt with, shall be punished as they deserve.... There are those who imagine that I am consumed with a burning desire to alter the laws of this country; that is not so.... The laws of England are good laws, wise and just and equitable.... It would be madness to expect a civilized country to revert to the barbarism of an age in which death was the penalty for every other crime....

[But] the age of Reason is not yet, and men who are animal in all but human semblence share the animal's obedience to corrective discipline, share too his blind fear of death—and are amenable to methods that threaten his comfort or life....

[The Four Just Men] represented a law—we executed expeditiously. We murdered if you like. In the spirit and the letter of the laws of England, we did murder.... I do not desire to extenuate the circumstances of my crime. Yet none the less the act I cannot justify to your satisfaction I justify to my own.[3]

By these few paragraphs, written in 1908, Edgar Wallace laid the foundation upon which the justice figures of the 1930s pulp magazines built their bloody structures. In less cadenced language, the identical thought energizes the later paperback series of 1970-1980. If the law is ineffectual, some figure external to the formal machinery of the law will rise to enforce equality of justice. He may be a dark gliding mystery like The Shadow, or a hunched terror like The Spider, or his disguised face may never be the same twice as The Phantom Detective or Secret Agent X. But the identical thrill for justice drives them all.

The sugar plum contains the usual concealed hook. If every man presumes to enforce his concept of justice, anarchy runs free. My death list may differ radically from yours. Worse, I might be on your list, a situation I deplore. Why do you think me a squalid monster bent on defacing the sun? I am a wholesome lad, a warm friend, a delight to the girls.

Please don't take it personally, but I can't trust you to amend the oversights of justice. Can I even trust myself? Then to whom shall we turn, you and I? The question is easier to answer in fiction, where we can usually find a man whose integrity is a polished shield. Who is wiser than you, or even me. Whose judgment, passionless and fair, unsoiled by pride, is motivated by altruism and dedicated to the public good.

He also does not make mistakes.

Perhaps it was easier to know what is right, back in 1908.

Society was still firm as German chocolate cake. Not yet crystallized were such disturbances as women voting and unions striking. The new technology, that rending devil, still squawked among fragments of its egg shell. If you, a believer in absolute justice, stepped outside the law to assure justice, you did so to improve, not to destroy. You acted on behalf of society, affirming its beliefs and principles, committing lesser crimes to avenge greater ones.

This attitude assumes a stable society where commonly accepted convictions blaze on every side. The 1908 verities were monoliths of gold. Some twenty-five years later, the verities had fractured to heaps of gilded pebbles. What happened? Blame it on jazz, bobbed hair and beer. Or the Wall Street bankers. Or the damn Democrats. One thing for certain—by 1930 there was no justice.

Unless you looked between the covers of 10¢ magazines, where the gun-wielding justice figures established their own system of correction, based on author's memories of how simple the complex past had been. In the 10¢ magazines, evil is enormously evil, the good supremely excellent. When the verities collapsed in late 1929—taking in their fall jobs, savings, the financial system and confidence in tomorrow—it was caused by malevolent men, somewhere unseen, plotting together: Business men, likely; bankers; gangsters; all coiling and twisting in avaricious slime. If society were too demoralized or too corrupted to maintain its own laws, then let some dark avenger rise. He would defend the people against that Vast Criminal Conspiracy of Them who kept the Golden Age from returning.

This simple analysis sufficed when the Depression had broken men's hearts. Earlier, in 1908, circumstances were different and popular literature reflected that difference. Although it was a time of deep social change, society was seen—from street level, at least—to be stable. The verities, unshaken, were hardly questioned. Government was benign. The Law was good.

Only occasionally a rascal would slip away from justice and have to be sent two warnings, followed by 9 mm termination from a silenced Browning pistol. In 1933 the caliber would be .45 and the avenger a jeering voice out in the darkness, who would enforce respect for the Law, if it took every round of ammunition in the city.

4-

The exploits of the Just Men appeared regularly throughout Edgar Wallace's career in a mixture of books, magazine serial parts and short stories. The material is collected into six volumes: four novels and two groups of short stories. The material is loosely chronological. The first two novels are closely associated in time; the others straggle through the 'Teens and 'Twenties. By dates of first book publication, these volumes are:

> *The Four Just Men* (1905)[4]
> *The Council of Justice* (1908)
> *The Just Men of Cordova* (1917)
> *The Law of the Four Just Men* (1921) (US,
> *Again The Three Just Men*)
> *The Three Just Men* (1925)
> *Again the Three Just Men* (1928) (US, *The
> Law of the Three Just Men*)

(To reduce the atrocious confusion among titles, the English titles will be used throughout these pages.)

The Law of the Four Just Men and *Again the Three Just Men* are short story collections. The bibliography is complex. Generally the material was first published in English magazines and books, then republished in the United States, so that any given item may have two or more copyright dates. The stories have appeared in numerous editions, both hardback and paperback, most of these omitting copyright dates. The result is a tangle of appalling proportions, which makes the student tingle with interest and bores the general reader. Having pointed the swamp out to you, we bow and turn away with a cryptic smile, murmuring unintelligibly.[5]

At the very beginning, before the opening of the first novel, there were four Just Men: Manfred, Gonsalez, Poiccart and Merrell. Of these, least is known about Merrell, who was shot to death by police around 1902. This occurred shortly after the Just Men killed Herman le Blois in Paris.[6] Merrell, seen leaving the le Blois residence by a detective, was shadowed for three days, the police hoping to follow him to the others. Discovering the surveillance, Merrell fled Paris, was trapped in a Bordeaux cafe and killed, following a gun-fight in which three policemen were shot. He remained unidentified and was buried in Bordeaux. Thereafter the group enjoyed no permanent fourth member, although on three occasions a fourth was temporarily enlisted.

It is hardly accurate to specify one individual as leader. The Just Men were intensely close-knit and, by long association, had come to understand one another so closely that they might have been animated by a single will. Perhaps at the beginning, attention focuses on Manfred. Later, Gonsalez becomes a leading figure. Initially, however, George Manfred, that articulate and subtle genius, holds center stage.

In the *Council of Justice* he is a tall, tanned man of about thirty-five. He wears a mustache and pointed beard, already beginning to gray. His forehead is broad, his eyes dark gray and grave. A powerful man of gripping personal presence, he has the features and poise of an aristocrat, an appearance heightened by the restrained excellence of his clothing. Occasionally he wears a monocle. He is probably English.

Frequently cynical, often sarcastic, his personality is brightened by a strong sense of humor. He smiles more than the others. Wallace reports that he likes poached eggs and spinach for breakfast, but is otherwise fastidious about food.

By contrast, Raymond Poiccart is unspectacular. In person he is a heavy man, massive, rather stout. His face, dark-complexioned, is habitually set in a morose expression (the word used is "saturnine"). He speaks little, is deeply suspicious of men and their motives, and is a chemist of unusual ability. He is French.

Gardening is Poiccart's deepest passion. To the raising of vegetables and flowers he dedicates his high attention. During the middle period of the Just Men's activities, he drops out for a two-year period to raise onions in Spain, amusing himself at night by collecting technical oddities of chemistry and the sciences.

He is also an artist of competence, surprising in a man of such heavy appearance. In the household set up by the Just Men in Curzon Street, London, at a later time, he plays the butler, stolid, polished, revealing nothing of his inner genius and gifts of strategy.

In that same household, Leon Gonsalez habitually plays the chauffeur and footman. A Spaniard, Gonsalez is intensely interested in automobiles—the other chauffeurs call him "Lightning." It is his relaxation to hurl a Spanz sports car at 60 mph along English back roads. He is equally fascinated by airplanes and pistols, handling each with superb skill.

Gonsalez is about 5'10" tall. His lean, pointed face is carefully clean-shaven. His hands are restless, his movements quick, almost jerky. It is habit, not nerves. The energy in him drives and it is not surprising that he went gray early.

The mind driving this body is quick and rather remote. His intelligence is dispassionate, almost cold-blooded, delighting in classification of facts. He is an enthusiastic physiognomist, studying personality traits as they are revealed by the shape of heads and features. He has translated Leguetius' *Theologi Physiognomia Humana* and published at least one book, *Crime Facets,* a collection of data on criminals and criminal types.

Wallace reports that Gonsalez was, at once, a "dilettante, scientist, and philosopher." He was also a clever disguise artist and a man with a weakness for nurses. This is not to suggest that he has considered marriage. "By the very nature of our work," he said in *The Three Just Men*, "we are debarred from that experience."

For all that, women are attracted to Gonsalez. The chill in his light blue eyes never seems to bother them and many are willing to feed him crumpets (a great favorite) for life. Which is the point at which he becomes remote and steps away smiling, back to his accumulating piles of hand-scribbled notes and the neat pair of gold-rimmed reading glasses. Gonsalez has killed more frequently than the others. It teaches wariness.

5–

These, then, are the people of the series—men of high

intelligence, quick-minded, and, as would be the usual thing in coming fiction, conversant with the newest concepts of science and technology. As a matter of course, they are all enormously wealthy and have pooled their fortunes into a single treasury.

No origins are given for any of these fortunes, a sorry oversight, since those of us wishing to become justice figures are naturally curious as how best to finance our operations. Great wealth frees you from the need to be grumping in the office precisely at the time The Scarlet Hand and His Hordes are looting the banks downtown. And it is desirable to pay cash for dynamite, airplanes and secret lairs rather than charging them or scratching them from the household budget.

With few exceptions, the major justice figures appearing from 1905 to around 1940 are wealthy. Their private careers were enabled by economic independence. Certainly reader identification played a part: Who wishes to identify with a hero as poor as yourself. In a larger frame, however, wealth provided a tacit explanation for the massive spending required of the justice figure during the course of the story.

Nick Carter never hesitates to purchase tickets at any point on earth. The Just Men casually buy a printing shop or set up a clinic. In later magazines, the adventurer Doc Savage will, as casually, demolish scores of airplanes, merely to baffle his opposition; and Richard Wentworth, the Spider, will not wince when his $75,000 limousine is destroyed monthly.

Great personal wealth removes those normal constraints of time and funds which bind the rest of us so tightly to the world. The story can unfold without tripping over routine transactions and economies.

At the same time, knowledge of the hero's extreme wealth seduces us to the belief that he is also wiser and less fallible, a postulate required to justify his activities beyond the law.

Technically the illusion of wisdom is established by showing the justice figure to be almost supernaturally well informed. Because science and engineering are arcane fields in 1905, sparking off astounding innovations in aircraft and automobiles and electric lights, our justice figures will be competent in technical fields, exactly like those wonderful boys in the earlier dime novels. They will have prodigious memories. Facts are known to them about most of the people of the story—

backgrounds, characters, the shadows on their pasts. The hero will not only be a licensed doctor, but will speak Arabic fluently, understand how a bucket shop is rigged, and can generate prussic acid gas on request.

He is a master of techniques, then, a library of facts. By analogy, possession of such knowledge, so varied and detailed, also assures excellence in making value judgments and dissecting ethical positions. The justice figure is required to make such distinctions before he ever presses the trigger. He is at once judge and executioner. Since the art of giving death is intrinsically more dramatic than giving judgment, you can hardly wonder that the intellectual content behind the hard action is usually fudged over.

Wallace was the first, and almost the only, writer to attempt to justify the position of the justice figure. A complete chapter in *The Council of Justice* is devoted to the matter. If the reasoning wobbles a bit, remember that, during the next twenty-five years, other writers did not bother to reason; they merely assumed the desirability of an extra-curricular justice organization and got on with the shooting.

6-

In his autobiography, *People* (1926), Edgar Wallace recalled that, about 1905, he had begun looking for alternatives to his profession of journalist. He had in mind writing fiction. He had attempted a few short stories "but they were not of any account." He had published a book af articles, titled *Smithy*, from The Tallis Press—an enterprise wholly owned and operated by E. Wallace.

The mild success of *Smithy* encouraged him to revise and expand a short story he had written, "and which had been rejected by every magazine in London," called "The Four Just Men."

The expanded form of this story—published in 1905 by The Tallis Press—told how the Just Men murdered an official of the government—for principle. Briefly, the story is this: Sir Phillip Ramon, Secretary of State for Foreign Affairs, is sponsoring a Bill through Parliament that will deport certain resident aliens to their country of origin. (In contemporary terms, this is about equivalent to the Secretary of State pressing for a law to deport Russian dissidents back to Moscow.)

The Just Men, feeling that this is improper conduct, proceed to issue their usual warnings. Ramon is suitably pig-headed, refusing to back down, although you wonder why he should reverse himself in the face of a threat. He does not retreat even after the Just Men demonstrate how easily they are able to introduce bombs into public places. But Ramon is not to be shaken.

The Just Men have enlisted (or, rather, blackmailed) the services of Thery, a criminal and skilled craftsman. He attempts to betray them at once, but they scotch him in time. With his reluctant aid, final preparations are made for the murder—execution, if you wish. The second warning is delivered. And at this critical time, a pick-pocket lifts the notes of their plan from Poiccart's pocket. The notes do the police little good, since they are in a cryptic shorthand. The pick-pocket, who knows Poiccart's face, goes to his maker with a dose of Prussic Acid gas—he didn't get two warnings, by the way.

The police close their ranks ten deep around Sir Ramon's person. But they might as well have saved the overtime. Ramon meets his doom in a closed room, a mysterious black mark on his hand. Curiously, Thery is also found dead with a similar black mark. He died, however, of his own error, not by action of the Just Men. The Three leave England safely and, we presume, the Bill withered away.

All of which makes an interesting story. What happened to the novel makes an even more interesting one.

To publicize the book, Wallace left unexplained how the murder of Ramon was carried out. On the cover of the novel appeared the following:

£500 REWARD A remarkable offer is made in connection with this novel. Apart from its interest as a most brilliant piece of story writing, Mr. Edgar Wallace has heightened its charm by leaving at the end one mystery unsolved. The Publishers invite the reader to solve this mystery and offer Prizes to the value of £500 (First Prize, £250), to the readers who will furnish on the form provided the explanation of Sir Phillip Ramon's death.[7]

The entry form, each neatly numbered, appeared at the rear of the book.

Unfortunately, several correct solutions were received over the next several years—apparently the competition was still open in 1908. Wallace found himself hard pressed for funds and eventually had to borrow money to pay the prizes. In *People*, he remarks that he sold 38,000 copies of the book and lost 1,400 pounds ($7,000).[8]

Eventually the solution was made public by a letter from Manfred in which he disclosed that Ramon's telephone had been hooked into a high-tension line and the Secretary electrocuted. (As was Thery, who bungled the connection at the other end.) In later editions of *The Four Just Men*, the explanation was written into the text, so you are not required to wait for Manfred to tell how it was worked.

By this, you may assume that the first appearance of *The Just Men* was a qualified success. For three years, nothing more about them appeared. Then, in 1908, Wallace published *The Council of Justice*, possibly to earn enough to pay off the debts of the first adventure.

The Council is an altogether extraordinary production—a pulp magazine novel in the 1935-classical vein, published twenty-five years before the form existed.

In brief, the Red Hundred (a klatch of dedicated anarchists headed by a fanatical woman) declare open war against England, and on the City of London in particular. They commit outrage on outrage. They initiate acts of terrorism against the suburbs, planting bombs liberally, killing people in batches. Against the city, itself, they mount an assault by balloons carrying high-performance bombs.

Opposing them are the Just Men, their ranks filled by a temporary fourth member, more reliable than Thery. During the first part of the book, the Just Men home in on the Red Hundred, disrupting their inner council, crippling their plans. When the shooting actually starts, in mid-book, it's the First World War, six years early.

We know the situation well. It is the familiar military action in our streets that, in the coming 1930s, was a trademark of the Popular Publications single-character magazines. Aerial weapons are used. Corpses litter the streets. Guns and bombs go off with bland disregard for property rights and traffic regulations. You can almost hear the insurance rates soar.

After considerable blood-red action in England, the story leaps to Spain for additional violence, before returning to England. Over the more warlike passages linger the familiar intonations of H.G. Wells. In one scene (cut from the American edition), a group of war balloons drifts toward London; these are brimfull of bombs to be sprinkled over the citizens. These devices are brought down by the Just Men, who send out falcons to rip the fabric, an improvisation that would have been right at home in the pages of the pulps.

Once down, the balloons are pounded to atoms by field artillery, so that the scene which begins with echoes of Wells' *War In The Air*, ends with echoes of *The War of the Worlds*. On the whole, the action is well-handled. Although the falcons require intense determination to believe, the contemporary mind can accept the balance of the novel without hesitation. What was lurid romance in 1908 is dispassionate reporting in the 1980s.

Since the Just Men are four against one hundred, they frequently advise the police of planned outrages. Surprising only to those unaccustomed to the conventions of popular fiction, the police are virtually helpless. It irks them no end to "be under obligation to men for whom warrants exist on a charge of murder."

Ultimately the Red Hundred begins to crumble. The Just Men prepare to leave England for their base in Spain. But at the last moment, Manfred is betrayed to the police.

There follow, almost as an epilogue to the main novel, several chapters describing his arrest, trial and sentence. He is to hang at Chelmsford Prison. Behind the scenes, Gonsalez and Poiccart perform marvels of intrigue. The suspense is maintained until Manfred stands on the trap of the gallows—and vanishes in a puff of black smoke.

The Council is a particularly full and satisfying novel. The character of Manfred is developed more elaborately than any popular hero of the next thirty-five years. Although essentially shown from the outside, he is given the opportunity, rare in any type of fiction, to make choices, exercise personal taste and express personal convictions. These are areas of the hero's personality usually denied to the reader, writers being so occupied with showing their hero doing things, they never get around to letting him feel anything.

It is rare for the lead player of an action novel to think in abstracts. It is even rarer for him to express himself literately. These abilities are not essential to describe X shooting Y, and is one reason for the curious flatness of pulp magazine prose; only one part of the character is shown. The other 86% is ignored in favor of more flame, more blood, more ammunition exploding.

The third book of the series, *The Just Men of Cordova*, was published in 1917. It picks up six years after the events described in *The Council.*

The Just Men have been relatively inactive during that period. Every nation in the world has issued warrants for their arrest. Politicians orate against them by day and the newspapers babble by night. Until this public shouting dies down, they have retired to obscurity in Spain, a country for which they have as high a regard as did Hemingway later. (So much so, that their practice is to speak Spanish between themselves, using English as a second language, and Arabic when they are in crowds.)

Manfred has settled into the life of Cordova, having assumed the name of de la Monte, an amateur criminologist and writer, who has published the book *Modern Crime.* Gonsalez, more inquiring, less settled, wanders the countryside, frequently in the disguise of a beggar, and pokes curiously into the Spanish underworld. Poiccart wanders in and out, his personal activities obscure.

As the novel opens, a certain Dr. Essley has engaged their attention. The doctor, deathly afraid of the Just Men, has appeared in Cordova to consult with a gifted local poisoner. This worthy fellow has developed a virulent vegetable alkaloid which, when administered by the touch of a feather, kills at once. As the doctor and the poisoner talk, one of the Just Men hovers outside with a microphone, listening to the conversation.

Now—title characters and villain having been introduced,

and woolly waves of mystery covering all—the scene shifts to London and the fortunes of Col. Black.

The plot that follows is densely tangled by four or five sub-plots. Stripped to its commas, the story tells of the downfall of Col. Black, a stock swindler and murderer. Overextended and facing ruin, he hopes to salvage his fortunes by 1) amalgamation with Sandford, a wealthy manufacturer, 2) marriage of his right-hand henchman, the dissipated Sir Issac Tramber, to wealthy Lady Mary Verlond, ward of the snappish Lord Verlond.

All Black's schemes fall through, done in by the invisible machinations of the Just Men. They have exposed Black as Doctor Essley—the one with the infallible poison—and warned him not to enter the Sandford premises, which are "under the protection of the Just Men."

Nonetheless, Black goes to the Sandford's, attempts to poison the daughter, is foiled, escapes and slips away from the police.

More escapes follow. Captured by the Just Men, Black escapes from them, too, killing Issac Tramber by accident and wounding one of the Four. But the police catch him a few seconds later and his star sets without hope.

It is not immediately apparent why the Just Men are in this novel at all. It would operate perfectly well without them. They are, in fact, an additional element added to a typical Wallace mystery-action novel. Except for the opening, two short appearances during the story, and the final chapter, the Just Men are there mainly by reference—the characters keep mentioning them and glancing over their shoulders. That creates the interesting impression of menace cocked to strike. When they do appear, it is sudden, shocking, suitably eerie.

Unfortunately, in this story, the Just Men are not very effective. They muff one attempt on Black's life (after giving him four warnings). In their final interview with Black, they fumble badly. He slicks away from them, Browning blazing, only to be arrested by the young policeman who is the novel's secondary hero.

All this is a far cry from their impeccably lethal actions of the past. The performance strongly suggests that a novelette has been padded into a novel by the introduction of the Just

Men and the addition of some of those early complexities in Spain. Since, however, the story was originally published as a serial, its problems may be related to the structure of that narrative form, which clips crisply along, each segment a specific length, each with a suspense hook in the final paragraph.

Whatever the cause, this is the weakest of the Just Men novels. Considered as a Wallace novel, it is fine and hauls the reader panting through the chapters.

Their next appearance, in 1921, is *The Law of the Four Just Men* (US title, *Again the Three Just Men*), a collection of ten short stories.

The scene is London. The time, about twenty years after Merrell's death—1919 or 1920.[9] The Just Men are still wanted, but they have been inactive for more than ten years and have passed into legend.

Poiccart does not appear in these stories. He remains in Spain, conducting the great onion enterprise. Manfred and Gonsalez have returned to England disguised as Spanish criminologists, with credentials from the Spanish Ministry of Justice. Manfred—known as Senor Fuentes—has shaved his beard. So disguised, he has become friends with Mr. Reginald Fare, an Assistant Commissioner of Scotland Yard.

(The convenience of having a friend in the high echelons of law enforcement was not lost on later writers. The situation swiftly became a convention of the form. Few secret justice figures, avenging by night, ever lacked personal ties with the Police Commissioner, whether he knew it or not.)

Under Fare's sponsorship, Manfred and Senor Mandrelino (Gonsalez) have toured Scotland Yard, lunched with Scotland Yard, dinnered with Scotland Yard, and learned all of that organization's improved practices.

The Just Men have not publicized their return. They live quietly. Over the period of a year, they noiselessly deal justice to deserving cases. Time has not stolen their edge. Says Manfred, masked and with pistol:

"I'm one of the Three Just Men—greatly reviled and prematurely mourned. Death is my favorite panacea for all ills."

In these brief stories, however, justice does not always mean death. In only three of the cases is it necessary to kill. One of those murdered is an authentic mad scientist who hates earth-worms and has devised a method of destroying them world-wide. A second victim is a brutal slugger who eventually bashes open a globe of compressed chlorine gas in the belief that it is his wife's head. The third is a particularly obnoxious wife poisoner against whom there is no proof: The Just Men manipulate him into prison and hang him there one night.

In less final cases, the punishment is adjusted to the crime. The blackmailer is stripped of his professional documents and gets hauled off to gaol by the police, acting on information received. The white slaver receives a memorable hiding with a whip. The owner of a crooked gambling hall discovers that a bottle of acid, introduced into his safe deposit box, has wiped him out.

The punishments have a wicked black glimmer about them, like night laughter in the crypt. Thus, that fellow who runs an opium house is fed drugged coffee, wakes in what seems to be a death-house cell with his execution scheduled the following day. (He is led to believe that a dose of *cannabis indica* has stimulated him to murder.) The farce is played to the end. Hood on head, rope on neck, he is marched off—and left shaking in the street, waiting for the trap to drop.

If these retributions have a malignant tooth, the stories, themselves, are entirely charming, pleasing as fresh-baked bread. Ten stories are not nearly enough; fifty would hardly be enough.

No ethical considerations distress their facile surface. The evil fully deserve the measure of justice they receive. The Just Men, effective, charming, lethal, catch our attention. They like one another; they are generous to others. They unravel interesting problems with a sort of terse originality.

The prose is lighted by cheerfulness. Wallace's language is uncluttered. His simple, smooth sentences glint with humor. Within the paragraphs glows an occasional unanticipated word, precisely selected, so that its presence is intensified by the accessible prose in which it is embedded.

The effect is effortless simplicity, as satisfying as a Mozart rondo. And, like the Mozart, it conceals a sting in those transparent shallows.

The Law is a collection of miniatures. But *The Three Just Men* (1925) is a massive whole, the most successful of the novels. It is a long, strongly organized story, tightly integrated, loaded with interesting characters, and lifted, chapter by chapter, to a conclusion of violence.

The technical problems flawing earlier novels are largely solved. The episodic structure of *The Council* is replaced by scenes linked in time and action, each thrusting the story on. The point of view, fragmented in *Cordova*, is now concentrated. The Just Men remain at front center throughout the story. As is usual in Wallace, the activities of the opposition are balanced against those of the Just Men, but all parts are subordinated to the primary plot.

In this novel, the position of the Just Men has fundamentally changed. No longer are they outlaws. This miracle occurred because of their activities during the First World War. At that time, they involved themselves deeply in intelligence work. One of them (not identified) infiltrated the German War Office and labored there for three months, gleaning richly. Their contributions toward winning the war were so grand that the British government has pardoned them, painting out all those past crimes. In return, the Just Men promise to keep the law in spirit and deed. They find it hard. Now they have the freedom of England, enjoying police protection and taxation like other citizens. What happened to all those other warrants in all those other countries is never explained.

Unwilling to rest on past glories, the Just Men have opened the Triangle Detective Agency. This is located at 233 Curzon Street in London's West Side—specifically, the City of Westminster, County of Middlesex. Their professional emblem, a silver triangle, is fitted to the door of 233, an exceptionally small house. Here, Poiccart plays the butler and Gonsalez the chauffeur.

These days, Scotland Yard comes knocking at the door in peace. Detective-Inspector Meadows is a frequent guest. And, if Assistant Commissioner Fare has vanished, the Just Men have ready access to other high officials.

So far are these former outlaws gone in respectability that, for three years, they have employed a number of retired police officers. These assist in such large-scale cases as the smashing of a gang of Spanish bank robbers; they also guard heroines from packs of gunmen.

Under this wholesome surface, the Just Men are as sudden as ever. Gonsalez, in particular, transgresses the Law's commandments with relish. They strike more anonymously these days, no longer leaving behind such symbols as a Roman IV impressed in wax. But when their blow falls, it is harsh still.

The Three Just Men relates the downfall of the excellent Doctor Eruc Oberzohn, Swedish scientist, plotter and food crank, who strongly resembles the traditional mad scientist of B movies.

Dr. Oberzohn loves snakes. In the basement of his villa, he keeps a full room of them, sliding about in glass boxes. He has perfected a sparkling murder technique. Using certain snake by-products, the Doctor can arrange that almost anyone may suddenly crumple without warning, a double puncture in his cheek. As a result, all London is in panic because of The Snake—but it's only Old Oberzohn and his henchmen working off their enemies list.

Oberzohn's finances are bad and fading. To correct this regrettable matter, he plans to steal the rights to a hill of gold in Biskarta, Angola. These rights belong to a beautiful young woman of charm, grace and gray eyes. She is named Mirabelle Leicester, and she knows nothing whatever about hills of gold. It is the Doctor's plan to trap her, get her to sign The Papers, following this coup either by the bump-off or by marriage to himself or one of his henchmen.

With Doctor Oberzohn, to think is to accomplish. Mirabelle is promptly trapped, tricked by Oberzohn's lieutenant, Captain Monty Newton and his mistress, Joan. (Out of a sense of delicacy, Joan identifies herself, variously, as Monty's sister and fiancee.)

Mirabelle is promptly rescued by the Just Men. This causes an attack on Curzon St. by the Doctor's hired gunmen. That flops. Then the gang attempts to kidnap Mirabelle from her country home. Unexpectedly they stumble upon Gonsalez and his pistol, resulting in a small war and another large failure.

Much annoyed, Manfred advises Oberzohn to refrain,

please, from trying to carry the girl away. Oberzohn responds by dropping a load of scrap iron on the Just Men's automobile. It is a serious misjudgment. Gonsalez instantly retaliates by burning down Oberzohn's business. There was no insurance and now ruin grins rudely into the Doctor's eyes.

But he does not learn from experience. Once more he sends the gang against the Just Men. Once more he loses valuable members. And now it is too late. Manfred has decoded the secret book, written so cleverly in Braille, and has learned all about the hill of gold. But just as he takes measures to protect Mirabelle's interests, she is captured again. The girl simply has no instinct of self-preservation.

She is locked in a secret room under the ruins of a factory near Oberzohn's villa. Having her in his power does not make the Doctor's financial problems any brighter. To cut down overhead, he sets his henchmen against each other. While they are engaged in hacking at each other, The Snake kills Captain Newton. It happens at a play, *The Ringer*, which was, by coincidence, written by Edgar Wallace. (And a highly popular play it was, too. Several pages of the novel tell us of the clever staging, the exciting action, the popularity of the event; you feel cheated that tickets are not now available.)

To the villa charge the Just Men, trailing a swarm of police like a comet's tail. Too late. Oberzohn has fortified himself in. Steel sheets slab the windows, electrified barbed wire rings the site around, machine guns and searchlights on the roof—to say nothing of a basement full of snakes.

A blast of gunfire begins. It is like the Second Day at Shiloh. And in the very core of London. By degrees, the police introduce military troops, a tank, a strafing aircraft. Under the cover of night, the Just Men force entry into the villa. They arrive a bare second before the snakes sample Mirabella. Oberzohn is captured, cackles that they can prove him guilty of nothing—well, hardly nothing.

Any idiot, other than a mad Swedish scientist, would know better than to tell a Just Man that nothing can be proved. Before his words die in the air, Oberzohn dies in his tracks. Gonsalez has learned the secret of The Snake deaths and demonstrates convincingly on Oberzohn.

The Snake, by the way, is an artificial cigarette in a holder.

Blow—and from the cigarette eject two icicles of frozen snake venom.

"A snake bit him," Gonsalez explains to the police.

With the publication of *The Three Just Men*, the form of the single-character action novel, still six-eight years away, came to focus. All basic elements had been invented. Only a few additional steps remained—to identify an audience, to place a shortened novel into a magazine with illustrated covers, and to triple the concentration of gangsters and death.

It is true that newsstands on both sides of the Atlantic reeled beneath the weight of Wallace novels packed with similar elements. Little was obviously new. For evolutionary processes are seldom spectacular. There is a minor rearrangement here; a tiny modification there. Suddenly a new form startles the eye. In relishing the new, who bothers to pick out the dime novel trace, the echoes of H.G. Wells, the translucent memories of Lupin and Colonel Clay.

Welcome to a brand new fiction form, half as old as time.

Once more the Just Men would walk. *Again the Three Just Men* (1928) (US title: *The Law of the Three Just Men*) is a final collection of thirteen short stories. Several of these were published during 1928 in the *S&S Detective Story Magazine*. They include "The Mystery of Mrs. Drake," which appeared in the March 24 issue as "Miser's Fate"; and "The Englishman Named Konnor," published April 14 under the title of "Only In Fun." The presence of other stories may hardly be doubted.

These adventures take place about 1925. Blackmailers appear, white slavers, swindlers, a few murderers, some highly capable confidence men. Through the stories moves Inspector Meadows, that tower of strength during the Oberzohn crisis. And the Just Men are mild—mild.

Complex schemes they penetrate with ease. How neatly they slip in that single bit of business which derails a mountain of criminal effort. They indulge little in violence now. Their efforts are less to avenge than to help the worthy in trouble.

They seem subdued. Poiccart stirs restlessly among the group's confidential papers. Manfred complains of getting old. The splendid Gonsalez, about whom so many of these adventures turn, shakes the problems until they unravel neatly.

"The truth is," says Poiccart, "we are fiddling with things.... We do a certain amount of good—yes. We right certain wrongs—yes. But could not any honest detective agency do as much?"

But the fires are only banked. On a boat crossing the Channel, Gonsalez faces a spy and traitor. Their conversation is brief, the execution silent. The story is "The Englishman Konnor." Of their later adventures, Wallace is discreetly silent. Too bad. We could have used another ten books. It was a shame to lose sight of them, just as matters were returning to the genuine formula, as before. But let us be grateful for what we have.

7–

Richard Horatio Edgar Wallace, 1875-1932, that platinum-edged phenomenon, was, at various times, a war correspondent (Boer War), crime reporter, publisher, editor, writer and occasional millionaire. And a compulsive gambler, as well, whose fortune was swallowed more than once by the horses.

His wealth was earned word by word. There were millions of words. He wrote with terrifying facility. When writing by hand proved too slow, he dictated. It is said that he could juggle half a dozen serials, a play or two, intermingled with short stories and business correspondence. Books spurted from his fingertips. Some years saw a dozen—perhaps more—hardbacks published, while the magazines on both sides of the Atlantic brimmed with 6-part serials.

His first books collected early newspaper work. But with the publication of *The Four Just Men*, mainstream writing began. It developed rapidly to a torrent of gold until his death in 1932, in Hollywood, California.

Primarily known as a "thriller" writer—that is, for high-tension mystery-adventure stories—he slid effortlessly into other fields. His work includes novels of social commentary (*Those Folks of Bulboro*), science fiction (*The Day of Uniting*), future war (*Private Selby*), humor (*Educated Evans*), adventure (*Sanders of the River*), true crime (*The Devil Man—* which coats fact with a syrup of fiction), autobiography (*People*), and history (*Kitchener's Army and the Territorial Forces*).

In mid-career he got into playwriting and pounded out a series of red-hot melodramas, including *The Ringer, The Terror,* and *On the Spot.*[10] The final three years of his life were spent in Hollywood working on scripts; *My Hollywood Diary* is an account of that period. It is believed that the last thing he did was the screen treatment for *King Kong.*

Wallace's writing begins at a time when the dime novel gloriously flamed. His work spans the first sprouting of the pulp magazines (overtowered by the majesty of *The Strand Magazine*), through their differentiation into specialized types, to the advent of the costumed hero. When Wallace died, *The Shadow Magazine* flamed brightly and the single-character magazine explosion was less than a year away.

Like Packard and Hanshew, Wallace drew directly from the dime novel tradition. He accepted the dime novel's pacing, its frequent scenes of bloody melodrama, and its techniques of whisking people from one peril to the next. He accepted the convention of plotted stories, where good and evil maneuver against each other, both out in the open. Like the dime novel, the scene is contemporary and dense with fresh technological devices.

Through Wallace's stories are scattered all those fine old gimmicks beloved of Sexton Blake and Nick Carter. He delights in trap doors and sinister muffled figures. Death traps tickle him. As do secret poisons, gangs with peculiar symbols, houses rigged with sliding steel panels, and signal buttons.

Strong physical movement drives his story line. He works the melodrama hard, using airplanes and automobiles, heroines in peril, whizzing bullets, maniacs with shining knives. Oh, yes....

The fast action rattles out with newspaper crispness, lightly scented by essence de silent movie. The whole package is wrapped in the English novel tradition out of H.G. Wells and H. Rider Haggard, theme and character interacting through an extended plot. In Wallace, it is rather more plot, and rather less character; but he is still writing novels.

You begin with the early Wallace fiction and watch technology unfold. Across the years, aircraft progress from science-fiction concepts to commercial schedules. The automobile, that astonishment, becomes an accepted nuisance. Silent movies appear. Red anarchists are supplanted by German spies, their Zeppelins, their submarines. The First World War begins as heroic jousting, ends with a generation buried and a depression welcoming the boys back home.

Crime alters with the times. Comes a rash of white slavers, saccharine smugglers, stock swindlers, private gambling houses, dealers in dope. Silent movies yield to sound. Commercial radio is born. Crooks hustle about in high-performance automobiles and evade Scotland Yard by airplane flights from small private landing strips.

For their part, the police organize themselves. They integrate communications across London, establish The Big Four and The Flying Squad, use radios and files of photographs and fingerprints (although there is still question as to whether fingerprints are all different).

One of the fringe benefits of reading Wallace is to watch the familiar devices of the present appear and fall into place. The stories may be tracked in time by the improvements in telephones and the advancing technology of the automobile. It is as fascinating as the changing attitudes toward smoking or the acceptance of women into the business world. The melodrama remains timeless—it could be moved intact to a modern action novel. But the changing technology, the altering mores of the period, are constantly in flux. It is rather like inspecting a closet packed with obsolete great-grandmothers's clothing. Possibly it is this not-quite-obsolete-enough atmosphere which has caused Wallace's novels to become unavailable in the United States.

It is a shame. They are almost as fascinating today as when they were first published. He was a master story-teller.

Wallace's influence saturated the pulp magazine fiction of the 1920s. In America his work was eagerly printed by *Argosy*

All – Story, Popular, Short Stories, Flynn's and *S&S Detective Story.* The Crime Club published an extended list of his books. He was a one-man demonstration of how to write mystery-action stories and get rich. His plotting techniques, his methods of establishing and maintaining suspense, his dime novel devices, even his costumed mystery figures, fed directly into mainstream pulp magazine writing.

Since the major thrust of Wallace's work occurred during the 1920s, discussion of it will be deferred to a later chapter. At the moment, it is enough to say that he was a major figure among those combining the dime novel tradition with that of the adventure-mystery novel. The end product was not entirely new. But it had a unique prose sound and caught readers' attention.

Wallace was one of the first writers to introduce overt violence into the popular crook story. Raffles, Cleek, Lupin, all of them shied from murder. But the Just Men and, later, The Ringer, kill without qualm, their victims deserving such an abrupt finish.

Most of Wallace's heroes use weapons. In their pragmatic world, there is no room for Cleek's attitudinizing or Jimmie Dale's lachrymose self-flagellation. The Wallace men shoot when required. No sentimental driveling. Since Wallace had seen action during the Boer War, he was closer to the reality of self-preservation than other contemporaries. They had to experience World War I before their ideas changed.

The later pulp magazines accepted Wallace's lessons. They slowly adopted the death-giving hero, compressed the story length, increased the gunfire and bloodshed, and reduced characterization to a few brief words. We cannot blame Wallace for the excesses of these magazines, but he certainly opened the way along which they would evolve.

8-

At the same time that the Just Men were attending to the oversights of the Law, another armed hero was making his debut far, far from London.

The scene was in West Texas, fifty miles south of the New Mexico line, near the Pecos River. By which you must understand that we are leaving the world of lethal sophisticates and turning to the equally lethal world of Indians and horses and manly men, under the big sky, where Judge Colt rules and you roll your blanket by smouldering embers at night, watching the stars like diamonds, your belly full of bacon and beans and coffee boiled right in the tin can, there in God's country among the sidewinders and Gila Monsters and cow critters. And you in last month's shirt.

Less poetically, it is 1906 in the cattle country. Through the magic glasses of Clarence E. Mulford we are about to meet a grinning, red-headed cowboy, short, wiry with a cheekfull of tobacco and a slight limp.

His name is Hopalong Cassidy. He is about to demonstrate the advantages of the quick draw through a library of books and magazines, moving pictures, television programs, comic books, paperbacks and billboards.

And incidentally he will energize about four generations of fast-gun cowboys, those splendid ornaments of the western pulp magazine.

VII—Fifty Miles South, Near the Pecos

1-

The face is almost young, the hair almost white. He looks out from the screen at the Saturday matinee, shrewd, patient, everybody's uncle.

His clothing is dark, more formal than jeans, a compromise between the rodeo and going-to-town best. For some reason, he often wears black gloves. A pair of heavy Colt single-action revolvers ride his hips.

He rides furiously from left to right across the moving picture screen, across the television tube. Curious partners accompany him. He closes in, fists battering the evil to their knees. And if, after all, that sneering wretch with the thin black mustache glides hand to pistol butt, forcing a showdown, then the black-gloved hands crook. A sudden movement. Fire, sound. Cassidy crouches watching, faint regret on his fine face, as the corpse falls.

Then to the bar room. Milk for mine. And a slice of that fresh home-baked-tasting bread generously spread with genuine oleomargarine. To be like Hoppy, you eat like Hoppy.

So the pleasant image of William Boyd, Hopalong Cassidy to the millions. From 1934 he was the Hopalong of the moving pictures; from the 1950s, Hopalong of television. He ignited the susceptible imaginations of at least three generations of boys.

Incidentally he sold milk, comic books, gun belts, small iron cap guns, smaller plastic imitation cap guns, bread, books, and a lot of hours of expensive television time. A rich commercial success. The Hopalong Cassidy portrayed by William Boyd was "...an absolutely ludicrous character."

Or so Clarence E. Mulford claimed.[1] Mulford wrote the original Cassidy stories for over thirty years. His opinion should hold value. He knew Cassidy back when the century was young. He lived with Cassidy through a swarm of novelettes and books and, if he saw only a few of the movies, his opinion is still interesting.

For one of the more eminent western writers of his day, Mulford enjoyed a placid enough background. Born February

3, 1883, in Streaton, Illinois, he was seized early by the itch to write. His first fiction earnings came as a shared first prize in a short story contest sponsored by the long forgotten *Metropolitan Magazine.*

In 1899, the family moved to Brooklyn, N.Y., placing Mulford about as far from the west as he could get. At the age of 23 he became a city clerk in the Brooklyn marriage license bureau. Nights, he wrote of the west.

For the Brooklyn clerk had contracted a passion for open prairies and tall sky. It stayed with him the rest of his life.

Just why this long-duration crush?

Who knows why anybody loves anything. We do know that the West, going West, living West was a major element of American thought during the 70s and 80s. When Mulford was a boy, every third publication babbled of The West, cataloging buffalo, Indians, intrepid horsemen, the Romance of the Prairie.

It was the last great freedom on the continent. The golden legend of the frontier had not wholly evaporated. Out there, somewhere, just beyond the Mississippi River, the traveler passed shimmering veils which burned away civilization's constraints. Left you capable of realizing your inherent abilities to grow, to accomplish, unfettered by petty rules.

For generations that theme had been puffed and ornamented by the dime novels, rattling out brightly colored adventures of Diamond Dick, Denver Dan, Wild Bill Hickok, Buffalo Bill, Pawnee Bill and all those Bills. These bubbles floated on an ocean of newspaper stories and magazine articles, vigorously illustrated, describing trips West by various Eastern writers.

All this interwoven with scraps of Harte and Mark Twain, fragments of Crane, samples of Parkman's *Oregon Trail* and memoirs by Colonel This and Major That, famous scouts and Indian fighters all.

Yes there was romance in the 1890 West. Bad men dancehall girls gold mines shoot-outs saloons Dodge antelope steaks Boot Hill stage coach saddle bags Sharps Winchester sage brush Colt, .45 single-action Colt wild tough perfect freedom be a man.

The actual situation differed mildly, as actual situations will.

Already fence crept the range. The Indians menaced rarely. The wide-open cow town, dusty jewel of wickedness, sat tamed with schools and newspapers from the East. The railroads slacked their expansion. The vast waves of settlement, now 50 years past, had calmed to more studied exploitation of the land. Numbers of men lived who knew, first-hand, what trail towns had been like and what they were now, and understood what "cowboy" meant in terms of a lonesome, dirty grinding job for tiny pay.

But the legend had engaged Mulford's mind and he was to seek after it, piece by piece, all through his life. He wrote of days already beyond recall—of the late 1870s, 80s, 90s. Perhaps there had never quite been such days. Perhaps he described events brighter than life, the characters more capable, the action gaudier.

On paper, it worked beautifully.

The stories bounded out—exuberant, filled with cockeyed fun, like a dormitory of boys joyously rioting.

That's the tone of the first stories: a froth of irresponsible fun. Only occasionally do the bubbles part. Something scalding and white-hot shows. Then the bubbles spin closed. The romp continues.

Buck Peters, Hopalong Cassidy, Red Connors, the other Bar 20 people, first appeared in a series of short stories—some hardly more than vignettes—that were published in the *Outing Magazine*, 1906-1907.

Outing, an Albany, New York, magazine, had been founded in 1882 to celebrate the glories of bicycling. By 1906 it had evolved to careful mingling of fiction, travel, nature and sports, with a circulation of 100,000. Its record was distinguished. It published Frederic Remington's western illustrations (they first appearing in 1887) and, later, the work of N.C. Wyeth and F.E. Schoonover. It featured articles by Dan Beard on camping, Lanier on fishing, Gene Stratton Porter on birds, George James on Indians. It first published Stewart Edward White's *Round-up Days,* and articles by Theodore Roosevelt, Zona Gale and William Beebe. In its pages appeared

Jack London's serial of *White Fang* (1905) and fiction by Owen Wister and Charles Alden Seltzer.

An educated guess would be that Hopalong Cassidy owed a great deal to *Round-up Days* and Wister's *The Virginian.*

They share a light conversational style. The sentences are simple. Anecdotes crowd the paragraphs. The characters have a bouncy craziness overlaying a rigid code of conduct. If Wister and White are more realistic, Mulford is lighter, far more facetious.

Within a year, Mulford's *Outing* fiction appeared in hardback, beginning a long series of books, most involving the Bar 20 people. For 20 years, while he worked in Brooklyn, Mulford elaborated the series. He added characters, married them off, made them widowers, transplanted the action from Texas to Montana, and strewed bad men, justly shot, through multitudes of trail towns. He sold to *Pearson's Magazine* in 1909, other magazines not yet identified, then collected the stories into additional books.

They were wildly popular. By the mid-1920s, a million and a half copies of his novels were in print, including translations into Scandinavian and Polish.[2] Huge royalties rolled in. But Mulford's prudence was unshaken. He worked 20 full years in Brooklyn. Then took his retirement in 1926, gathered up his royalties and bought a home in Freyburg, Maine (even more distant from the West than Brooklyn is). At the age of 43 he prepared to write full time.

He did so until 1941. That year, when he was 58 and inclined to peppery opinion, he quit writing altogether in protest against high federal income taxes. The gesture did him no more good than it did Edmund Wilson, some 25 years later.

When the writing ceased, he took up the hobby of

...big caliber revolver shooting (hand-loading my own maximum cartridges) over ranges of 300 to 500 yards, which forced me to buy fifty-five acres of land, with a high hill for backdrop.[3]

He donated to the Library of Congress an immense collection of Western books—histories, documents, journals—card files of 17,000 historical events, and a vast assembly of western artifacts. If he had not seen the West until the mid-20s, he had assiduously researched. He had a passion for authenticity, you see, and exactness.

He died in Maine, May 19, 1956, at the age of 73.

Cassidy was even older by that time. But Cassidy was doing fine in G&D reprints, in a short-lived pulp magazine, and on television.

That western air preserves a man.

2-

He is that wild young red-head skylarking in the bunkhouse. He has the stripped leanness of the early twenties. He is of medium height, with a curious disproportion between his narrow hips and heavy shoulders, broad and sloping. For some years, already, his legs have been bowed, a legacy of too much horse-riding and too little milk.

Morning at the corral: He steals a friend's hat, fills it with rocks, and sinks it in the horse trough. He wears rough, worn clothing, rather soiled, a faded bandana tied around his neck. Low on his legs ride two Colts with walnut handles. At 23 he is already known for blinding speed getting those hulking single-action pistols out, and for his astounding artistry with them. He is a Pagannini of the .45. His nervous system is precisely tuned to the use of weapons. At close range, he knows intuitively where the bullet will go. At longer ranges he hardly has to aim. In addition to the Colts he uses a .50-calibre Army Sharps. Later he will change to a lesser caliber. He is a fairly good rifle shot; it is with the pistol that he excels—with either hand.

In the saloon, laughing riotously, he helps carry out a struggling friend and roll him in the dirt. That done, he has a small drink—he does not drink much—then lights a cigar and sits at cards.

Either he is very hot or very cold at cards. His luck wobbles wildly. Good luck or bad—it makes no difference. It isn't gambling he cares for; it is the suspense of the draw, the competition, the reading of the other players. It is known that he will bet on anything and on either side.

In addition to cigars, he smokes hand-rolled cigarettes. Also chews tobacco. He drinks beer, whisky. He swears. No malice frets him. He sparkles with irresponsible good nature. He is reckless, curious beyond explaining, and demonstrates a convincing talent for tumbling into trouble.

Yes, a sprawling cub of a boy. He likes round-about ways through the desert. He likes the high ground. Behind the tumble and play, there watches, softly murmuring, a cold strategic mind, the mind of a Jackson or Alexander. At this time it is young, silly with bright blood, not quite seasoned by experience.

His name is William Cassidy. Called Hopalong or Hoppy by his friends. The nickname refers to a slight limp. He was shot in the right thigh several years back, while aiding Sheriff Harris of Albuquerque. Being young, he is intensely sensitive to direct remarks about his limp or references to cripples which might be construed as sneer.

Cassidy is 23 (the same age as Mulford) when the series opens.

It opens with a story of violence. You will find it in the first three chapters of the book *Bar 20* (1907) which collects the 1906-1907 *Outing Magazine* stories. As is usual for the time, the short stories and sketches are disguised as a 25-chapter novel. The book actually contains about 8 short stories and 4 sketches—as far as can be gleaned from the book without inspecting the magazine.

The story takes place near the Bar 20 ranch. This is located about 50 miles south of the Texas-New Mexico border, near the Pecos River. At the north, the Bar 20 is bounded by the C 80. On the boundary, Skinny Thompson (Bar 20) has words with Shorty Jones (C 80) and Shorty ends up with a dead horse.

Another C 80 hand, investigating, ends with a bullet in him. Just an average morning. Now matters escalate. In Buckskin, the near town, Shorty guns a Bar 20 man. With that, the air fills with the slither of steel coming free of leather. Twelve C 80 men hole up in the Houston House, a combination barroom and hotel. Bar 20 scatters around outside. And the gun work begins.

Over the space of an afternoon, the Houston House is methodically shot to splinters. Eventually all 12 C 80 men are killed.

The scene of the wrecked barroom was indescribable. Holes, furrows, shattered glass and bottles, the liquor oozing down the walls of the shelves and running over the floor; the ruined furniture, a wrecked bar, seared and shattered and covered with blood; bodies as they had been piled in the corners; ropes, shells, hats; and liquor everywhere over everything.[1]

Such a bare outline might suggest that the story unfolds in purple gloom, drums muttering behind eerie clouds. Not the case at all. The story is casual, sunny, impudent. The Bar 20 men, casually clowning, sky-lark, grin at the bullets' whine. They bleed, but off-handedly:

"Where'd they git yu."
"In the off leg. Hurts like blazes. Did yu git him?"
"Nope. I jest came fer another cig; got any left?"
"Up above. Yore gall is shore apallin.' Help me in, yu two-laigged jackass."[5]

Cassidy shoots his initials into the saloon door (with bullets at 5¢ each and wages $30 a month). In punishment, he not only gets shot in the laig but receives a permanent part in his hair. However, he has the pleasure of leaning out in the middle of the action and dumping a handful of hot cartridge cases down a friend's neck.

In the course of the shooting, we meet most of the Bar 20 regulars: Buck Peters, the foreman, a mild-looking man, slow to speak, never flurried, a highly competent cattleman and gun-fighter, and Cassidy's prime teacher.   Red Connors, Cassidy's closest friend, although you'd doubt it to hear them harangue each other. Another redhead, he is older, more taciturn, and is as astounding a performer with the Winchester rifle as Cassidy is with the Colt.

Johnny Nelson, a great pie-eater, is the baby of the outfit, still in his early teens, hot to make his name shine and do marvels.

And there are the lesser names that will grow familiar over the years: Lanky Smith, Skinny Thompson, Pete Wilson, Billy Williams, and others.

They were, Mulford tells us—

... not lawless, nor drunken, shooting bullies, but "naturally peaceable," rubbing elbows with men who were not.[6]

The violent reputation of the cowboy, Mulford explains, is because Eastern riffraff in large quantities has come out among them, forcing the cowboy to obey the law of self-preservation. Which neatly explains away the Houston House debate—and, besides, as Mulford points out, when the cowboys caused damage, they paid for it.

Curiously, none of the Bar 20 boys recognize that among them moves a living legend. They view Mr. Cassidy's antics with delighted or annoyed eye, depending on circumstances:

"That mus' be that fool Hopalong."

So says his friend Red. No respect. It's eating all that beef does it. But it is a singular attitude to hold toward the hero of the piece and the subject for a yard of books.

One month later: the second story. A drunken Indian, humiliated when a horse throws him before witnesses, collects three other tribesmen and goes wild. They ambush and wound Johnny, flee with the Bar 20 in pursuit. Near the border, the Indians take their stand. Buck is wounded. Cassidy, hit badly by a ricochet, becomes delirious, as he always does when wounded. The Indians get wiped out and honor is restored.

Third story, six weeks later: Cassidy, convalescing, rides north to visit his friend Sheriff Harris. Harris is murdered while standing in a saloon talking with Hopalong. In this story one of the long-term characters is introduced—Tex Ewalt, a part-time badman, slick professional gambler and dressy dude from Santa Fe. One day, Hopalong and Ewalt will be friends. Not now. Decidedly not now.

Next story. Cassidy goes roving down to Mexico to visit lovely Carmencita, delightful Carmencita, Carmencita of the flashing black eyes. He wooed her passionately before the sisters locked her away from him. That was five years ago, when he was an impressionable 19, riding with the Bar 20 in pursuit of a Mexican rustler with the unfortunate name of Tamale Jose.

Red got a bullet in him that time; T. Jose got dead; Cassidy got a 500-peso reward placed on his head. So here he is back.

Some things haven't changed: the reward is still outstanding. Lovely Carmencita, however, now weighs 673

Argosy, Apr. 3, 1920. *Argosy* was the first of the pulps. This issue contained four serials, a novelette, and four short stories, a mass of fiction offered weekly for 10¢.

The Popular Magazine, Aug. 1906. Long before the specialized western action magazine, the western story drew its legions of readers. Daily ranch life was often the subject, since the form had not yet hardened to a contest between good and evil.

pounds and has a hot-tempered husband with an itching stilleto. Cassidy punches his head, shoots up a cantena, wounds the sheriff, and romps off with the sheriff's pistol. Some time later, he rides back to return the gun and cuts cards with the sheriff to see if he is to be a prisoner in the jail.

One month later. Introducing Frenchy McAllister, a good solid man with a grudge. Some years earlier, his wife was murdered by an outlaw; his revenge will come in a later story.

But now at the old bunkhouse, punchers skylark and commit heavy-handed jokes. (The back and forth chatter in these stories often occupies 25% of the space and is sufficiently engaging that you wish it longer. The boys rag and joke each other continuously; it sounds properly authentic.)

After the fun, Cassidy takes off on a prospecting trip. Winds up near a town run by a tough gang. Immediately, he wounds a claim-jumper, blacks the sheriff's eye and kicks him from a saloon. That night, the gang attacks his shack, where Hopalong is comfortably sited with a gallon can of peaches. They regret their hasty ways.

The next story, occupying Chapters 12-15, tells how Red and Cassidy visit the town of Cactus Springs. There, Travennes (head of the local vigilantes and part-time crook and cattle thief) attempts to frame them for horse-stealing. A serious lapse of judgment. Before the story is over, Cassidy and Red collect 11 prisoners, 19 pistols and leave town fast. They return as swiftly with a group of friends, and proceed to demolish Cactus Springs to the final board and nail. Numbers of hardcases end up dead, including the sanguine Mr. Travennes.

The next story occupies seven chapters and concerns the tracking and eventual destruction of a pack of rustlers. That group is headed by a certain Slippery Trendley—the one who murdered Frenchy McAllister's wife in Montana 20 years before. Bar 20 combines forces with six other ranches and 75 men descend upon the rustler nest, wiping it out in an all-day fire fight. Trendley falls a prisoner. He is given over to McAllister, who kills him in sundry painful ways, undescribed and undiscussed.

In the final story, love comes to Cassidy. Going to town to compete in what is apparently a festival of western arts, he

meets a wide-eyed young dainty, name of Miss Laura Deane.
The festival has also drawn Tex Ewalt, there for dark purposes.
Over the past months, Cassidy has been responsible for the
death of about 50 of Tex's friends, and the time has come, he
thinks, to put an end to this attrition.

Unfortunately, for him, Cassidy learns that delicate Miss
Laura is an actress who is practicing the rewarding profession
of clipping cow punchers for their rolls. Mr. Cassidy is properly
put out. He expresses his hurt feelings in the pistol contest,
performing shooting feats prodigious. His performance ends
as he shoots bits of attire from about Tex—his buttons, his belt,
his spurs, his self-respect.

And so ends the initial set of stories. And so, way back
there in 1906-1907, the mould was created that would be filled
by generations of pulp western fiction. Mulford is one of the
major shapers of the field. From the Bar 20 boys and the
amiable, lethal Cassidy, radiate innumerable legions of hard-
riding, hard-shooting, devil-may-care heroes battling
infamous greasers and renegades, rustlers, gamblers and
assorted sneaks.

Almost every western filmed for 30 years used the Mulford
scenes: bar room shootout, the in-town gunfight, the chase, the
battle among the rocks, the facing down of the tough overlord
of crime.

So familiar are the scenes, these exhausted excitements,
that you can hardly conjure up a time when they sparkled crisp
and fascinating. Seventy-odd years of repetition dulls them.
They are grand cliches, suitable only for television parodies.
Strange, then, that even after 70 years, Cassidy should glow
with vitality. If his imitators seem thinner, the stories duller,
the gun play ever more predictable, it's no great puzzle. Even
the best wine can be diluted only so much.

3-

The early Cassidy stories contain much movement,
climaxing in finales of extended violence, where large groups
of men gather to blaze away at one another for 2,000-3,000
words. The action is leavened by liberal injections of comedy,
mock-serious elements, a certain facetious turn of style. The

prose switches from sunshine to blood in three words. Dialogue is extensively used. The sentences are clear and short. The simplicity of prose sound is unmarred by complexity, either of construction or thought.

Fundamental differences exist between these stories and those by Owen Wister published in *Harper's* about five years earlier during 1902. Those were collected as *The Virginian*, a very large book disguised as a novel. (It is not.) It would appear that Mulford owed many of his backdrops, much of cowboys' cheerful attitudes, to Wister's work. The use of these materials is quite different.

Wister's fiction has guns in it, and blood sometimes runs. But he is more consistently concerned with those deadly weapons of ethical and moral decisions made according to certain hard rules of conduct understood by the westerners and only imperfectly understood by the Eastern narrator of the stories.

Almost every story in *The Virginian* turns some delicate point of personal perception. The complexities of the hero's character—he is from Virginia: hence the title of the book—his relations to others, his love affair with The Girl, her reactions to him, are neatly examined, emotion by emotion, nuance by nuance.

Physical action occurs; psychological action dominates. Surprisingly this doesn't make the story either dull or obscure, but is so skillfully handled the fiction never drags. A case in point is one story, about half through the book, concerning the exercise of authority.

The Virginian, as acting foreman, has completed a cattle drive and is now returning to the home ranch by rail with his crew of men. The villain of the piece, Trampas (the same for whom the Trampas Walk is named), burns with indignation that the Virginian has been placed in authority over him. He seeks to induce the crew to jump the train with him and take off for the gold fields.

To undermine the Virginian's authority in the eyes of the crew, one of Trampas' henchmen engages the Eastern narrator in a long, elaborately constructed story that is disclosed as a tall tale in the last sentence. The idea being that by proving the narrator a gullible fool, the Virginian, being his friend, is also a fool and unworthy of respect.

To regain authority, the Virginian repeats essentially the same hoax on Trampas. At a train stop, he concocts an elaborate yarn massed with corroborative detail, about the practice of frog farming in Texas. Trampas is gradually taken in by this exotic fancy. His credulity is not believable, considering the circumstances. For purposes of the story, he does believe, and put out he is when the Virginian bursts the hoax in his face.

Since Trampas has been conned more slickly than the puncher conned the tenderfoot, the balance of authority is reestablished. Everyone is tickled, except Trampas. The mutiny dissolves. The Virginian is again in control.

Sounds bald. It's neatly done, though. And isn't it a far cry from the Ride-Ride, Shoot-Shoot stories categorized as westerns.

In this story, as in other parts of *The Virginian,* the point turns upon those perceptions that we are all aware of but which rarely appear in literature less formal than that of Henry James. These perceptions permit communication between people at delicate levels and without speech. You are aware of these communications constantly in daily life, almost never in literature. So the relationships between people in Wister's books are relatively unusual ones for a popular story. All rings psychologically true. The observation of authority shifts and power structures between these men is precise and cleanly drawn.

Except that Trampas could never have accepted the frog story.

The way that Wister handles these materials points the way to the next western novelists: Charles Alden Seltzer and B. M. Bower (both contempories). Zane Grey, Max Brand, and William Macleod Raine.

Chronologically, B. M. Bower was first. The name is a pseudonym for Mrs. Bertha Sinclair-Cowan (1874-1940). She was brought up on a Montana ranch, where she saw the real wild west day by day. She lived among horses, cowboys, and immense landscapes.

When she began to write, her descriptions of life on the range were entirely authentic, with that casual precision and lack of melodrama possible only to one who has been part of it. In the course of a long professional life, she turned out sixty or seventy books, publishing extensively in *The Popular Magazine* and *Argosy*.

Her most famous series characters, the cowboys of the Flying U Ranch, first appeared in *Chip of the Flying U,* a novel published complete in the October 1904 issue of *Popular*. It appeared as a book in 1906.

Numerous Flying U stories followed in *Popular* from November 1904 to 1909. Additional stories have been noted in 1912, 1913, and 1928, and, in *Argosy,* in 1933. Collections of Flying U stories include *The Lonesome Trail* (1909), *The Happy Family* (1910), *Flying U Ranch* (1914), *The Flying U's Last Stand* (1915), *Rodeo* (1929), *Dark Horse* (1931), and *The Flying U Strikes* (1934).

Each book clusters fairly closely related chapters, more or less complete in themselves, into a loose-jointed novel. The mark of Wister is on them. Here and there, the prose is pimpled by schoolgirl cuteness, where the author unfortunately yields to the impulse to call the men of the Flying U, the "Happy Family" or the lady doctor, the "Little Doctor." Since these are ranch stories, numerous cowboys appear: each is named, none is developed. The interaction of developed personality which characterized Wister's work is entirely absent. Backgrounds, equipment, behavior seem sharply realistic. You have the feeling that the author strains to establish a story thread and narrative action into the low-key situation of a few men taking care of many cattle.

The characters introduced in *Chip* are generally consistent through the series, with some few later additions. Patsy, the cook; Jack Bates, Cal Emmett; Happy Jack; Slim, who is fat; Shorty, a sort of foreman; James G. Whitmore, the Old Man; and Claude Bennett—who is the Chip of the stories.

He's called Chip because of a fiendish appetite for saratoga chips, called potato chips these days. You can tell that he's the lead figure immediately: face is thin, refined, straight nose, square chin, and a reticient, no-nonsense way about him. His horse is named Silver. He has no Indian companion.

Chip and the Flying U tells how Della Whitmore (the Old Man's daughter) arrives at the ranch, her gradual love affair with Chip, and how they got engaged. Supposedly they got engaged; he kisses her in the end and, after that, the man's got to do the right thing doesn't he?

It is a testy romance. True to the conventions of 1904, they get along poorly at first sight. Then she grows to dislike him—the first symptom of love—but be sympathetic: she's only 23 and just out of an eastern medical school. Thus her honorary title, The Little Doctor, a touch that causes the Great Big Reader's gorge to rise. She also has grey eyes, can shoot a rifle, ride a horse, repair men and horses, while being just adorable. The first group of stories focuses on her. Later, she vanishes and the Flying U group, itself, is the main subject.

We begin with Della's arrival at the ranch. The cowboys promptly rig a fake lynching to horrify her. But she does not panic. Instead she borrows Chip's rifle and shoots a coyote, amazing all and earning their initial respect. She rapidly strengthens her position by treating Silver's broken leg, uses a stomach pump on the children that ate up her medical supplies, and nurses Chip for sundry fracture and dislocations caused by a horse falling on him.

During his convalescence, they discover that Chip is a natural artist in the manner of Remington. In a matter of pages, the cast stands reverently before his painting and a state senator has purchased it, paying a lavish fee. There follows a mild complication as to whether Chip or Della painted the picture, but it is only a tiny small complication, dissolved by the story's end. After this, Chip believes that Della loves a visiting eastern doctor, another trifling alarm, since the doctor turns out to be a woman. And now Della rides off alone because it is the end of the book and time to wrap up the love story. Out on the prairie, she gets unhorsed and jabs her foot full of cactus spines. Chip picks them out, every one, and boldly kisses her to sweet submission. The story ends with sugar syrup trickling from the paragraphs.

What has happened to the familiar devices of western fiction? Where are the barrooms, tough guys, rustlers, and guns? Not here, certainly. Guns, in fact, hardly appear. One rifle is fired at the coyote. And, when Silver's leg is broken,

Chip goes to his bedroll and takes out his pistol, a realistic if unexciting place to carry a .45. But even so, he doesn't have to shoot his horse.

After Bower cleared this initial oosh of romance from her system, the stories pick up wonderfully.

In "The Mutiny of the Six" (*Popular,* February 1904), Dunk Wittaker, part owner of the Flying U, has developed the land hungries. Plotting to annex the adjacent ranchland, he hires a no-good cowboy to conceal calf hides on that property. These can later be found, rustling claimed, and the people next door forced off their property.

A fragment of his plan is overheard by Cal Emmett of the Flying U. He relays his suspicions to the other cowboys and so, when the hides are found, no one is believed guilty but Wittaker. After Dunk attempts to place the no-good on the payroll, the Happy Family quit together. Astounded by this wholesale mutiny, Dunk tongue-lashes Chip, right out there in front of everybody. "Perhaps he mistook Chip's passive attitude for timidity."

Chip pinched off the lighted end of his cigarette from the habit born of long riding over the range land, where carelessness with fire is a crime, and then. . . took two swift strides and made a quick move. Dunk fell over the pile of bedding and lay in a most undignified posture, with his head down and his feet waving impotently in the air.... Chip's boot helpfully sought a good target and landed with effect. Dunk rolled off the bedding. . . scrambled to his feet, and immediately sprawled again in the grass.... Dunk did not get up. He lay upon his left side, and looked up craftily.... His right hand stole backward. . . but he reckoned without the boot. It was there, just where it was most needed, and Dunk had two raw knuckles to remember it by. When one would draw a gun, one should do it quickly.

In other words, Chip knocked Dunk down, kicked him, knocked him down again, then kicked the partly drawn gun from Dunk's hand. The description of the action is understated as you may notice, and given a lightly humorous touch. It is the western way. The tone of the prose is unfortunately self-consciously literary. The action is obscured by a wordy haze and vapors of righteousness rise all about.

Shortly thereafter, The Old Man arrives, buys out Dunk's share of the ranch, the evil minion confesses, and the boys of the Flying U take up their jobs again.

The Flying U Ranch (1914) picks up a little over a year later. Chip and Della now have a little boy toddling about the horses. They play no particular part of this story, since they quickly go to Chicago to take care of the Old Man, who has been hit by a automobile in that wicked city. Sheepherders have bought the spread next to the Flying U and begin studied trespass of the premises. It is all a sinister plot on the part of Dunk. Matters build for about 200 pages. Happy Jack is severely wounded—to the universal horror of all, for, regardless of what you have read about the west, guns and gunfire are shocking intrusions into normal life. Eventually, the Happy Family and Dunk's minions meet head on.

Two—possibly three—guns are displayed. No shooting. Dunk is bluffed into leaving the territory—a new Flying U hand pretends to recognize him as a wanted outlaw and, glory be, it appears that Dunk is. So he lights out, the sheep menace collapses, and the Old Man will get well after all.

Most of the Flying U group reappear in the novel "Rodeo," published as a 4-part serial, October 7 - November 20, 1928, in *The Popular Magazine*. It's about twenty years later. The Flying U boys have been swallowed up by the city now, and appear in coats and collars. Back to the ranch for a reunion, they rapidly get cross-grained with the Kid, Chip and Della's son. He is in the throes of a delayed teenage or something, for he is remarkably touchy about honor, competence, etc. etc. Claims that the new generation of cowboys are just as good as the old timers.

One thing leads to another and he feels abused and unappreciated, a mental condition not uncommon with young men. Off he goes to Chicago to participate in a rodeo, thus proving whatever it was he wanted to prove. It is not quite a Frank Merriwell story, because the Kid, for all his callow blatting, is well realized and his feelings, however greenly damp about the edges, are nicely handled. He succeeeds in proving himself, over many an improbable chapter, by winning the big race, accidently catching a thief who stole his shirt and, incidentally, $30,000 in box office receipts. As a blazing climax, he finally wins through for his team, even though his knee had been severely injured and people thought he was drunk.

The story is episodic, interesting, and just a little painful to those remembering the foaming passions of their early twenties. But the Kid endures through all these coming-of-age rites, finally, and enters early manhood flat on his back, the injured knee bandaged, the Little Doctor and Chip hovering proudly over him, the Happy Family agreeing that he done good, and the only girl in the world (a pink and white vision) round-eyed in the background. What more could a brash young man require?

During 1933, a few additional Flying U stories were published in *Argosy*. These are brief, competent, compressed and tightly told, having the tougher texture and unsentimental outlook of the 1930s. The events described are from the early days at the Flying U, probably before the arrival of The Little Doctor, and Chip is a central figure in all of them.

"Bad Penny" *(Argosy,* December 2, 1933) tells how the saddle bum, Penny, slips off from a cattle drive to get drunk. He is badly needed. The Flying U is operating short-handed and struggling to deliver a herd to the railhead. Lurching back drunk late at night, Penny accidently sets off a stampede. It is a stroke of luck that saves everyone's life and saves the herd, too. For a cloudburst hurls a howling flood through the place where they had bedded down. Chips removes Penny's bottle and primes him with the story that he came rushing back to warn them of disaster. So it all ends well—at least, until Penny gets thirsty again.

"Law On the Flying U" (September 16, 1933) concerns a nice young fellow who has stolen his brother-in-law's horse. The brother-in-law is a horse beater and the young man loves horses, understands horses, is driven to a frenzy by the mistreatment of horses. He took that horse to save it. When the sheriff and brother-in-law come riding up to the Flying U, Chip and the boys, with considered imprudence, aid the fugitive's escape. For once a gun does go off; it belongs to the sheriff and is fired accidentally. The evil brother-in-law gets hit, which serves the horse beater right.

The Flying U stories are low green hills rolling at the feet of

hulking mountains. More powerful story-tellers would follow
B. M. Bower. Her scenes are small-scale, her prose tame, the
adventures more pastel than scarlet. And more vivid
characters than Chip and the Happy Family would energize
western fiction. The world of the Flying U is neatly small-scale,
filled with a calm pale light that dispels melodrama's hotter
tints. In Bower's tidy pages, the dime-novel west, that
passionate fantasy, has no place. Her focus is upon the small,
living stuff of daily operations on a cattle ranch. She was there,
as Mulford was not, and she knew that world in every familiar
detail, not as a researched fact but as a thing lived with and
seen under all the varying lights of the sky until it has grown as
commonplace as the heart's pulse. She had been there, and her
fiction was shaped to her own, quiet, personal experience.

Although Bower's work lacks the bloody drama of her
contemporaries, her place in the early development of western
fiction is not negligible. By a narrow margin, she first created
an extended series about a ranch and its population of
continuing characters. The dialogue of her cowboys is
reasonably realistic, although quietly edited to remove flights
of glowing profanity. Her bunkhouse conversations and table
talk echo in Mulford's 1906 *Outing* stories. She demonstrated
that it was possible to address the West in terms other than the
Realm of Myth. And if her characters were men, rather than
gods, they were men you would be proud to know.

Chronologically, the major western writer to appear after
Bower was Zane Grey. About a year after the first Flying U
stories, in 1905, Grey published *Betty Zane* and *The Spirit of
the Border,* both frontier novels. His first formal western,
Riders of the Purple Sage and *Desert Gold,* appeared in 1913.
(By that time, Mulford had published five books and a stable-
full of Bar-20 episodes.)

Grey was a sentimental-realist. His novels are packed with
intensely observed detail, his backgrounds glossy as waxed
linoleum. He had been out there and could speak with authority
about land shapes, the glint in a pony's eye, the pattern of
shadows among cactus spines.

Much less realistic are the attitudes of his characters. Fat
streaks of sentiment flaw them, reflecting the conventions of

fiction at that time. Whenever a woman is involved, the sentiment becomes dense enough to cause physical anguish to contemporary nervous systems. If this is a fault now, it was not so then. Grey enjoyed vast popularity. His serials ran in numerous magazines: *Popular* (1909), *Munsey's* (1914), *Argosy* (1915), *Blue Book* (1917). Then, leaving the pulps, he permanently entered the slick magazines: *Country Gentleman* (1917), *Harpers* (1920), the *Ladies Home Journal* (1921-1924), the *American Magazine, Colliers....*

Grey sold copiously to that market and, in consequence, his influence on the pulps was considerable. For one thing, he was earning massive checks by writing westerns, for the slicks paid much more than the pulps could offer. For another, he demonstrated repeatedly how to meld a brightly detailed, realistic shell on a melodrama of action. His characters were sympathetic and warm, fleshed out and subject to human limitations. Like Wister, Grey set his stories in specific historical time and the events can be calibrated in years, often very closely.

These characteristics were swiftly seized upon by writers who were, at once, technically more skilled than Grey, and considerably less informed—a deadly combination that drove authenticity out the door and historical accuracy out the window. It is not recorded that readers objected.

4-

Max Brand (that most prominent of Frederick Faust's pseudonyms) carried the lessons of *The Virginian* and Zane Grey a long mile further. Their dramatic situations frequently turned on actions stemming from an unwritten code of western conduct, rules of behavior that were, at once, rigid and atrociously sensitive. Brand accepted that code as a fixed convention and upon it, built stories in which dramatic tension was developed through the clash of opposing moral systems.

It may seem curious to speak of pulp magazine fiction in these terms. The conventional image of this fiction is shallow narrative in which cardboard images commit mayhem and the blood spurts out. In this action world, violence is common as gravity and a blow in the face represents the totality of human relationships. Or so it is claimed.

The stereotype contains enough truth to make it dangerously false. Pulp magazine fiction varied wildly in quality. What was offered to the readership depended upon the magazine, the date of publication, the editorial policy at that date, and the writer's skill. There is no sensible way to speak of a "typical pulp story" without defining your remarks in terms of these factors. The prose offered by a 1935 *Horror Stories* differs essentially from that of a 1921 *Adventure* or a 1950 *Dime Detective*. The stories in these diverse publications can be compared because they are fiction and, therefore, subject to consideration by those standards applying to other literary productions. However, the content may vary from the sexual sensationalism of *Horror Stories* to an intense drama of ethical decision in *Adventure*.

In an article on the love pulps (Scribner's, April 1938), Thomas H. Uzzell remarked that:

These readers possess no fertile imagination; their dreams must be written out for them. The dreams must not be too complex—motivation must be simplified to merely instinct responses. It is this inviolable rule of simplification which gives the pulp story its mark of triteness. The cliche and the familiar complication are necessities, not lapses. They are symbols which the reader can easily grasp; they enable the reader to understand a story without thinking it out.[7]

The identical criticism may be extended to "Buffalo Bill's Fair, Square Deal," or *Prison Stories* or the *Lone Wolf Detective Magazine*. The audience varies; the simplification remains constant—for certain magazines at certain times under certain editors. It is not a universal truth, applying to all pulps and all editors at all times.

It is true that, like most magazines, the pulps published some reprehensibly inadequate stuff during their lives. Many also published some of the better fiction of their time. During the 1910s and 1920s, the leading pulp magazines attained levels of excellence that exceeded the quality routinely offered by the slicks or by the popular hardbound books.

The opinion is subjective but it is based on the observation that you can read a 1915 magazine, or one from 1923, or even from 1932, and generally get through it. On the

Love Story Magazine, Aug 10, 1921. The third issue of the magazine, published twice-a-month, whose success established the love story magazine form.

The All-Story, March 1908. Six serials, one novel, and eleven short stories crammed into 192 pages, plus advertising. In this magazine, later merged with *Argosy*, developed the scientific romance and the early science-fiction adventure.

Sea Stories, Feb. 1922. The first issue of a special subject pulp that offered 144 pages of action on the world's waters.

Argosy All-Story Weekly, Sept. 18, 1920. Whistling Dan Barry, a nature spirit in cowboy clothing, appeared in three serials that mixed poetry, violence, and racking emotion in satisfying proportions.

other hand, it is almost beyond human ability to read through a 1915 *Cosmopolitan* or *The Green Hat, Black Oxen,* or *Red Pepper Burns.* A 1919 Max Brand novel is still as crisp as a Michigan apple, contemporary as tonight's news, when compared to these. And Brand is far from simple, whatever has been written about him.

Brand was a genius. He thought he was a poet, but he was something more. It is to this something more that our subsequent remarks are addressed.

The tension in a Brand novel frequently results from the conflict of qualified good with not-so-qualified evil. Many technical difficulties face writers who seek to convert symbols into living characters. Brand didn't always succeed, but he usually came close. He wrote tight, skin-crawling suspense stories about these opposing forces and he polished that story form until it glittered like a chrome icicle. His characters make sharp-edged decisions about the way they are going to behave (that constitutes the moral part). These decisions provide the emotional energy for the balance of the story. The action is determined—even predetermined—by a character's choice of behavior, simplified and contrasted for effect. The story traces out the consequences of that value judgment.

As early as 1918, Brand had developed many of the symbols and character types that would fill his later fiction. With these, he played increasingly complex variations, at first with the joy of a master improviser—later, more mechanically.

The best of the characters (both hero and villain) perform with really inhuman competence. Their abilities far exceed human physical limits. Their shadows stun. Their glances split rock. They are figures belonging more to myth than to narrative fiction.

Few of them begin larger than life. At first introduction, they appear as human beings. Only later do they begin to alter on the page. The process is rather creepy. As you read, their abilities grow almost diabolical. Gradually, the people of the story invest them with an aura of omnipotence once enjoyed only by Greek god-spirits. Without quite knowing what happened, you find yourself in the company of demi-gods, Beowulfs wearing pistols and rough shirts. They materialize in prose glittering with detail, heated by emotion raised to poetic intensity.

The prose tingles and snaps. Vigorous, fresh, it is as transparent as water. But not simple. Every action is motivated. Every character makes decisions and each must endure the consequences of his decisions. Each character is gnawed by the conflict between his wishes and the necessities of his experience. The story advances from the first interactions of the first characters. It continues, a fugue for full orchestra, ever more complex, modified by decisions of increasing desperation, to a climax whose savagery may involve no bloodshed at all. But there will be psychological tension screaming in harmonics almost beyond the ear's capacity.

The motivation is complex, detailed, emotional. The structure is that simplest of all narrative forms, the chase. But with differences. Mulford, a capable craftsman, fills his fiction with chases. But Brand is an artist. There is a difference in quality and in excellence.

Brand's first major series character was "Whistling Dan Barry," whose first appearance was in the six-part *Argosy All-Story Weekly* serial, "The Untamed" (December 7, 1918, through January 12, 1919). Two sequels followed: "The Night Horseman" (7 parts, September 18, through October 30, 1920), and "The Seventh Man" (6 parts, October 1 through November 5, 1921). Two years later, these were followed by the long serial, "Dan Barry's Daughter" (6 parts, June 30 through August 4, 1923), a sequel to the sequels.[8]

Dan Barry is only outwardly human. Spiritually he is feral—a wild thing, part child, part nature demon. Consider him a nature elemental, if you will, a vital force risen from the high deserts that has briefly clothed itself in a human body. From time to time, Brand refers to him as an avatar—a throwback to a more primitive state of man—an idea often mentioned by Jack London. But Barry is hardly that human. His status is established immediately, in Chapter 1 of "The Untamed," when he stalks and kills a rattlesnake with his bare hands. It is roughly the way he will deal with problems in the novels: directly facing into them, no discernible emotion, blinding physical agility, and death at the end.

He is no more concerned with human emotion than is the

wind or sky. His closest friends are animal: Black Bart, part dog, mostly wolf, a ferocious killer, black, huge, powerful, recognizing only Barry's authority; and Satan, a satin-black horse taken from a wild herd by Barry—he walked out to the herd, holding a halter, and led the horse away. It was not a capture but an enlistment. Satan, too, is entirely vicious, dangerous to all but his master. His master, it would seem, is dangerous to all.

These three are linked by tight cords of respect and understanding. Together, they are a single unit, communicating by gestures, more rarely sounds, hardly ever words, beings from some terrible Eden.

In person, Barry is slight, young, rather fragile, with slender hands. Almost womanish in appearance, he is diffident, meek-voiced. To those around him, accustomed to more burly forms, he is easily under-rated. For a time. Like any other wild thing, he will not tolerate himself to be touched. He moves with a soft padding step, a human cougar. And is as efficient, remorseless a killer as the cougar. He is one of the mostly deadly killers appearing in literature. More so, even, than Tarzan, for Barry operates purely at the instinctual level, with a few traces of those intellectual processes which humanized Tarzan.

Barry is as much a throw-back in muscular strength as in mind. His muscles (Brand remarks) reflect those primitive times when man's muscle fiber was three-four times more powerful per ounce. For all his slightness, Barry is far stronger than his contemporaries.

There is equal difference in his physical quickness and the power of his blow. Again the feral trace shows within his eyes. These are normally brown, until anger works in them. Then they go flickering to phosphorescent yellow, quite terrible.

What distinguishes him from all other men is his whistling.

It is his hallmark, a thin trilling fantasy, welling up spontaneously, a tissue of melodic fragments and improvisational runs:

...a delicate thread of music.... It was a happy sound, without a recognizable tune... as if a violinist, drunk, was remembering snatches of masterpieces, throwing out lovely fragments here and there and filling the intervals out of his own excited fancy.[9]

It was, as Brand elsewhere says, "the song and the summons of the untamed."

Nature elementals have no families. Barry is without history. Joe Cumberland, the rancher, found him as a boy walking across the desert, confident, whistling. He would admit to no parent. He was walking north, following the high track of the wild geese.

Cumberland brings the boy home and keeps him there— with difficulty—raising him in the company of his daughter, Kate. As "The Untamed" opens, Barry has entered his young manhood. So far Cumberland has been able to keep the boy from much contact with other men. Most particularly he has kept Barry from fighting, for he well knows the boy's latent nature. If once Barry fights, he will revert to those cougar-like traits barely concealed in his heart.

At this point in his development, Barry encounters a gang of outlaws. They are led by Jim Silent, an early version of the familiar Brand figure, The Large Man. That figure is characteristically huge of frame, immensely powerful, authoritarian, and deadly quick with weapons. (With minor modifications, Silent will later transform to Jim Silver, hero of a different novel series.)

Through a series of events partly accidental, partly psychological, Silent feels his authority endangered by Barry. Accordingly, he slaps Barry across the mouth and the taste of blood instantly undoes all Old Joe Cumberland's teaching. The yellow-lighted eyes flare:

Dan was laughing.... Yet there was no mirth in it. It had that touch of maniacal in it which freezes the blood.[10]

Attacking Silent bare-handed, Barry almost kills him before being felled with a chair. Silent rides away from the gang, his confidence severely shaken. Barry follows. Relentless, unyielding, he has shucked off all considerations other than revenge. Only Silent's death will take away the taste of blood in Barry's mouth.

Increasingly panicked as the chapters pass, Silent attempts to kill Barry by ambush, by complex trap, finally by maneuvering him into a false position where he will be outlawed. Earlier, Silent has captured Kate, planning to use her against Barry.

Finally a scheme is partly successful. Barry has trapped and jailed Lee Haines, a rider with Silent. Led to believe that Haines is Kate's lover, Barry rescues him from jail and a roaring mob. Gets himself shot in the process. He finds shelter with the family of Buck Daniels, a Silent man whose life was saved by Barry. Throughout Barry's illness, Buck conceals him from Silent. When it is evident that he wants Kate, Buck rides to Silent's camp and frees Kate, although he realizes that he is throwing away his life to do so.

At the moment Silent prepares to gun down both Buck and Haines, Barry comes whistling in through the night. In a vicious gun fight, most of the gang is killed. Silent escapes to town and issues a challenge to Barry.

It is a thoughtless gesture. Barry rides in the next day and strangles him.

After the bodies have cooled, it's time for the happy ending. Kate waits starry-eyed. But the wild geese fly. Dan's heart lifts on a cold thin wind and, as the book closes, he melts away, with wolf and horse, back to the desert.

Across the white circle of the moon drove a flying wedge of wild geese.... A faint honking was blown to them by the wind, now a distant jangling chorus, now a solitary sound repeated like a call.[11]

It is Jack London's wolf call transposed to the upper air. The symbol repeats throughout the Dan Barry and the later Jim Silver books. The geese pass crying and the hero's heart answers that high cold music. The call of the untamed. The call of the wild. Name it what you wish. It's the wilderness speaking in its own language to ears that will hear.

The second Dan Barry novel, *The Night Horseman,* is one of those extraordinary books you read with a rising chill. It rings every nerve. To this commentator, it seems one of the great minor novels of American literature. In its pages, true enough, you find that "shock of recognition" (Edmund Wilson's glorious phrase) that strikes you when you are in the presence of literature. The book appears to be unknown to literary critics, as you may have anticipated. Those organizing seminars on American literature do not refer to it. But reader demand has kept it alive since its first appearance in print. Although neglected by those who should know better, *The Night Horseman* is superb. It was first published as a 7-part serial in *All-Story Weekly*, September 18-October 30, 1920. It is part horror story, part chase, part spiritual thriller, touched with parody, full of psychological penetration, emotionally exhausting.

It opens with humor. Dr. Randall Bryne, Ph.D. surgeon, genius, goes west for his health. In appearance, Bryne closely resembles those bulge-eyed men of *Amazing Stories* covers.

Dr. Bryne's function is multiple. He provides certain comic flashes to relieve the story's suffocating emotional tensions. He also provides an extreme contrast to the purely instinctual life of Dan Barry.

No sooner has the doctor arrived on the scene than Kate appears, takes him to the ranch where Joe Cumberland lies dying. He is, the doctor realizes, essentially dead, living only by force of will. He is waiting.

They all are waiting: Kate, Cumberland, Buck Daniels (now hopelessly in love with Kate). The entire ranch is gripped in brooding oppression. The doctor is baffled. Each person is waiting, his feelings intensely strong, each different. For what? The doctor cannot find out. Hints. Odd clues he cannot understand.

Skillfully the tension is built. Out there a doom figure approaches. Who knows when? Horror's yellow light glares across the prose. From out there will come something strange, which half paralyzes Buck with terror, sets Kate quaking with emotions too dark for analysis, keeps Cumberland alive, waiting.

Fearing that Cumberland will die, Buck rides out to find Barry. He leaves with bitter reluctance. He feels that Barry's presence can only destroy Kate.

In a distant town, he finds Barry idling away the days, waiting patiently to fight the massive killer, Mac Strann, whose brother Barry has shot. Regardless of Cumberland's need, Barry refuses to leave. That feral nature is in control. He has lost awareness of time. He has almost forgotten the people of the past. In desperation, Buck slaps Barry's face, flees across the plains toward the ranch, knowing that he has transformed Barry into a yellow-eyed killing machine who will follow.

At the ranch, Kate conceals Buck. When Barry enters, ready to kill, she diverts him to Cumberland. Barry administers to the sick man, gripping his hand, pouring out spiritual energy so intensely that a medium would have observed a crackling blue river flare between them. Dr. Bryne is nonplused.

While Barry is so occupied, Mac Strann, who has been trailing behind, fires Satan's stable, shoots Black Bart. He does this to lure Barry back to town where he will attack and Mac Strann can kill in self defense.

Doesn't work that way. Satan is saved. Barry remains to nurse Black Bart back to life. Kate is desperately seeking some way of reaching the human essence lost in Barry. She hopes to do so by gaining Black Bart's acceptance. It is a fearful problem. Black Bart has forgotten her utterly. He is too savage to approach.

Nevertheless, she approaches.

There follows a scene of extraordinary terror. Within reach of Black Bart's fangs, Kate kneels and dresses his wound. She is reeling with fear. The possibility that she will be torn to rags is immediate. The prose shocks, writing of force and technical virtuosity. It is like gripping a live wire. Later against this scene is played a similar one when Buck and Barry finally meet and Buck must find some way to reach Barry's buried humanity or be shot to death.

In a powerful scene, Kate and Buck do finally touch Barry's human elements. He begins to sense time. He even remembers old relationships again.

But he is not to be turned from chasing down Mac Strann. This unfortunate has finally yielded to the panic afflicting those Dan Barry hunts and he flees through a cloudburst. Barry saves him from drowning in a boiling creek in order to kill him personally. Mac Strann refuses to fight and turns away. Barry is amazed:

Twice men had stood before him, armed, and twice he failed to kill. Wonder rose in him; wonder and great fear.... Were the chains of humanity falling about him to drag him down to a tamed and sordid life?... The strength of men could not conquer him; but how could their very weakness disarm him?[12]

Returning to the ranch, he seizes Kate, rides off with her into the storm. She doesn't protest much. Buck, horror-stricken at her fate, grasps Joe Cumberland's hand as the old man dies. It is not Dan Barry's handclasp. But Cumberland thinks it is.

So the novel ends, dense with ambiguity. All characters have changed. Even the hero. As for Doctor Bryne—he returns to the East, his life deeply modified. The purely intellectual life, he finds, is not nearly enough.

The instant of his conversation gives the novel its title. The doctor, much disturbed for love of Kate, walks hotly into the night to cool his mind:

"... looking back," he says, "I saw a horseman galloping with great swiftness along the line of the crest, very plainly outlined by the sky, and by something of the smoothness in the running of the horse, I knew that it was Barry and his black stallion. But the whistling—the music! Dear God, man have you read of the pipes of Pan?...

"He was gone... but something had happened inside of me.... The ground no longer seemed so dark. There were earth smells—very friendly—I heard some little creature chirruping contentedly to itself.... And then I looked up at the stars... and for the first time I was contented to look at them and wonder at their beauty without an attempt at analysis or labelling."[13]

The symbol is powerful and, for Dr. Bryne, marks the moment of his rebirth. The symbol does not quite catch the central essence of the novel. Remember that Barry meant horror to some and death to others. Unity with Nature and nature's elementals does not mean a condition of perpetual sweetness.

This strong novel is followed by a six-part serial in *Argosy*, October 1 through November 5, 1921. Titled *The Seventh Man*, it does not rise to the emotional heights of *The Night Horseman*. Instead it proceeds as inexorably as classical tragedy. As in formal tragedy, each event occurs because of the personalities involved. Again, the action is determined by each character's choices.

In brief, a young miner, Vic Gregg, quarrels with his sweetheart and kills a supposed rival. Fleeing a posse, he takes refuge with Dan and Kate Barry (now five years married), and their young daughter, Joan. Barry decides to lead the posse on a false trail and rides out on Gregg's horse, Gray Molly. During the chase, a random bullet kills Gray Molly. Barry believes the killing to be deliberate, that the animal was slaughtered in spite. He determines to avenge the horse's death by killing every man in the posse. Which suggests that he does not well discriminate between human and animal life.

The vendetta proceeds. So successful is it that the posse is obliterated, but Barry is outlawed, in consequence. By this time, the methodical murdering has stripped from him the five years of civilized life with Kate. Reverting entirely to the feral, he carries off his little daughter, Joan, to a cave back in the hills.

Kate follows. She realizes that she has lost all influence with him. But she hopes to rescue Joan from a life lived at the instinctual level.

With some difficulty, she locates the cave and steals back her daughter. Barry comes close behind to reclaim the child. When he appears, Kate shoots him dead.

Now the mystic brotherhood of man-horse-wolf is broken. Black Bart and Satan return to the wild. The novel closes with the high, cold calling of geese.

A later novel, *Dan Barry's Daughter* (1923) traces Joan's later life. If loose ends bother you, be pleased to know that love eventually frees her from the lure of the wild goose call.

An exceptional series. Beside it, the other *Argosy* stories seem trivial and gray. You are not aware of reading a western novel. Only that it is a story full of passion and caring for people. The narrative force, glowing under pressure, numbs your judgment. If inconsistencies in Barry's character show from novel to novel, if the villains collapse into panic rather abruptly, if the wild geese cross overhead so very often, the tight, lyrical Brand writing overrides all flaws.

So far back, so long ago, Brand set standards of excellence which, only infrequently, would be reached again in pulp magazine fiction, including his own.

Brand was a major event in the pulps. He demonstrated

convincingly, over and over, how to present a realistically detailed story that presented perceptive and intelligent people interacting emotionally. He transformed the more leisurely Wister-type story to one seemingly in constant motion, using the chase and the impending retribution as suspense elements to maintain tension. He modified the Zane Grey style by removing the attitudinizing and most of the coincidences.

The Brand stories exist at a singularly pure level, free of time's limits, in a world more open, more dangerous, more intense than our familiar present.

5-

A world which, in fact, Clarence Mulford never really left.

Between Mulford and Brand (with the luminous figure of Grey, glittering with success, ever wafting on before, like golden thistle-down), the basic shape of the familiar western novel was laid down in the early years of the 1920s.

Mulford had stamped this field as his own in 1906. Within a few years, he had shaped the west of newspaper accounts and dime novel excitements into a personal mythology, strongly action-oriented and stiff with selected detail. Mulford was a powerful visualizer. His early books are bright with detail so ingratiatingly described that it seems observed at first hand. The stories brim with specific images: the shapes of saddles, the structure of saloon doors, the weight and range of a Buffalo Sharps, the disadvantages offered by the front sight of a Remington rifle when fired at extreme range.

Only later (perhaps while reading Zane Grey), might it occur to you that Mulford's details lack a certain body. Call it "immediacy." The facts are neatly selected and assembled, but they seem vaguely remote, as if he were describing scenes observed through almost transparent glass.

It is the effect you get when working through other mens' eyes. Remember that all Mulford's work was hardened by research. His sources were excellent; his images were synthesized from the myths and folklore of his time. But he did not have direct experience. He was not polished by the actual and that lack showed.

It is also true that, of the early western novelists, Mulford is the least sensitive to personality interplay. Customarily he views from the outside. His people are seldom guilty of complexity. Their emotions, if warm, are single, simple nouns: admiration, envy, respect, anger. Their relationships are equally simple. You quickly get the impression that the Bar 20 is a big loose family, fiercely defensive of each other, not just a group of hired men watching the boss' cows.

The relationship which appears most frequently in Mulford's work is a sort of father-son thing between the main characters. This shows first between Buck Peters and Hopalong. Over the years (as you may have guessed) the usual role reversal occurs and Hopalong begins to act paternally to the older Buck. Elsewhere in the series, Cassidy will act as the father surrogate for Johnny Nelson and, in turn, for Mesquite Jenkins. He remains in this position until the series ends. But then he's the hero, you see.

Mulford writes in bright primary colors, using few pastels. Action is his subject: Action, movement, friendship under danger. Lots of freedom, lots of violence. All of this salted down with humor.

Consider the first group of stories. They occur over a year's time. During that period, Cassidy works as a cowboy on the Bar 20. Or does sometimes. He also rides all over the West, from Texas to Mexico to New Mexico back to Texas, a disconcerting distance on horseback. In the course of riding, he contrives, during various adventures, to kill between 25 and 35 men.

You might think that such wholesale slaughter would burden his mind. It doesn't. He ends the stories as cheerfully cock-eyed as he began. He is a death-giver of a stature to daunt even a Just Man.

But he does not seem to have thought about it. Unlike Manfred, Cassidy is untroubled by his ambiguous moral position. No part of his intelligence is given over to intellectual finessing. His is the strategic mind. It is flexible, pragmatic, unclouded by the need to justify his actions. He is a splendid fighting machine, untroubled by guilt or remorse. His responsibility ends when his weapon is reholstered. Leave the dead in the street and turn to the next story. It is the enforced callousness of the series hero who is never permitted to feel his own terrible history.

Over the decades, he will become more of a justice figure, carrying a badge, enforcing the law. For the present, neither justice nor law enters into the matter—other than that rough justice paid to stealers of other men's cattle. Hopalong is less an abstract justice figure than a duelist who actively resists the least encroachment upon his concept of personal honor. He is exquisitely touchy and strangers press him to their peril.

The exploits of Hopalong Cassidy explore many of the characteristic story elements that later dominated pulp western fiction. He extended the dime novel image of the roving, gun-quick westerner of high personal integrity and touchy personal honor. He was the first continuing character to routinize death by six-shooter, and almost certainly the first whose adventures built repeatedly toward the terminal, resolving gunfire, an inverted form of purification rite.

Through these early stories, he lives only in the shining present, untroubled by the past. Sufficient for today are adventure, action, beef for breakfast, a respectable horse. Perhaps a cigar that doesn't crumble between the fingers; certainly friends who can be relied upon. All these elements structured within a code of personal honor, sternly rigorous.

The elements of a rich full life.

You thought matters more complex, didn't you?

6–

We have considered the Bar 20 stories at length because they are prototypes of the story type that would jostle through magazine pages for the next forty years. Mulford was there first. His influence, like light among cut glass, gleams and glitters, although it's hard to see the origin of the beam.

Success provides its own sequel. Since the Bar 20 stories were highly successful, we can assume that they bloomed into further stories. And they did. They would shortly grow into an endless chain, endlessly generating.

It is a long series—a mixture of short stories, novels, novelettes. Most share one or more characters. Cassidy does not always appear, although his name is dropped at careful intervals. Each major series character is featured as the lead in at least one novel, and others of the original Bar 20 group wander through the stories, the familiar faces always present. The series is as much the history of a group of friends as the biography of any one character.

In real time the stories were written from 1906 to 1941. In fictional time, they extend from about mid-1870 into the early 1900s. The narrative line is loosely chronological. Most stories contain a brief summary of the immediate past. There is frequent reference to events in very early stories. As a result, the stories fit into rather precise time slots. In 35 years of writing about Cassidy and the Bar 20 group, Mulford created a sprawling but self-coherent history.

Much of the earlier material published leaped about in time. *Hopalong Cassidy* (1910), the second book, occurs after the events narrated in the third book, *Bar 20 Days* (1911). The fifth book, *The Coming of Cassidy* (1913) returns to the primal atom as it describes how William Cassidy first joined the Bar 20. Although Mulford bounds freely back and forth across time, the incidents dovetail with a pleasing precision into the overall history.[14]

Individual novels and stories were frequently reprinted in the pulp magazines. Title changes were frequent.[15] Reprints fell sharply off in the 1940s, but during the early 1950s there was a revival of interest in Hopalong, fueled by the television series. This led to *Hopalong Cassidy's Western Magazine* (1950-1951), a three-issue publication offering three new Cassidy novels. These were not by Mulford who was resisting the income tax at that time, but by Louis L'Amour. The stories are excellent, accurate continuations of the series and closely follows Mulford's style. (These novels will be discussed later.)

As mentioned, those stories covering the earliest days of the Bar 20 were published in *The Coming of Cassidy* (1913), itself made up of fifteen short stories. These had appeared in *Red Book* (1908), *Field and Stream* (1911), and *Pearson's Magazine* (1912-1913).

The stories, varied and interesting, shine with humor, their crispness unmarred by sentimentality. Four women move through the series and about these hang no cloying vapors. The punchers treat them with apprehensive respect. And the women, in turn, do not faint or bleat. One of them is a crook and one an idiot. But at least they are positive figures.

The individuals of the stories are equally positive. Grinning, hard-boiled, crude gentlemen, riotous nobility, they pound cheerfully across the pages. Some are wrong-headed. Some short-tempered. Their codes of behavior are prickly with a sense of honor that shames these sniveling times. They drink terrible whisky. Live on biscuits, beans and bacon. Are uneducated, unrefined vulgarians.

But if one called you friend, you'd be proud to acknowledge him. A man is something more than acceptable grammar and a clean shirt.

The Bar 20 was Buck Peters' child. He was about 30 when he drove a buckboard down onto the Snake Creek. He was stocky, compactly built, already an expert at the cattle business, and acting as the agent for an eastern syndicate. At Buck's recommendation they bought a thirty-mile long, rather thin strip, between the west bank of the Pecos River and both banks of Snake Creek. Possession of the water led to possession of large quantities of back range.

Buck built a sod house and, in the spring, received 2000-plus cattle from his bosses. From the drive crew delivering the cattle, he proselyted two men—one of them Red Connors. A week after that Cassidy arrived.

He was Bill Cassidy then, a hot-tempered teen-ager, riding north. Red had driven off for supplies, leaving Buck alone with one man and 2000 steers for company. Three unemployed buffalo herders attempted to take over this desirable setup about the time that Cassidy arrived. Shortly afterward two buffalo hunters were dead and one wished he were. The Bar 20 legend begins with this.

The next several stories introduce most of the main characters of the series: those two inseparable friends, Skinny Thompson (6'4") and Lanky Smith (5'2"): Billy Williams; big slow-witted Pete Wilson, the strongest man Red ever knew; Johnny Nelson, still young enough to be concerned with being too young and hell with the infrequent girls; and some numbers of other citizens who passed this way, played their parts, and moved on.

In the sixth story, Bill Cassidy changes his name. He had ridden into Clay Gulch to price some cattle offered for sale by the Crazy M ranch. Once there he interferes with an attempt to

murder Sheriff Toby Harris. Several plotters fail to live and so
will sin no more. Harris comes out brilliantly. Cassidy takes a
slug in the right thigh, shattering the bone. Harris lifts him up,
assists him across the street for help.

Harris: "Hop along Cassidy, You'll be a better man with one good laig than th'
whole gang was all put together."
Cassidy: "Th' bone is plumb smashed. I reckon I'll hop along through life. It'll
be hop along, for me, Hopalong Cassidy."[16]

Other stories ring the changes from the grim to the comic
(for Mulford is a fine comic writer). Hopalong has an adventure
with a crooked gambler. The ranch undergoes a horrendous
winter and Peter Wilson is introduced—Pete is fleeing from an
ex-wife who just may wish to come back to him.

Then six of the boys, returning by train from the cattle
market, encounter a band of train robbers: the story is fast and
very funny. There follow several adventures of Sammy Porter,
a young man even younger and brasher than Johnny Nelson,
whose neck is saved by Cassidy and who saves Cassidy's neck.
Finally there is the story of how Johnny wooed unwisely and
too well and how the Bar 20 boys played a practical joke on him
that was as subtle as a cement biscuit.

It is an interesting set of stories, even for those who do not
like westerns. The tone of the relationship between the men of
the ranch is set early and it is worth quoting Red on the subject.
Of the eight permanent members of Bar 20, he said:

"We ain't eight men—we're one man in eight different kinds of bodies. G-d help
anybody that tries to make us less."[17]

Bar 20, previously examined, narrates adventures in
divers places. *Bar 20 Days* (1911) and *Trail Dust* (1934)
continue adventures during the early days. *Bar 20 Days* is a
particularly wild and joyous collection of short stories and
includes extraordinary adventures.

Among these is the visit that Cassidy and Nelson pay
Galveston. They get shanghaied aboard a gun-running ship,
an error the Captain is to regret. After the two get themselves
awake, they club two mates, secure guns, hold up the ship at

rifle point and turn it back to port. After which Cassidy punches the Captain's head and gets his own beauty sadly damaged. The opening pages are pure farce, as Hopalong and Johnny search through town for something to weigh down their empty holsters—they had to give up their pistols before the authorities would let them out on the streets.

A second story takes us to a canyon haunted by a ghost seeable only by Mexicans—until Johnny Nelson sees it. Various violent complications follow. During the course of these, we are introduced to a fearsome drink called The Flying Ghost, compounded of gin, brandy, whisky, guaranteed to "show more ghosts per drink than any liquor south of the Rio Grande." This story was reprinted in the June 1935 issue of *Greater Western Magazine* as "The Ghost of the Canyon."

Other stories concern a siege by Apaches, an account of how Cassidy accidentally got drunk and was declared a horse thief, and a Johnny Nelson adventure in which he ends up full of bullet wounds inside a hut being shot to splinters.

In the final story Tex Ewalt reappears. He schemes to murder Cassidy from ambush, a plan that fails. Instead, Tex ends with a bullet in his knee cap. Immediately afterward, Cassidy saves him from a flash flood, an act of courtesy that turns their relationship around. From this point onward, they become warm friends. Tex drastically alters his way of life and a new name is inscribed on the side of the angels.

Hopalong Cassidy (1910) is a novel packed with subject matter: sinister plotters, range war, rustlers, young love and a memorable firefight violent as a World War.

A pack of rustlers plans to create a range war between the Bar 20 and the H2. The villain of the piece is Antonio, a slippery double-crossing wretch who embraces "with his husk of soul the putrescence of all that was evil."

Such over-writing is not characteristic of Mulford, who enjoyed spare prose. *Hopalong Cassidy* was his first novel, however, and the initial chapters are filled with high-cholesterol sentences. As Mulford warms to his work, the prose tone recedes to plainer language.

Through the earlier chapters, Antonio is reasonably successful in stirring up trouble. This is partly because the H2 owner, Meeker, is a hot-headed idiot, his personality necessitated to make the plot work. He has a lovely daughter, Mary, who becomes fascinated by Hopalong, and she stirs him even more intensely than Carmencita, back when she weighed 101 pounds.

For some chapters, it appears that the young folks may never get married. Then Antonio oversteps himself. The two ranches, suddenly awake to common peril, join forces to crush the rustlers, holed up on Thunder Mesa. There follows an extended battle, described almost bullet by bullet. First the rustlers are engaged at a distance. Then the mesa is invaded and a bitter night battle is fought hand to hand.

Comes the dawn. The participants are sprawled around bleeding or dead. (The Bar 20 is as badly shot up as the rustlers.) The few remaining bad guys are tied up, waiting execution. Now occurs one of the scenes suggesting that Mulford was well aware of *The Virginian*. The rustlers and the victorious ranchers chat amiably together, exchanging views on the battle. They share a frugal meal, casual as a social coffee after the meeting. Then the rustlers are taken off and hanged.

The risks are known. Quarter is not asked and not extended. If you win, you acquire someone else's cows. If you lose, you get a high place among the cottonwoods. Expressionless, the rustlers go to their doom. Part of the western mystique, so far as that is understood by eastern writers of cowboy novels. If you can't change circumstances, act as if they do not hurt. An attitude learned, possibly, from their Red Brothers.

A similar scene appears in *The Virginian*, although Wister develops and dramatizes it quite differently. One of the Virginian's former friends, now gone bad, has been captured in the act of stealing cattle. He was one of a group of three. The others have escaped and he will not admit that there were others.

He is guarded all night. In the morning, they give him coffee, then ride him out to the cottonwoods. At no time has he spoken to the Virginian.

As in Mulford's scene, here is self possession in the face of the inevitable; friendly interchanges between prisoner and captors; punishment dealt without rancor and without sentimentality.

Unlike Mulford, Wister charges the scene with emotional tension. Dramatic overtones are explored and changes rung on them, for Wister studied the emotional knots between people. When action appeared, he used it not for itself but as another device to depict emotion in stress.

So, in this story the attitudes of the various groups and individuals are examined through all sorts of variations. Shifting emotional tones color the pages. Slowly you learn of the Virginian's intense regret that his friend has come to this end and that his friend refuses to speak to him. For his part, the thief does not dare address the Virginian for fear of losing his self-possession. The entire scene is a shuddering dream of sorrow, horror and despair, packaged in prose as smooth as a black marble floor.

Wister's work intensively dramatizes the rite of death. It quakes with emotional energy. In Mulford's version, the drama remains but the emotion is effectively stripped out. The story is a cored apple, hollow within. The exterior is presented in fine detail: Men risk their lives; others narrowly escape death; all endure pain humorously or philosophically. But all are presented so stoically that they do not seem to participate emotionally in the action. With some personal effort, you can recapture the probable emotions of those involved, for Mulford is not entirely barren. But he is arid.

In later novels Mulford will develop a rather richer emotional life for his people. To the last, however, he will not seem comfortable doing so. That leads to certain gigantic omissions in the presentation of his characters. By the end of the series, Cassidy will have personally killed some 200 men. It seems cavalier to dismiss slaughter of this magnitude with the remark that they needed shooting.

The justification Mulford gives for this bloody history is a familiar one to those following the fortunes of the justice figure. No side-stepping is involved. As always, Mulford is bluntly straightforward:

... the West was wild and rough and lawless; and [Cassidy], like others, through the medium of the only court at hand, Judge Colt, enforced justice as he believed it should be enforced.[18]

7–

After the action at Thunder Mesa, the victors limp home. During the fight, Frenchy McAllister has been killed, resulting in major changes to the story line.

Frenchy had bought the double Y spread at Tin Cup, Montana. Buck has a half ownership, with the full share coming to him on Frenchy's death. Now a property owner, Buck resigns as the Bar 20 foreman and aims his horse toward Montana. Hopalong replaces him as foreman, amid general rejoicing. It is a good time to get promoted, because the glowing Mary has agreed to marry him in the Fall.

On this optimistic note the first novel ends.

Now we may briefly follow out the rest of the series.

Buck sets up shop in Montana and, in a short time, is on the verge of ruin, victim of range jumpers and rustlers. It is told in *Buck Peters—Ranchman* (1912). His request for aid arrives at the Bar 20 at an opportune time. The railroad has now crossed ranch property, fences encroach, and the trails are closing. Civilization looms. The Bar 20 gang is only too ready to pull up stakes and head north, with Mrs. Cassidy and Tex Ewalt, to visit violent justice on those deserving same.

The Man From Bar 20 (1918) picks up the history after they have lived in Montana for several years. The novel features Johnny Nelson, who has fallen into disfavor with all the wives and is fleeing the state for less domestic scenes.

Wives? Yes, there is something magical about Montana air. Red, Buck, Lanky are married. Tex will soon be. Hopalong now has a son, William Jr. Johnny admires him and has taught him to chew tobacco. The wives consider Johnny a disruptive influence and, since they keep looking at him with icy meaning, he finally saddles his black mare, Pepper, and heads south.

He is, as the novel opens, a powerfully built man just under 30, standing 5'10," weighing 160 pounds, with a size 16 neck. Time has calmed his peppery temper and diminished his rashness. Still he is deadly swift with the short guns, shooting from the hip by instinct. He is left-handed, but, as he says, "eats and shoots with both."

Arriving in New Mexico, he takes a job with Logan of the

CL Ranch. He is to be a trouble-shooter against local rustlers, whose wicked activities provide the plot for so many of these adventures. The assignment leads to a series of interesting situations, heavily flavored with gun smoke. These climax when he is cornered on the top of a butte by a batch of gunmen and an annoyed grizzly bear. The bear is killed, if barely. The gunmen also die, most peculiarly, sliced down by the old mountain man, Luke Tedrue, who comes gliding up by night, gripping his Bowie knife.

Following the blood-letting, Johnny and Tedrue confront the remaining rustlers in a cabin and a bloody fight concludes the novel.

By the 1921 *Bar 20 Three*, Johnny has fallen prey to the wicked eyes of Margaret Logan. (He had saved her ranch in the 1920 *Johnny Nelson*.) He has settled down, thoroughly married, as foreman of the SV, near the town of Gunsight, the scene of several brave stories.

About this time, Hopalong and Red get the itch to travel and ride south to visit Johnny. Age is dimming Red. His hair has faded to a sandy tone, the last trace of a flaming crimson mop. Years of battle have left other traces. He shows less exuberance. His eyes have a cold squint, hard as glass. (This is nearly the first time Mulford mentions their "cold, hard" eyes, adjectives he will work intensively over the next years. It would appear, after all, that death giving does result in character changes.) Red rides silently, slouching in the saddle, at long intervals grousing sourly at Hopalong. In a scabbard by his leg rides his Winchester rifle with which he can shoot all the periods off a page.

Beside him rides Hopalong, cheerfully careless as ever, forever peering about, alert as a jay. Mulford describes him as "nonchalant," another favored word. But other character traits have matured by now. The reckless clowning of his youth has passed. His cool, strategic mind is nearly mature. He trusts few men, we are told, and those few he trusts completely. Still proud, still easily amused, he is the fastest and most accurate pistolman in the southwest.

As father of a splendid child, he has also developed caution. It happens to us all. He carries a .45 Sharps Special rifle, the Buffalo Sharps. It weighs 17 pounds, throws a huge slug 1000 yards. When there is nothing else to talk about, he can war with Red about the alternative merits of their rifles.

They arrive at the SV in time for bad news. While in the town of Mesquite, Johnny sold a cattle herd and was robbed of the money. Cassidy and Connors promptly ride to Mesquite and are slung into jail by a crooked sheriff. That night Johnny demolishes a significant portion of the jail and frees them.

Off they head toward the desert and, in a series of thrilling coincidences, locate the rustlers at work and the oasis where all stolen beef is located. The rustlers (who are also robbers, card cheats and bullies) are busily thinning out stock at all the ranches and currently are planning a massive raid at the Question Mark spread.

Learning this, Red and Johnny ride to warn that ranch. Cassidy remains to spy out details of the robbers' roost.

Despite all these precautions, the rustlers raid successfully. This mightily irritates the Question Mark crew. They ride into Mesquite with the intent of reducing it to powder. The rustlers, lead by that malevolent master mind, Kane, hole up in a gambling hall that has been fortified like a medieval castle.

Two days of concentrated shooting. Little to show for it. Now enters Cassidy, hot, disgusted, short-tempered. In half a thought, he sets fire to the gambling hall and the end is near.

Kane flees with a few trusty henchmen. These attempt to doublecross him and seize his wealth, but Cassidy and the boys close in from the darkness. Johnny recovers his money and the three split a reward.

This novel first appeared as a serial in *Short Stories* (1921) and was reprinted in the March 1935 issue of *Complete Western Book Magazine* under the title of *The Bar 20 Trio*.

Hopalong Cassidy Returns (1924) is a short story collection containing material published in *Argosy*, December 9, 1923, through January 28, 1924, in weekly installments. The stories are a Continental Divide for the series; on one side stands Cassidy, the young, irreponsible marvel; on the other, the ice-eyed living legend.

What has happened is that Mary Cassidy and William Jr. have died of the fever. So it is stated. What actually killed them is that doom which haunts the families of series heroes.

Hopalong takes their deaths bitterly hard. Rigid with grief, he rides south. Red Connors goes with him, leaving his cwn family to travel along for fear that his friend will simply throw away his life in some moment of despairing rashness. That fear will ride with them for more than a year.

The first story of the group introduces a new character, Mesquite Jenkins. He will remain with the series until its end. Mulford was partial to young men as central characters. As his people mature, get married, become foremen, he tends to move them to the rear of the stage and introduce new fighting blood. It is Mesquite's function to replace Johnny Nelson, although Johnny continues as a secondary character.

Not yet 20, a stocky boy, Mesquite stands 5'7" and weighs about 150 pounds. Every ounce is lethal. He is a natural killer, taut, touchy, sudden, as restful a companion as a black mamba.

Mesquite idolizes the Cassidy of western legend and is riding out to find him, somewhere out there in the West. While on the trail, he gets inveigled into a robbery and murder. He knows nothing about the murder.

The men he fell in with nauseate him—rather too late. Breaking away from them, he rides off full of apprehension, feeling that a sheriff is going to get him any second. When he blunders into Hopalong and Red by accident, he instantly assumes that they are hunting him and wounds Cassidy by error. Red shoots Mesquite by design. Doesn't kill him, however, which is the only mistake not made in ten smoking pages.

Red drags Hopalong off. Mesquite drags himself off. Eventually Johnny Nelson finds the boy and takes him back to the ranch.

If the coincidences bother you, breathe slowly and think of calm things.

Back at the SV, Mesquite slowly heals and is put to work. In due time, all problems are resolved and Mesquite, of his own will, restores his share of the stolen money. The other robbers end up dead.

The remaining stories tell their adventures as the three of them ride back to Montana. Red is coldly suspicious of the deadly young man with the frozen eyes. Cassidy, however, grows to treat Mesquite as a son. It is as much the appearance of Mesquite as the long ride with Red which stabilizes and eventually dissolves Cassidy's despair.

As Mulford pointed out, Cassidy "was born with suspicion for the obvious method of procedure." His mind has grown elliptical. No longer does he pound into town, shouting and whooping. Now his moves are made in silence, meticulously, precisely prepared, with elaborate feints that would bring a nod of approval from an Indian.

Unsuspected abilities stir in him. To those who have earned his trust, he patiently teaches the lore of 200 gunfights. He has trained Johnny and now he begins to train Mesquite.

Watch a man's eyes, not his gun. The eyes tell you when he's going to shoot.

Black your belt buckle. No use giving your opponent a shiny target.

In lighted areas, stay back from windows and doors.

Get to the high ground and stay still.

Set up simple signals and make d--n sure everybody knows them.

Carry more water than you need.

Keep cold. Keep emotionally uninvolved. Don't fight in anger. Let anger energize, not drive.

Assess the situation as it really is, not as you wish it to be.

The goal is icy objectivity. He preaches the doctrine of coldness to them, continuously, thoroughly, over years.

He has become a Deputy Sheriff in Twin River County, Montana. The Sheriff is Buck, a figurehead; Cassidy does the work. Perhaps the Doctrine of Coldness helps him on the job. More likely it is an attitude he has adopted to protect himself from further emotional savaging. Frozen objectivity is one way to keep anguish for the lost family from spilling out.

Experience tells us that only time quenches these fires. Beneath Cassidy's controlled exterior, demon flames storm. Only a little tension spills the fury out.

[On his face] was a malignancy like the mask of hovering Death. The cold eyes peered out from beneath closely narrowed lids. The thin lips were pressed

together.... There was such a suggestion of lynx about [him] that some of the on-
lookers glanced instinctively to see if there were tufts on his ears.... Here was
Death, poised to strike.[19]

It is hardly the picture of chilled repose.

Hopalong is legend now, his name known all over the west.
Stories of his battles have magnified and expanded in the
telling. Even in Mulford's eyes, he has become a partial myth-
figure. His forethought and quickness of perception, his
reflexes, his pistol work, all exceed the far edge of human
ability. He stands inhumanly gleaming, unable to err. It's a far
piece from that fool Hopalong.

1925. Mulford reached a high point in word production.
During the year, a series of articles was published in *The
Frontier* on aspects of the Old West. Then a 12-part serial,
"Hopalong Cassidy's Pal" in *Argosy*, the story being
published as a hardback in 1926, titled *Hopalong Cassidy's
Protege.*

A second serial ran in *Short Stories* (April 30 through June
25, 1926), "Bar 20 Rides Again." It got into hardback the same
year, and later reappeared in the January 1935 issue of *Real
Western* under the title "Snake Buttes."

The novel is mainly about Tex Ewalt, although it is
strongly gingered up by the presence of Hopalong and others of
the fine old crew. Seems that Johnny Nelson, far off in New
Mexico, has got all shot up. A criminal genius named Nevada
has organized a rustling gang along military lines, has shot
down half the effective range strength in a single stroke, is
stealing cattle wholesale and concealing them in the almost
inaccessible Snake Buttes area.

Down from the Montana ranch moves a war party of ex-
Bar 20 men. Only two regulars remain behind: Buck to cover
the ranch and Mesquite, gone to his mother's funeral.

The move to New Mexico is conducted in the new Cassidy
fashion. Assuming that there will be spotters at train junctions
and telegraph offices close to the rustler operations, they skirt
the area. They ride the train in a long loop south, buy horses,
and ride back north, having collected every last scrap of data
available about the Snake Buttes region.

This wary approach is intensely interesting. The date,

remember, is 1926. The pulp magazines of the period were packed with the stomp-in-and-blast-'em-out-type story, an operating procedure which fills the paperbacks of today.

How different it is in Mulford's 1926 fiction. Cassidy's intelligence reaches a thousand miles, assessing the hidden mind south. His response to Johnny's plight is immediate. The mailed blow is initiated, but, until the moment of impact, it is unseen. The player on the other side is never permitted to know that a counterstroke is in motion.

We have an action narrative, then, in which, like the Lone Wolf novels some ten years before, the dominant element is planning. The Bar 20's preparations, movements, approach are thought through and executed with military precision and something of the real world deepens the shallow pool of the pulp magazine western.

Cassidy's movements are in counterpoint to the main focus of the novel, which is on Tex Ewalt. The two narrative lines are synchronized. Suspense is maintained by keeping the lines separated until the final pages. Then they rush together into climax.

While the Bar 20 rides south by extraordinarily bad trains, Tex Ewalt has resurrected his old image of a gambler and ice-hearted gunman. Sending his wife to visit with Rose Peters at the Double Y, he travels south. In a series of finely calculated moves, he joins the gang at the Buttes under an assumed name. Once there, he is able to stimulate a series of lethal arguments by which the gang whittles itself down. Finally he arranges a signal fire, calling in the Bar 20, waiting some dozens of miles away. They slide into the Snake Butte camp by night, cold as death and as efficient.

Next morning, Nevada steps from his bed, opens the front door, and finds Cassidy waiting outside, slightly crouched in the fresh morning sunlight, squinting, cold, infinitely dangerous. Nevada draws his weapon, although not quite rapidly enough. It is an unfortunate way to begin a day.

A rather less intellectual novel, *Mesquite Jenkins—Tumbleweed*, was published in 1932. The Bar 20 people do not appear. The story, weighing about a quarter of an ounce, tells how Mesquite comes rolling along (like a tumbleweed drifting across the trails) just in time to keep rustlers from wiping out the ranch of a fairly ineffectual young man and his beautiful beautiful sister.

Mesquite is not quite up to par in this novel. Nor is his criminal opposition, presently observed to be shot dead. As the final body falls, Mesquite saddles and bolts. His young heart is pierced by love. He fears that he is going to propose to the girl any second. If she accepts, Mulford is going to have to create still another young, unmarried character for Cassidy to take under his wing.

So Mesquite bolts in a dense haze of symbolism involving tumbleweeds. The image is milked to agony but the novel was reprinted in the October 1933 issue of *Complete Western Book* as "Rollin' Cowboy."

Mesquite again plays the lead in the fine novel *Hopalong Cassidy Takes Cards* (1927), reprinted in 1950 as a Popular Library paperback.

Like most of the later Mulford novels, it is a taut, well-written story of suspense, filled with interesting shadows and depths. Cassidy again appears as a strong secondary character, manipulating the action from outside. The less you see of him, the more you wish to see.

Cassidy (now the Sheriff of Twin River) has sent Mesquite north to check out some peculiar rumors. Once in the region, Mesquite takes a job as a livery stable attendant under a particularly drunk old man. He rapidly discovers that the livery stable is the focus for a gang of horse thieves. At the proper time he sends for Hopalong, who drifts in by night, silent, cautious, competent.

Shortly after, thirty men close in on the thieves and take them without a shot being fired. The ending is taut and brittle, developing its effect through dramatic tension rather than gunfire.

The final novel, *Hopalong Cassidy Serves a Writ* (1941) was published the year Mulford gave up writing. Thereafter the Bar 20 remained alive only in reprint editions, the popular motion pictures, and, finally, the television series. As a result of the popularity of the television program, Cassidy once more entered the novel form.

In the summer of 1950, Best Books, Inc., brought out a new pulp magazine that would perhaps catch a few readers from among the legions of television watchers. *Hopalong Cassidy's Western Magazine* was a 25¢ quarterly of 162 pages. It contained a short, original novel and four short stories that had previously been published by Better Publications, Inc.[20]

The first issue, "Rustlers of West Fork" (Fall 1950), mentions all the long-familiar names: Buck, Johnny, Mesquite, Lanky. Hopalong, almost unchanged, moves directly to front center stage:

...trim, bowed legs, the broad sloping shoulders, the lean waist and choppy walk of the horseman. ...the guns he wore... were walnut stocked and worn by much handling.[21]

Cassidy is now carrying money from Buck to Dick Jordan, an old friend. He discovers that Jordan, now crippled, and his daughter, Pamela, are essentially prisoners on their own ranch. Some very tough types have moved in and taken over.

But not for long, you will be pleased to hear. Cassidy fights the Jordans free, leads them to safety over the mountain in a vicious blizzard. Once over the mountain, he stomps into town and closes up the saloon in which the gang is accustomed to lounge.

At this point he is joined by Johnny and Mesquite, who have heard that he is having fun and ridden off to join him. The three descend upon the gang's ranch and clean house, cutting down seven toughs in as many minutes. The main crook is shot entirely to pieces by Cassidy in three paragraphs that read as if printed on transparent ice.

A few pages later the final gunman dies violently and Cassidy rides off to new adventure. Incidentally, he gives up a perfectly lovely and willing girl for no particular reason other than that this is the first issue of a new magazine. Why tie down the hero at once?

The theme is the familiar one of the justice figure, modified to meet the rigidities of the western action story: A roving figure stumbles upon an obvious wrong. He is from the outside world, smooth as an angel, untouched by the complexities and passions of the immediate problem until he involves himself. He renders judgment and enforces this with great violence. Then he withdraws from the situation, returns to the outside,

Adventure, Dec. 18, 1918. Distinguished adventure fiction, emphasizing character and locale around the world, brought the magazine a towering reputation for excellence.

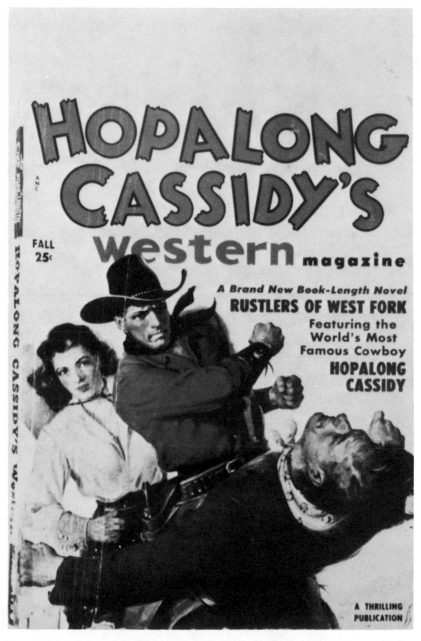

Hopalong Cassidy's Western Magazine, Fall 1950. Success of his television program brought forth a new series of Cassidy's adventures written by Louis L'Amour.

moves on.

It is the overall narrative skeleton of *Mesquite Jenkins—
Tumbleweed*, 1932, and also *Buffalo Bill's Tomahawk Duel*,
1905. In his final novels, Mulford had considerably modified
this form. He eliminated the random character of the
encounter, decreased the violence and gunplay, increased
elements of problem solving and planning. The pulp magazine
stories were not, however, patterned upon the later Mulford
novels but those of the middle and late 1920s in which gunplay
was emphasized. And the magazine also reflected
contemporary techniques of narrative structure, dramatic
emphasis and character building, all polished by years of
western pulp fiction publication. The combination was
pleasing.

The magazine novels were signed by Tex Burns,
pseudonym for Louis L'Amour. His prose is given a Mulford
sound, is dense with Mulford details, is paced and shaded in
Mulford's style. L'Amour had read the previous books with
sympathy and appreciation. But the magazine novels do not
merely rework the past fiction; they carried it forward, fresh
and vigorous, a continuation of Cassidy's history by one of
western fiction's modern masters.

The Winter 1951 issue, "Trail to Seven Pines," again
features Cassidy in the role of the roving cowboy. Unsupported
by the familiar Bar 20 faces, he enjoys such dramatic events as:

—hearing shots and finding a dead man stripped of
identification;

—leading a relief party to the assistance of a wounded
man, only to discover that he has been freshly murdered;

—twice escaping an earthquake;

—fighting two separate, deadly batches of killers on his
own;

—fighting an insane gunman out among the dramatic
lava beds.

The novel is well done but the magazine did not succeed.
Few magazines succeeded in the 1950s, a time of savage
market contractions, when the final great extinction of the
pulp publication form was underway. After the Spring 1951
issue, "Riders of the Broken Range," *Hopalong Cassidy's*

Western Magazine was cancelled. The novels themselves were published by Doubleday almost as rapidly as they were written, slight title changes being made. They were published as *Hopalong Cassidy and the Rustlers of West Fork* (1951), *Hopalong Cassidy and the Trail to Seven Pines* (1951), *Hopalong Cassidy and the Riders of High Rock* (1951) and a fourth novel which had not seen magazine publication, *Hopalong Cassidy, Trouble Shooter* (1952). These books were decorated with pictures of William Boyd as Cassidy on the backs of the dust jackets. Mulford's opinion of Boyd's characterization has already been expressed.

Even the William Boyd tie-in was not powerful enough to lure readers from the television screen to the printed page. After the 1952 novel, the long silence began. Bar 20 was lost to fiction at last. It melted away, an insubstantial dew, the rides completed, the range at peace, the pistol holstered and cold at last, a delicate mist of dust gray-white across the walnut handle. Gone.

8-

Mr. William Cassidy, known as "Hoppy" only to his closest friends, is one of those few early giants whose presence decisively shaped a portion of the pulp fiction medium. So far in the past did these giants appear, so long have they exerted their authority that their true stature has been lost in the details of the years. Very small hills can obscure the mountains on the horizon. So giants like Cassidy, Nick Carter, the Just Men are obscured by generations of those more modestly endowed.

Hopalong Cassidy died about 1911, being then almost 60. The cause, although unknown, does not seem to have been violence.[22] That was long ago. The endurance of the character has been phenomenal, particularly since few who recognize his name have read a line of his adventures.

His fictional life spanned the pulp magazine era from almost the first wail to almost the final sigh. During that period, his stories grappled with legions of reflections of themselves—roving cowboys in singles and doubles, all gun-swift and honorable, bringing justice where they found the need; ranches staffed with hard-nosed men, quaintly named; unlisted hordes of toughs and thieves; shoot-outs in saloons and mesas. All this done in breezy, colloquial language, the sentences stripped, the dialogue sounding as if transcribed from speech.

All those sounds and images that troubled Mulford's thoughts during those nights in Brooklyn, so long ago, so many chapters before.

Afterward

While Mulford toiled on the chapters of Hopalong Cassidy, another young man, not far away, sweated over a series of stories about a new kind of detective. In a few years, he would have on his hands the most popular fictional detective in the United States since the golden days of Nick Carter.

A thousand writers, peering slyly back at Sherlock Holmes, would attempt to shape an investigator who would tread new territory. Arthur Benjamin Reeve would do so. His detective, Professor Craig Kennedy, would set thunder rolling. The scientific detective, already established by Dr. Thorndyke and Luther Trant, would become a major literary type and would hurl forth such names as Scientific Sprague, Dr. Bentiron, Dr. Goodrich, the Scientific Club and a spangle of others.

The interest in science applied to detection was paralleled by an equal interest in the occult, for to most readers science was a mystery as obscure as the dark arts of Egypt. The occult investigator developed to a highly specialized breed of detective. John Silence, Carnacki, Semi-Dual, Jules de Grandin all faced problems whose causes were rarely of this world. Robert Howard's later occult adventurers, Solomon Kane and King Kull, did little investigating but much fighting with forces unmeasured by the scientific detectives.

The broader fields of fantasy foamed with new faces. After John Carter showed the way to adventure on Mars, the interplanetary, interstellar adventure raced through the magazines: Polaris ventured strangely on Earth, as did, in their own ways, Buck Rogers, Taine and the explorers of the Golden Atom. Within our sun's system some adventured after John Carter to The Radio Planet, The Planet of Peril, The Light Country. Others leaped through interstellar space with Jason Croft, the Interstellar Patrol and the crew of the Skylark.

Most of these adventurers were, one way or the other, endebted to Edgar Rice Burroughs, whose creations of John Carter and Tarzan established new adventure forms and heroic figures so irrepressibly vital that, six generations later, their images shine in current fiction.

Scientific investigators and occult detectives. Literate ants, battle-wise heroes, star flights and winged heroines.

The subjects for the next volume.

Notes

Chapter II: *Glory Figures*

[1]McIntosh, Gerald J., "Real People in *Tip Top*," *Dime Novel Round-Up*, No. 403; and "Rounded Up for the Round-Up," *Dime Novel Round-Up*, No. 421.

[2]Leithead, Edward J., and LeBlanc, Edward T., "*Rough Rider Weekly* and the Ted Strong Saga," *Dime Novel Round-Up*, No. 478.

[3]One of whom was Thomas W. Hanshew, soon to leave dime novel writing and remove to England, where his Cleek stories would become a popular rage and decisively influence mainstream pulps twenty years later.

[4]Breihan, Carl W., "Jesse James and the Gallatin Bank Robbery" *Real West*, pp. 33-34, 48-50, October 1971.

[5]Deutsch, James I., "Jesse James in Dime Novels: Ambivalence Towards An Outlaw Herd," *Dime Novel Round-Up,* No. 517. This is a sound discussion of the Jesse James dime novels and the good/evil hero figure.

[6]McIntosh, Gerald J., "Following in the Merriwell Trail," *Dime Novel Round-Up*, No. 474. The DNR contains a substantial amount of information concerning the Merriwell mystique. Other issues covering facets of the Merriwell story are Nos. 391, 396, 421, 425, 426, 445, with numerous others, before and after.

[7]Dizer, John T., Jr., "Boys Books and the American Dream," *Dime Novel Round-Up*, No. 426.

[8]Unfortunately this book was not available for examination and it is not known in which decade the novel is set. Apparently the daughter was practicing the new sexual freedom without benefit of the pill and got caught. It is reported that the book was not a success.

[9]Standish, Burt L., "Flaming Hate," *Top Notch*, May 1, 1930. The speaker is Frank Merriwell Jr. The sentiments are Merriwell from any generation.

[10]The bulk of the series was written by Luis Senarens, who picked up the series after the third issue when Harry Enton dropped it. At that time Senarens was fourteen years old. For more on the complex history of The Steam Man and the *Frank Reade Library* refer to E.F. Bleiler's "Introduction," *Eight Dime Novels,* Dover, 1974, p. xiii. Senarens later became editor of *Mystery Magazine,* a long-lived cross between a pulp magazine and a dime novel, first issued in 1917.

[11]Innumerable books have explored the developmental lines of science fiction in elaborate detail. To cite one or ten or twenty is to slight the many. A few useful works, still generally available to the casual reader, include Moskowitz's *Under the Moons of Mars*; Goulart's *Cheap Thrills*; Carter's *Imaginary Worlds*; Bleiler's Introduction to *Eight Dime Novels* (Dover); Roger's *A Requiem for Astounding*; Knight's *In Search of Wonder*; and Ashley's three-volume *The History of Science Fiction*, with examples and commentary. These books serve as a beginning. But only a beginning. There is as much commentary as there is science fiction.

Chapter III—*Nick*

[1]E.F. Bleiler, *Richmond: Scenes in the Life of a Bow Street Runner,* "Introduction to the Dover Edition," pp. xii-xiii, Dover Publications, Inc. New York, 1976.

[2]Quentin Reynolds, *The Fiction Factory,* p. 63, Random House, New York, 1955.

[3]J. Randolph Cox, *Nick Carter Library,* Dime Novel Roundup Bibliographic Listing No. 502, Vol. 43, No. 7, July 15, 1974.

[4]In developing these data, extensive use has been made of the Nick Carter bibliographic listings prepared by J. Randolph Cox. Each listing provides an introductory essay on the Nick Carter novels, a discussion of the authors involved, and a detailed citation of titles, reprints and other information concerning each publication. The work is based on Street & Smith's editorial and business records and is authoritative and indispensable. The excellence of this material is such that your faith in present scholarship is refreshed and renewed. The additional bibliographic listings in the series are as follows: *New Nick Carter Weekly,* No 516, Vol. 44, No. 9, December 1975, *Nick Carter Stories: Nick Carter Stories and Other Series Containing Stories About Nick Carter,* Part I, No. 526, Vol. 46, No. 4, August 1977, *Nick Carter Stories: Part II,* No. 542, Vol. 49, No. 2, April 1980.

[5]Nick's early training is discussed in a letter from Nick Carter, dated March 3, 1910, which is reproduced in its entirety in the *New Nick Carter Weekly,* No. 710. The strong parallels between Nick's training and that received some years later by the hero of *Doc Savage Magazine,* Clark Savage, Jr., is a tribute to the tenacity of memory within the halls of Street & Smith. Apparently they never forgot anything, never let an established character rust away, never discarded a successful fictional background. Someone always remembered.

[6]In certain critical articles, Sim Carter is referred to as "Seth." That name, however, does not appear in the Nick Carter series.

[7]The description of Old Thunderbolt is from the *Nick Carter Library,* No. 17, November 28, 1891.

[8]*New Nick Carter Weekly,* No. 427, March 4, 1905.

[9]Dr. Quartz first appeared in the *Nick Carter Library,* No. 13, October 31, 1891. Moriarty was not mentioned in the Sherlock Holmes adventures until 1893.

[10]*New Nick Carter Weekly,* No. 382, April 23, 1904.

Interlude:*The Vanishing*

[1]Quinn, Laura, "Popular Fiction: Penny Dreadfuls, Boys' Weeklies, and Halfpenny Parts," Department of English, University of Minnesota. This pamphlet, highly recommended, may still be available from the Curator of the Hess Collection, 109 Walter Library, University of Minnesota. In discussing boys' popular fiction during the Victorian Era in England, Quinn traces major thematic strains which have persisted into the present. She indicates that the popular fiction heroes of the penny dreadfuls "are heroes because of their autonomy, their deftly and rigidly maintained independence of the social

network from which real-life heroes can never extricate themselves.... Much popular fiction fosters what we might call the myth of the autonomous agent which implies that the hero of the story is the sole source of the order which results from the resolution of the tale's conflicts. The autonomous agent is above the complex of social relationships and institutions which determine and delimit 'real-life' behavior."

This is precisely the condition which exists in the single-character pulp magazines of the 1930s, especially The Shadow, Doc Savage, The Spider and the Phantom Detective. Both Savage and the Spider occasionally are forced to conform to the letter of the law. This invariably results in such unbearable social consequences that only when they regain their autonomous status is stability restored.

Chapter IV—*Rogues and Bent Heroes*

[1]Grant Allen, *An African Millionaire* (1897), reprinted by Dover Pubs., Inc. (1980). A biographical sketch of Allen's life and work is contained in the "Introduction" by Norman Donaldson.

[2]Chris Steinbrunner and Otto Penzler, *Encyclopedia of Mystery and Detection*. This valuable reference volume gives considerable detail on Raffles and the lives of Hornung and Atkey. It also provides an extensive listing of Raffles films, omitted here, probably to the detriment of the text, since the interplay between the silent/sound movies and the popular magazines was direct, intimate and, to date, unexamined.

[3]This book is a five-part, episodic novel that begins with a retelling of Bunny's initial meeting with Raffles.

[4]The May 1903 story, "By the Black Deep," has not been collected in book form, per Steinbrunner and Penzler, *op. cit.*, p. 14.

[5]*From A Surgeon's Diary* was published as a softbound volume in 1975 by Ferret Fantasy, Ltd., London, England. Additional bibliographic information concerning the Romney Pringle magazine stories and books may be found in the paperbound *In Search of Dr. Thorndyke* (Popular Press, 1971), by Norman Donaldson, pp. 52-57.

[6]Maurice LeBlanc, *The Exploits of Arsene Lupin* (1907). The quotations used in this discussion are from Chapter 1 of this volume, unless otherwise specified.

[7]LeBlanc, *The Teeth of the Tiger* (1914).

[8]Thomas W. Hanshew, *Cleek, the Man of Forty Faces* (1910) from which these quotations have been extracted.

[9]The device of Cleek's plastic face was frequently used in later pulp magazines. The most prominent adaptation was in *The Avenger*, a single-character magazine published 1939-1942. During a portion of this time, 1939-1940, the face of Richard Henry Benson, the Avenger, was paralyzed and could be shaped like dough and tinted like a number painting. Later, he was cured of this affliction.

[10]An essay on Cleek and Hanshew, lavish in detail and researched in depth, may be found in the *Dime Novel Roundup*, Nos. 483 and 484 (March 15 and April 15, 1973), by J. Randolph Cox.

[11]Perhaps the Katzenjammers also borrowed their technique from still earlier work. J. Randolph Cox has mentioned this unorthodox use of flypaper

in some of the Frederick R. Burton stories contained in the 1896 *Nick Carter Library*.

[12]Louis Joseph Vance, *The Lone Wolf*, Chapter XIII.

[13]Nor do the Lone Wolf paperbacks of the 1970s have anything to do with the original Lone Wolf character.

Chapter V—*Alias the Gray Seal*

[1]Maurice B. Gardner in the "Letters" column, p. 47, *Xenophile*, No. 24, July 1976, remarks that he wrote to Packard shortly after World War II "... not knowing he had passed on, and his widow answered my letter. She [mentioned] that her husband had been working on a new Jimmie Dale story at the time of his death, but to my knowledge the story was never completed."

[2]Arthur Guiterman, *The Bookman*, June 1920, "Frank Packard and His Miracle Men," p. 468.

[3]Compare this dialogue with the following extract from the *Nick Carter Weekly*, No. 247, September 21, 1901:

"... I got here on the dead jump and never looked at the t'ing before I opened it before Jimmy, and he seed dere wasn't nothin' in it."

[4]Herbert Asbury, *The Gangs of New York* (1928), Chapters XI, XII and XIII, dealing with gang structures, tong wars and a glimpse of the transition into the Prohibition Era. This book describes the real underworld of 1900-1925. (And earlier chapters provide much detail concerning the period from the Civil War to 1900.) That the images of the 1900-1915 underworld persisted into the popular fiction of the 1930s suggests that they had already entered folk myth. The conversion was much assisted by the scenes used in the early moving pictures.

[5]A few "automatic revolvers" were manufactured in the early 1900s. This is a revolver that cocks itself after every shot. While there was such a weapon, there is no reason to assume that Jimmie Dale used one. Packard is extremely sloppy with his gun nomenclature. He uses "revolver" and "automatic" as interchangeable words. It is not clear what weapon Dale carried—probably a double-action .38 revolver before the First World War, and a .38 automatic after he resumed operations. Perhaps.

[6]The entire East Side is shrieking "Death to the Gray Seal," a cry which will echo in the later Shadow novels. As a battle cry, this has a honorable history and may be found, lightly changed, as far back as 1901 in the *Nick Carter Weekly*, No, 247:

Tough Thug: "It's Nick Carter and his gang!"
"Immediately there were shouts and cries, amid which could be heard the words:
"Kill him! Kill them all! Down them! Death to all of them!"

It is suspected that similar outbursts were recorded in still earlier fiction. As well as real life.

[7]By 1914 there appears to have been considerable cross influence between the moving pictures and popular fiction. The very early silent movies drew

directly from the short stories of the day. The Cleek stories, for instance, were filmed instantly on publication. Complex patterns of cross-influences with the media quickly developed. The silent movies would borrow images from the dime novels and stage melodramas and fill the screen with sinister Chinese, dope addicts, dreary dens, villains, pursuits, mysterious cloaked figures. These would then be picked up by popular fiction with small variations; in turn, the movies would reborrow the modified images and present them so vividly that the writers would then.... It is suspected that many of Packard's Badlands interiors derived from the silent films of the day. The entire subject cries for more research.

[8]The later pulp magazine fiction adopted the images but discarded the symbolism. Thus early Shadow novels (1931-1935 period) present tough drinking dens and other gangland interiors with no attempt to do anything more literary than present some very hard people scheming over grog. In the Phantom Detective magazine novels (from around 1933-1937) similar interiors appear, although stylized to the point of becoming cardboard backdrops. The Spider magazine novels are perhaps the only pulp fiction which retained elements of Packard's moral symbols.

[9]Don Hutchinson, "Jimmie Dale: Pulp Archetype," *Xenophile*, March-April 1976, pp. 12-14. This article suggests that R.T.M. Scott, who wrote the first two Spider novels (1933, October and November), was influenced by Packard's work. It is certainly possible. But the major influence Packard exerted on *The Spider* magazine was through Norvell Page, who took over writing the series with the December 1933 issue. Page faithfully reproduced Packard's time structuring, emotional outbursts, tormented hero, and diction—including a lavish expenditure of exclamation points!

[10]Guiterman, *op. cit.*, pp. 468 and 470.

Chapter VI—*The Death Givers*

[1]Edgar Wallace, *The Council of Justice*, Ward, Lock & Co., Ltd. (1916), Introduction, p. 6.

[2]*Ibid.*, p. 190.

[3]*Ibid.*, pp. 227-228. Manfred's speech lays out the legal and moral position that later will be adopted by more inarticulate 1930s justice figures. Of all these, only the murderous Spider (*The Spider* magazine, 1933-1943) showed any sensitivity to the issues involved. In no magazine is the issue faced as bluntly as by Manfred. Of particular interest is Manfred's contention that the Law's faults are in great measure due to "spurious humanitarianism"— "Bleeding hearts" and "coddling crooks" being phrases of the same weight but later currency. It is interesting to compare Manfred's remarks in 1908 with the commercial humanitarianism shown in the newspapers of the 1920s and the legalistic humanitarianism of the 1960-1980s. The position in the 1930s was less that of unchecked sentimentalism reducing punishment than the breakdown of those social mechanism protecting the citizen. If the police could not protect you against gangsters and bank presidents, who could?

[4]The editions of *The Four Just Men* most readily available in the United States are by Burt and Triangle (a reprint of the Burt edition). These contain heavily abridged versions of *The Four Just Men* and *The Council of Justice*. Manfred's speech, however, is preserved in full.

[5]Charles Kidde, *A Guide to the First Editions of Edgar Wallace*, The Ivory Head Press, Morcombe, Dorset, 1981, paperbound, 88 pages. This valuable reference clarifies many of the problems in first issue English and American hardcovers.

[6]Le Blois, described as a poet-philosopher, was shot for corrupting the "youth of the world with his reasoning." Considering this charge, it would be appropriate if the Just Men had forced him to drink hemlock.

[7]This immense paragraph appeared on the unillustrated cover of the first edition of the book.

[8]Edgar Wallace, *People,* Crime Club, Doubleday, Doran & Co., 1929, pp. 180-182.

[9]The story states that Merrell was killed twenty years ago. This rounds out the actual lapsed time. Merrell was alive in 1902 and, since the *Law of the Four Just Men* was published in 1921, the events of that story probably occurred in 1919. That places Merrell's death 17-18 years before.

[10]Several Wallace plays were later written into novels by his secretary, Robert Curtis. Titles include *The Green Pack* and *The Man Who Changed His Name.* The novels are interesting if not intensely seasoned with the Wallace touch. Their theatrical origins show through the text and you can feel the first and second act curtains. As in any play, there is much talk and little physical movement.

Chapter VII-*Fifty Miles South, Near the Pecos*

[1]*Time Magazine*, May 21, 1956, p. 95.

[2]*Time Magazine*, December 16, 1935, p. 42.

[3]Stanley J. Kunitz and Howard Haycraft, Editors, *Twentieth Century Authors*, H.W. Wilson Co., 1942, p. 995.

[4]Clarence E. Mulford, *Hopalong Cassidy's Rustler Round-Up* (retitling of *Bar 20*), Grosset & Dunlap, undated, Chapter 3, p. 22.

[5]*Ibid.,* pp. 20-21.

[6]*Ibid.,* p. 29.

[7]Thomas H. Uzzell, "The Love Pulps," *Scribner's Magazine*, April 1, 1938, p. 41.

[8]William F. Nolan, "Max Brand's Pulp Fiction Characters," *Xenophile*, No. 32, May/June 1977, p. 11.

[9]Max Brand, *The Seventh Man*, Chapter XLI, Dodd, Mead & Co., 1921.

[10]Brand, *The Untamed*, Pocket Books, New York, 1976, p. 35.

[11]*Ibid., pp. 184-185.*

[12]Max Brand, *The Night Horseman*, Pocket Books, New York, 1967, p. 237.

[13]*Ibid.,* p. 213.

[14]All Mulford's works have not been examined. It is not improbable, given his writing techniques, that Cassidy appears or is mentioned in other volumes not directly in the Bar 20 series.

[15]Around 1950, when television had revived Cassidy, Grosset & Dunlap reprinted five or six novels under gussied-up titles. These books seem to have been printed from original page plates or copied from them. Thus *Hopalong Cassidy's Rustler Round-up* carries the tell-tale imprint *Bar 20* at the top of each left-hand page throughout the book.

[16]Clarence E. Mulford, *The Coming of Cassidy*, A.C. McClung & Co, 1913, p. 172.

[17]Mulford, *Hopalong Cassidy Returns*, A.L. Burt & Co., 1924, p. 211.

[18]Mulford, *The Coming of Cassidy*, p. 173.

[19]Mulford, *Hopalong Cassidy Returns*, p. 121.

[20]Of these four short stories, two were reprinted from the *Masked Rider Western*, January and May 1944; one was reprinted from *Range Riders Western*, December 1939; and one from *The Rio Kid Western*, April 1945. Of interest is the first short story, "Texas John Alden" by Patrick Ervin, a pseudonym of Robert Howard. The story is another wonderful experience of that great man, Breckenridge Elkins, the Gent from Bear Creek.

[21]*Hopalong Cassidy's Western Magazine*, Vol. 1, No. 1, Fall 1950, p. 7.

[22]Mulford, *The Coming of Cassidy*, p. 148. Mulford stated that Hopalong carried his nickname "to the time he died, and after...." That may be idiomatic usage meaning "a long time," but the implication is that he died prior to the writing of the book, which is dated 1913. 1911 is perhaps a good working date. Red survived him, a tough old boy, vivid of speech, full of anecdotes. You cannot press this sort of reasoning about dates too far, because discrepancies begin to boil up all around you and strange, indeed, is the logic required to explain them away.

Selected Bibliographic Listings

Allen, Frederick Lewis. *The Lords of Creation*. New York and London: Harper, undated.

Allen, Grant. *An African Millionaire*. New York: Dover Publications Inc. 1980.

Asbury, Herbert. *The Gangs of New York*. New York: Knopf, 1928.

Ashden, Clifford (pseudonym of R. Austin Freeman and John Pitcairn). *The Adventures of Romney Pringle*. London: Ward, Lock & Co., 1902.

-----*The Further Adventures of Romney Pringle*. Philadelphia: Oswald Train, 1970.

-----*From A Surgeon's Diary*. London: Fantasy Ltd., 1975.

Bleiler, E.F. *Eight Dime Novels*. New York: Dover Publications Inc., 1974.

-----"Introduction to the Dover Edition of *Richmond; Scenes in the Life of a Bow Street Runner*. New York: Dover Publications, Inc., 1976.

Bower, B.M. (pseudonym for Mrs. Bertha Sinclair-Cowan). *Chip of the Flying U*. New York: G.W. Dillingham Co., 1906.

-----*The Lonesome Trail*. New York: G.W. Dillingham Co., 1909.

-----*Flying U Ranch*. New York: G.W. Dillingham Co., 1914.

-----*Rodeo*. Boston: Little, Brown, 1931.

-----*The Flying U Strikes*. Boston: Little, Brown, 1934.

Brand, Max (pseudonym for Frederick Faust). *The Untamed*. New York and London: G.P. Putnam's Sons, 1919.

-----*The Night Horseman*. New York and London: G.P. Putnam's Sons, 1920.

-----*The Seventh Man*. New York and London: G.P. Putnam's Sons, 1921.

-----*Dan Barry's Daughter*. New York and London: G.P. Putnam's sons, 1924.

Breihan, Carl W. "Jesse James and the Gallatin Bank Robbery," *Real West*, Vol. XIV, No. 97, October 1971.

Burns, Tex (pseudonym for Louis L'Amour). *Hopalong Cassidy and the Rustlers of West Fork*. New York: Doubleday, 1951.

-----*Hopalong Cassidy and the Trail to Seven Pines*. New York: Doubleday, 1951.

-----*Hopalong Cassidy and the Riders of High Rock*. New York: Doubleday, 1951.

Carter, Lin. *Imaginary Worlds*. New York: Ballantine. 1973.

Clurman, Robert (editor). *Nick Carter, Detective*. New York: Macmillan, 1963.

Cox, J. Randolph. "Introduction to 'The Impossible Theft' from the *New York Weekly*, October 5, 1895." Reprinted in *Nick Carter, the 100th Killmaster*. New York: Award Books, 1975.

-----*Nick Carter Library*. Bibliographic Listing: *Dime Novel Roundup* Supplement, Vol. 43, No. 7, July 15, 1975, Whole No. 502.

-----*Nick Carter Weekly*. Bibliographic Listing: *Dime Novel Roundup* Supplement, Vol. 44, No. 9, December 1975, Whole No. 516.

-----*Nick Carter Stories: Nick Carter Stories and Other Series Containing Stories About Nick Carter*, Part I. Bibliographic Listing, *Dime Novel Roundup* Supplement No. 10, Vol. 46, No. 4, August 1977, Whole No. 526.

-----*Nick Carter Stories: Part II*. Bibliographic Listing. *Dime Novel*

Roundup, Vol. 49, No. 2, April 1980, Whole No. 542.

-----"Cleek and His Forty Faces; or T.W. Hanshew, a Dime Novelist Who Made Good," *Dime Novel Roundup*, Vol. 42, No. 3, March 15, 1973, Whole No. 483; and Vol. 42, No. 4, April 15, 1973, Whole No. 484.

Deutsch, James L. "Jesse James in Dime Novels: Ambivalence Towards An Outlaw Hero," *Dime Novel Roundup*, Vol. 45, No. 1, February 1976, Whole No. 517.

Dizer, John T., "Boys Books and the American Dream" *Dime Novel Roundup*, Vol. 37, No. 2, February 15, 1968, Whole No. 425; and Vol. 37, No. 3, March 15, 1968, Whole No. 426.

Donaldson, Norman, *In Search of Dr. Thorndyke*. Bowling Green: Bowling Green Popular Press, 1971.

-----"Introduction" to *An African Millionaire*, by Grant Allen.

Fletcher, David. *Raffles*. New York: G.P. Putnam's Sons, 1977.

Gardner, Maurice, letter concerning Frank Packard, *Xenophile* No. 24, July 1976.

Goodstone, Tony. *The Pulps*. New York: Chelsea House, 1970.

Goulart, Ron. *Cheap Thrills*. New Rochelle: Arlington House, 1972.

Greene, Hugh. *Cosmopolitan Crimes*. Penguin, 1972.

Gruber, Frank. *Zane Grey*. New York: Belmont Tower Books, 1978.

Guiterman, Arthur. "Frank Packard and His Miracle Men," *The Bookman*, June 1920.

Haggard, H. Rider. *King Solomon's Mines*. London, New York: Cassell, 1885.

Hanshew, Thomas W. *The Man of Forty Faces*. London: Cassell, 1910.

-----*Cleek of Scotland Yard*. Garden City, N.Y.: Doubleday, Page, 1914.

-----*Cleek's Government Cases*. Garden City, N.Y.: Doubleday, Page, 1917.

Henry, O. (pseudonym for William Sidney Porter). "A Retrieved Reformation," *Roads of Destiny*. New York: Doubleday, Page, 1909.

Hornung, Ernest William. *The Amateur Cracksman*. New York: Scribner's, 1899.

-----*Raffles*. New York: Scribner's, 1901.

-----*A Thief In the Night*. New York: Scribner's, 1905.

Hutchinson, Don. "Jimmie Dale: Pulp Archetype." *Xenophile*, March-April 1976.

LeBlanc, Maurice. *The Exploits of Arsene Lupin*. New York: Harpers' Bros., 1907.

-----*The Confessions of Arsene Lupin*. London: Mills & Boon Ltd., 1912.

-----*Teeth of the Tiger*. New York: Grosset & Dunlap, 1914.

-----*Arsene Lupin Intervenes*. New York: Macaulay Co., 1929.

Kidde, Charles. *A Guide to the First Editions of Edgar Wallace*. Dorset, 1981.

Leithead, Edward J. and Leblanc, Edward T. "Rough Rider Weekly and the Ted Strong Saga," *Dime Novel Roundup*, Vol. 41, No. 7, July 15, 1972, No. 478.

McIntosh, Gerald. "Real People in *Tip Top*," *Dime Novel Roundup*, Vol. 35, No. 4, April 15, 1966. Whole No. 403.

-----"Rounded Up for the Round-Up," *Dime Novel Roundup*, Vol. 36, No. 10, October 15, 1967, Whole No. 421.

-----"Following in the Merriwell Trail," *Dime Novel Roundup*, Vol. 41, No. 3, March 15, 1972, Whole No. 474.

Mulford, Clarence E., *Bar—20*. New York: The Outing Publishing Co., 1907.

-----*Bar-20 Days*. Chicago: A.C. McClurg & Co., 1911.

-----*The Coming of Cassidy—And The Others*. Chicago: A.C. McClurg & Co., 1913.

-----*The Bar-20 Three*. Chicago: A.C. McClurg & Co., 1921.

-----*The Bar-20 Rides Again*. Garden City, N.Y.: Doubleday, Page & Co., 1926.

-----*Hopalong Cassidy Serves A Writ*. Garden City, N.Y.: Doubleday, Doran & Co.. 1941.

Mott, Frank Luther. *A History of American Magazines 1885-1905*, Vol. 4. Cambridge, Mass.: Belknap Press of Harvard University Press, 1957.

Moskowitz, Sam. "A History of 'The Scientific Romance' in the Munsey Magazines, 1912-1920," *Under the Moons of Mars*. New York: Holt, Rinehart, Winston, 1970.

Noel, Mary. *Villains Galore...The Heyday of the Popular Story Weekly*. New York: Macmillan, 1954.

Packard, Frank. *The Adventures of Jimmie Dale*. New York: Geo. H. Doran, 1917.

-----*The Further Adventures of Jimmie Dale*. New York: Geo. H. Doran, 1919.

Perowne, Barry (pseudonym for Philip Atkey). *Raffles Revisited*. New York: Harper & Row, 1974.

-----*Raffles of the Albany*. New York: St. Martin's Press, 1976.

Quinn, Laura. "Popular Fiction: Penny Dreadfuls, Boys' Weeklies, and Half-penny Parts." University of Minnesota, Department of English.

Reynolds, Quentin. *The Fiction Factory or From Pulp Row to Quality Street*. New York: Random House, 1955.

Standish, Burt L. "Flaming Hate," *Top Notch*, May 1, 1930.

Steinbrunner, Chris, and Penzler, Otto. *Encyclopedia of Mystery and Detection*. New York: McGraw-Hill, 1976.

Uzzell, Thomas H. "The Love Pulps," *Scribner's*, April 1, 1938.

Vance Louis Joseph. *The Lone Wolf*. London: Nash, 1915.

-----*The False Faces,* London: Sheffington, 1920.

-----*Red Masquerade*. New York: Doubleday, Page 1921.

-----*The Lone Wolf Returns*. London: Hodden & Stoughton, 1924.

-----"The White Terror," *The Saint Mystery Magazine*, Vol. 22, No. 4, August 1965.

Wallace, Edgar. *The Council of Justice*. London: Ward, Lock & Co., (undated).

-----*The Just Men of Cordova*. London: Ward, Lock & Co., 1917.

-----*People*. Garden City, N.Y.: The Crime Club, Doubleday, Doran & Co., 1929.

-----*The Law of the Three Just Men*. Garden City, N.Y.: The Crime Club, Doubleday, Doran & Co., 1931.

Wister, Owen. *The Virginian*. New York: Macmillain, 1902.

Index